ROSE CROIX

Dr Robert Crucefix 33°, the first Sovereign Grand Commander, 1845-1850.

ROSE CROIX

The History of the Ancient and Accepted Rite for England and Wales

Brig. A. C. F. Jackson, CVO, CBE, 33°

LEWIS MASONIC Books

First published in England

© 1980 A. C. F. Jackson

Revised and enlarged edition 1987,
Reprinted 1993

Published by LEWIS MASONIC, Ian Allan Regalia,
Coombelands House, Coombelands Lane,
Addlestone, Surrey.
Members of IAN ALLAN GROUP

ISBN 0 85318 151 9

British Library Cataloguing in Publication Data

Jackson, A. C. F.
  Rose-Croix.
  1. Ancient and Accepted Rite *(Masonic Order)*
  —History
  I. Title
  366′.1′0942   HS596.A5

Printed in Great Britain by
Latimer Trend & Company Ltd,
Plymouth

Contents

Appendices

Illustrations

Foreword

An account of the origins and growth of the Ancient & Accepted Rite in England and Wales is long overdue and the Supreme Council welcome the publication of this book. The author, who has been a member and student of the Rite for 40 years and is well known as an esteemed Past Master of the Quatuor Coronati Lodge, has covered a wide field in his researches and has succeeded in recording the interesting results of his labours in a clear and instructive manner.

While this book is not in any sense an official publication and the views expressed in it are solely those of the author, the Supreme Council has no hesitation in commending it to all those at home and overseas who have the interests of the Ancient & Accepted Rite at heart.

☦ **Ralph Hone, 33°,**
Sovereign Grand Commander.

Acknowledgements for the Illustrations

The portrait of Augustus, Duke of Sussex by Pelligrini is reproduced by gracious permission of Her Majesty the Queen. The prints of Prince Louis de Bourbon-Condé and the Duc Decazes are by permission of the *Bibliothèque Nationale* of Paris. The oil painting of the birthplace of the Charleston Supreme Council is reproduced by permission of the Supreme Council Southern Jurisdiction USA. The picture of Frederick the Great is reproduced by permission of the Trustees of the British Museum. The portrait of William Tucker is reproduced by permission of the brethren of Lodge of Virtue and Honour No 494, Axminster. The photograph of the Grand East and the seals of the Supreme Council of 1819 are reproduced by permission of the Supreme Council for England and Wales. The seals of the French chapters and lodges came from the collection of Monsieur Charles Haudot of Strasbourg. The remainder of the illustrations, i.e. examples of early Rose-Croix jewels; jewels of the intermediate degrees; the early 18° apron of the Netherlands Supreme Council; the authorisations to the Duke of Leinster and to the Duke of Sussex, dated 1819; the apron worn by Dr George Oliver; and the portraits of Thomas Boothby Parkyns, Dr George Oliver, Waller Rodwell Wright and Dr Robert Thomas Crucefix, are reproduced by permission of the Board of General Purposes of the United Grand Lodge.

Rephotographing of some of the portraits and the seals was done by Ann's Studio, Hermanus, and the redrawing of the seals was carried out by Miss Rosemary Luyt of Hermanus, South Africa.

Introduction

THE ANCIENT and Accepted Rite of Freemasonry came to England in 1845 when a Supreme Council for England and Wales was formed, but the development of the Rite had begun more than a hundred years earlier. The object of this book is to tell the story of how the Rite started, how it came to England and Wales and how it developed into its present important position.

The Rite is now a world-wide organisation which has attracted the attention of masonic writers of all nationalities and much detailed research has been, and is still being, carried out about its origins and development. Only one small book has been written previously on the Rite in England, that by the Rev A. W. Oxford in 1933. This touches briefly on early history and omits all reference to the interesting subject of how parts of the Rite were practised in England for some 70 years at least before the Supreme Council was formed. The older histories have naturally been overtaken by newer information and this makes it possible now to reconstruct a reasonably connected story of the early development of the Rite in the XVIII century and its expansion in the XIX century.

There are, however, two difficult periods where evidence is still incomplete. The first is from about 1755 to 1765 when there were many quarrels in the French Grand Lodge and its high degree off-shoots. This period is now being studied by members of the French Research Lodge, *Villard de Honnecourt*. Considerable information about events at that time has come from the comparatively recent rediscovery and publication of a contemporary pamphlet, *Mémoire Justificatif*, written by a member of the French Grand Lodge. This document, which has not previously been available to English mason-ic writers, though obviously giving a one-sided story of the quarrels, explains many previous obscurities. The second period is that im-mediately preceding the formation of the American Supreme Council in Charleston i.e. from about 1795 to 1801. Here information is scanty and conflicting.

In addition, modern writers do not always agree about the interpretation of events. In certain cases, it has not been felt necessary to adjudicate, and the reader must decide for himself which point of view he accepts. When a modern work is referred to extensively, permission to quote it has been obtained. This does not apply to the many references to papers in *Ars Quatuor Coronatorum*, the transactions of the Quatuor Coronati Lodge of Research No 2076 EC as, by convention, any member of the Lodge has the privilege of referring to the work of other members, subject to suitable acknowledgement. All books and papers quoted are given in the Bibliography. When references are frequent, the name of the book or the author is given in an abbreviated form which is shown in the Bibliography. As a result, the distraction of frequent notes is avoided.

The Rite, in many Supreme Councils overseas, is known as the 'Ancient and Accepted Scottish Rite'. The word 'Scottish' did not appear in the original patent of the Supreme Council for England and Wales. Nevertheless, it is found in some official documents in the last century. It is possible that the use of the word 'Scottish' in the title was encouraged by its appearance in all the documents issued in connection with the Lausanne Convention of 1875. The word is in the title of the *Rules and Regulations* of the Supreme Council for the years 1874–78 and then disappeared, by which time the Convention and everything associated with it were gladly being forgotten. The word was officially dropped from the title in 1909. The title, in this book, of the Ancient and Accepted Rite is abbreviated to A & A Rite. It is abbreviated to A & AS Rite when referring to Supreme Councils which have the word 'Scottish' in their title.

The expression 'High Degree' is used throughout to distinguish a masonic degree which has a numbered title higher in numerical order than the three Symbolic degrees, i.e. the First or Entered Apprentice, the Second or Fellow-Craft and the third or Master Mason, including the Royal Arch. This expression is used for convenience and is not intended to imply any superiority, other than numerical, over the Symbolic degrees or the degrees of any other Masonic Rite.

All translations into English, unless otherwise stated, are by the author. It should be noted that the word for 'Scottish' or 'Scots' as an adjective in France until about mid-XVIII century, was '*Ecossois*'. This, and any other archaic French spelling, have been eliminated and the word appears always as '*Ecossais*'. Both words have, of course, identical meaning. Certain proper names have a different spelling in foreign languages, but the English spelling is always used, except in quotations, e.g. 'Adoniram' which in French is '*Adonhiram*'.

Acknowledgements

Through the courtesy of the Board of General Purposes of the United Grand Lodge, the author has had access to the following previously unpublished material in the Library of Grand Lodge:

(a)   The notebook of John Knight of Redruth, Cornwall, *c* 1811, recording high degree working in England from about 1790.
(b)   The original papers dealing with the abortive French attempt to form a British Supreme Council under the sovereignty of the Duke of Sussex in 1818.

Through the courtesy of the Supreme Council for England and Wales, the use of:

(a)   The recently rediscovered Francken Ms of 1771, which contains, amongst other writings, the first known copy of the 1762 Constitutions of the Rite.
(b)   A previously unpublished manuscript of *c* 1790, containing early French rituals.

In a book of this type, which has taken three years to produce, the author has had correspondence with a number of masonic writers who have given him much valuable assistance and replied to his many queries. He would, however, like specially to mention the Secretaries of the Pilgrim Lodge, of the Lodge of Peace and Harmony, of the Prince of Wales's Lodge, of the Royal Sussex Lodge of Hospitality, the Grand Secretary-General of the Grand Lodge of Belgium and the Grand Secretary General of the Supreme Council for Ireland.

He also received valuable assistance from Bro F. W. Shepherd, who was able to fill gaps in the story of John Knight and early Masonry in Cornwall: from the Great Vice-Chancellor of the Great Priory of England and Wales for permission to use the long extract from the pamphlet on the Order: to Madame de Lussy of the *Bibliothèque Nationale* of Paris for important information and for some of the illustrations: to M. Charles Haudot for photographs of early French seals: to Colonel F. W. Seal-Coon, J. Fairbairn-Smith and Paul Naudon for allowing their published books to be heavily drawn upon: to M. Alain Bernheim who assisted with critical correspondence and for his invaluable article in the transactions of the French Research Lodge, *Villard de Honnecourt*.

The author would also like to express his thanks to the following members of his own masonic circle for considerable assistance and advice, George Draffen of Newington, Colonel Eric Ward, Michael Spurr, A. R. Hewitt, T. O. Haunch, J. M. Hamill and C. N. Batham, the last three in their special capacities in the Library of the United Grand Lodge, and in the Quatuor Coronati Lodge, without whose constant assistance, this book could never have been written. Finally, the author wishes to express a special debt of gratitude to R. A. Ingham Clark, Grand Secretary General of the Supreme Council for England and Wales, for his encouragement, guidance and help at intervals over many months.

Introduction to Second Edition

In my conclusions to the first edition of this book, I suggested that there was still much to discover about the history of the A & A Rite generally and of its development in England and Wales. During the last five years, additional information has become available, and I have also to thank those of my readers who have produced new facts or have pointed out errors. The result has entailed many changes which inevitably make the 1980 edition of *Rose-Croix* out of date.

I am now confident that the correct story of the first period about which there was uncertainty—that from 1755 to 1765 when there were many quarrels in the Grand Lodge of France and its high degree offshoots—can be told. Credit for this is chiefly due to French masons, as one would expect. They have been able to fit in the facts in the rediscovered contemporary pamphlet, the *Mémoire Justificatif*, written by Brest de la Chaussée who was an officer of the Grand Lodge at that time. This, with what was already known, virtually completes the story.

Equally important progress, due largely to detective work on the 1771 Francken Ms. by my colleague, Alain Bernheim, now indicates the correct date and authorship of the 'Constitutions of 1762', a story which I have amplified in *AQC* 98.

All this new evidence casts doubt on the deductions made by previous masonic historians about what happened during the later period from the death of Francken in 1795 until the announcement by the Supreme Council at Charleston of its inauguration, in 1802, by a manifesto to world-wide masonic bodies. For want of better material earlier writers have been forced to rely on facts, now known to be of doubtful authenticity, or on documents which were much embellished many years after they were written. There is still clearly much to be done in getting the correct facts and sequence of events in this vital period of the history of the A & A Rite. We must hope that the discovery of new material will give correct answers to the present contradictions.

Equally incomplete is the story of the arrival from France of the high degrees in Britain. The position is gradually becoming clearer but there is still much evidence missing. This, in some ways, is a joint problem, affecting the Orders of the Temple in England, Ireland and Scotland as well as the A & A Rite. It may be that when the history of the former is written, we shall, in the A & A Rite, learn more about our past.

JERSEY   ACFJ
1987

PART ONE
The Development of the Rite

1
THE BIRTH OF ECOSSAIS MASONRY

By about 1730, the three degrees of Craft masonry were being worked in Britain and in many parts of Europe. During the next few years, other degrees start appearing. They usually had names which included the word 'Scottish' or 'Scots', or in France '*Ecossais*'. These are the degrees which, in due course, developed into the Ancient and Accepted Rite, and it is with their story that this book is concerned.

The question as to when and where these new degrees started has never been satisfactorily settled. There are two main theories. These 'high degrees' could have begun in England about 1730, or earlier, and been taken into use in France some five years later. This fits with the dates of their first appearance in both countries, listed in detail in Appendix I. The alternative is that the high degrees were invented in France soon after the publication of Dr Anderson's *Book of Constitutions* in 1723, partly as a reaction against the new theism of the English Craft and partly as more suitable for the French character. This theory further suggests that the new high degrees were called *Ecossais* to distinguish them from the older *Anglais* (English) masonry which had started in France probably about 1725. If this idea is accepted, it follows that a few English lodges got interested, for a short while, in the new French degrees and practised them. These lodges would naturally call the new ceremonies 'Scottish' or 'Scots' as a direct translation of their French names.

The Chapter expands these alternatives by giving an historical account of the start of the development of high degree masonry in the two countries.

The English Theory

The XVII century was a transitional period in English masonry. It had seen the end of Operative masonry and the entry into lodges of men who had no ties with the Mason trade. These non-operatives were accepted into lodges with the same ceremonies that had been used for centuries by operative masons. The *Old Constitutions* and the *Old Manuscript Charges* formed the basis of these ceremonies, and well-thumbed copies, written during the century, are certain proof that this is correct. It has always been a matter for conjecture why these non-operative masons, frequently men of influence, social position and scholarship were interested, or why they remained masons after taking part in the crude operative ceremony of their initiation. The traditional history in the *Old Constitutions*, with its many anachronisms, and the *Old Charges*, with their slightly ridiculous codes of conduct designed for medieval workmen, not to 'take your fellow's wife violently nor his daughter ungodly nor his servant in villanie' or not to play cards and dice, can only have appeared as comical to them as they do now to us.

The second half of the XVII century was, however, a period of extraordinary interest in the past. In his *Illustrated English Social History*, G. M. Trevelyan writes:

> The ecclesiastic-political controversies of the time, in which all sides appealed to the practices of the past, set a premium on historical research ... It inspired the researches of clergymen and religious laymen alike ... The publication of medieval texts, and the study of Anglo-Saxon and Medieval antiquities by these men between 1660 and 1730 were astonishing alike in quality and volume.

Intellectual exercise was a relief from contemporary worry. Friends met to talk and discuss their common interests. Masons' lodges were clubs where men of similar tastes could meet without interference, and certainly without fear of the political informer. Meetings, one assumes, were mainly for intelligent conversation and mild conviviality. 'Making ceremonies' were few and possibly considered as no more than the out-of-date relaxation of some of the members. This was the background to the development of the Craft rituals which culminated in the production of the Hiramic legend in the early decades of the XVIII century.

The old operative masonry possessed a store of written legend which can be found in the many surviving *Old Constitutions* of the Order. Some of the stories appear in several manuscripts: others, like that of Noah and his sons, in perhaps only one or two. The new class of scholarly men, then in lodges, would have been aware of these legends and they would also have known of the early history of the Jews, given in the Bible and by other Jewish writers, of whom Josephus is now the best known. It is from such sources that the theme of the Hiramic legend was evolved. It seems equally reasonable to suggest that other themes were discussed and developed in some lodges, and these produced the stories of the early high degrees. As will be seen later, these were all Biblical, centring around the building of King Solomon's Temple and its rebuilding by Zerubbabel.

It would be unwise to take this speculation too far, but it does provide an answer to the appearance of what are now called high degrees in some English lodges at a period when many lodges had not adopted the Hiramic legend. The tendency has been to assume that the high degrees were a sequel to the three Symbolic degrees. A study of the dates will show that they may have been contemporaneous—at least with the Third Degree.

It is also worth noting how unsatisfying the Hiramic legend, with its unfinished result, must have been to many masons, and that it would not have been unnatural for men of intelligence to want to take the story further. This continuation of the Hiramic legend is exactly what the early high degrees relate. As the high degrees died out in England, so did the Royal Arch assert itself. The similarity between some of these early high degrees and the legend of the Royal Arch is remarkable. A study of the degrees of the Ancient and Accepted Rite will show that they cover the whole story of the latter. It is possible that they were, in fact, the Royal Arch in an expanded and rudimentary form.

The first mention of high degrees in England, that can be confirmed, is of regular meetings of a lodge in London at the Devil's Tavern at Temple Bar in 1733 (see *AQC* 59). The lodge met twice a month and is referred to in three contemporary documents as 'a Scots Masters Lodge'. Two years later, the Bear Inn Lodge, at Bath, held a well authenticated meeting at which the Master, both Wardens and nine brethren were made 'Scots' Masters. This seems to have been an isolated event as the next meeting of the lodge, at which 'Scots' Masonry is mentioned, was not until 1747, and then similar meetings were held, with the last as late as 1758. Another early mention of these degrees is How's *Freemasons' Manual*. He says that the French lodge, St George de l'Observance No 49 chartered by the Grand Lodge of England in 1736 stationed in Covent Garden, worked 'sublime degrees' in a body attached to their lodge. In fact, in 1736, this Lodge was 'Unanimité, changing its name in 1771. How's statement is unfortunately not corroborated. In 1740, the Lodge of Antiquity in London met and nine brethren were made Scots Masters. In the same year five Master Masons were 'Rais'd Scotch Masters' in Lodge No 137 at Bristol. The last two incidents are the only ones recorded by these lodges.

These few references to 'Scottish' masonry in England give the impression that the meetings were unusual occasions at which special ceremonies were carried out, possibly by visitors. We know nothing of what took place, but there is no suggestion that anything was being invented or developed. It will be seen, from Appendix I, that the English references to high degrees decrease after 1740, except for the occasional meetings. The lodges at Bath and Bristol were visited several times about 1737/38 by Dr. Desaguliers, a Past G.M. of the Grand Lodge, with other distinguished visitors. It therefore seems most unlikely that he would not have been aware of the meetings of Scots Masters that were being held. With so many meetings of Scots Masters there cannot have been anything clandestine about the existence of the degree. That it ceased to be conferred after a few years is suggested by the ignorance of Dr Thomas Manningham, Deputy G.M. as shown in the letter, dated 1757, given at the end of this chapter. There was, however, some form of high degree, called by variations of the word 'Harodim' which continued in the north-east of England until about the time of the Union of 1813. This does not seem to have had any effect on the development of the A & A Rite in England.

The high degrees had no great appeal to the average Englishman at this time. Masonry in England was, as it still is, mainly a middle-class institution. In the early days of the Grand Lodge, some of its rulers, apparently younger members of the upper classes, did try to make masonry more flamboyant with carriage processions and the wearing of masonic clothing in public. These ideas met with ridicule and stopped abruptly. There is no doubt too that, by the 1740s, the high degrees were tinged in many English minds with a Jacobite hue. Any chance that they might have spread ended when the '45 Rebellion, led by the Pretender Charles Edward, threw England into a mild panic. The north-east was a Jacobite centre and that, in all probability, was the reason for the continuance there of the Harodim degrees after the other high degrees had disappeared or been replaced by the Royal Arch as it developed.

An elaborate legend connecting Freemasonry with Scotland appears from the earliest times in the high degrees. It tells of masons, driven from Jerusalem after the destruction of the Temple, escaping to Scotland and staying there until they left to take part in the Crusades. Whilst in Scotland, they lived at 'Heredom', a mountain north of Kilwinning. These masons were usually known as 'Elect' or *Elu*, though in some French rituals as 'Harodim'. In all cases, they seem originally to have been the Menatzchim or Overseers of the Tradition-al History of the Third Degree. There have been many different spellings of the word 'Heredom', and it appears frequently in high degree masonry. The whole concept is legendary but, as it appears so frequently, its usually accepted derivations may be given:

'Harodim' is a Hebrew word, the plural of Harod—one who rules or acts as an Overseer. The word seldom appears in English degrees of the A & A Rite, but is frequently found in French versions. It appears, however, in other English rites.

'Heredom' seems to be a made up word but the following suggestions have been advanced as its meaning. It figures in English and French high degrees.

> *Heres domus*, the Latin for house of the heir, or first-born.
> *Hieros domos*, the Greek for holy house.
> *Har Edom*, the Hebrew for (Holy) Mountain of the Earth.

The meaning of the word is explained by G. E. W. Bridge as follows:

> ... The original intention of the authors of rituals in which Heredom appears is not known, but they all belong to what may be termed the 'Holy Mount of Attainment' class. Heredom in Masonry may be regarded as one of the Sacred Mountains along with ... Sinai, Tabor, Moriah, &c. with, in the Rose-Croix, possibly a special reference to Calvary?

The appearance of the word 'Heredom' in the earliest traditional stories of masonry could be an explanation for the word 'Scottish' in English high degree masonry. The legends could equally have been of French origin, and therefore provide no solution to the problem of where high degrees started, but it is another reason for the high degrees in either country having a Scottish name.

The French Story

Some French authors consider that masonry may have come to France long before the formation of the Grand Lodge in 1717. They suggest that it may have arrived as early as the second half of the XVII century through the Scottish regiments in the service of the French kings. Such masons must have been non-operatives from Scottish operative lodges as there were no speculative masons in France by this date, but their presence would have connected masonry, in the minds of Frenchmen, with Scotland. There have always been strong ties between Scotland and France from the time of Robert the Bruce, and the many Frenchmen who visited Scotland would have been aware of the existence of Scottish masonry.

This theory does provide a reasonable explanation for the high degrees to be associated in French minds with Scotland, but it is hardly proof of their origin. An equally tenable one can be developed about the Irish. It is known that non-operative masonry existed in Dublin in the second half of the XVII century from a speech made in

1688. Soon afterwards (July 1690) was the Battle of the Boyne and some 16,000 of the defeated Irish Army went into voluntary exile in France with James II. They were formed into Irish regiments in the service of the King of France. Inevitably there would have been masons among them. In fact, there is a tradition that a lodge was at work in an Irish unit in the year 1688 and that it lasted for about 100 years. There is no proof that this story is true, but it has never been disproved. From these facts we might get the degree of *Maître Irlandais* (No 7° in Appendix III).

English Craft masonry moved to France soon after the formation of the Grand Lodge, and the first lodge in France could be about 1725. It was composed of Englishmen and, for a number of years, the English-speaking element predominated in most French lodges. There were many Scotsmen in these lodges. Thus the word *Ecossais*, for whatever type of masonry being worked would not have been misplaced; and it would certainly have been popular with the large number of Scottish Jacobites in the service of the Stuart Pretenders.

In its early days, masonry, unlike in England, was often an entirely upper class affair, particularly outside Paris, and was patronised by the nobility, those around the royal court and their hangers-on. It was as a result of this background that one gets almost the first reference to high degree masonry. *Le Journal de l'Avocat Barbier*, of March 1737 writes of French courtiers making up a Masonry somewhat different from the English and using such expressions as *chevalier*, *chevalerie* and *chapitre*. This is convincing as the type of language that the upper class Frenchman would use in his normal life. There seem to have been high degree lodges, of which we know nothing, in Paris about 1743 as, in one of them, the Baron von Hund, later the founder of the Rite of Strict Observance in Germany, claimed to have been received into a masonic system which, in its higher degrees, was a continuation of the Templar Order. Findel refers to a lodge of Frenchmen working a Scots degree in Berlin in 1743, but which may even have opened two years earlier.

Up to 1743, masonry in France had ostensibly been unlawful, though many of those taking part were too important to be suppressed. The police in Paris did, however, take severe action against masons who were in no position to complain. In 1743, the anti-masonic Cardinal-Minister Fleury died and most of the repression ended. In the same year, the Grand Master, the Duc d'Antin, died and was replaced by Prince Louis de Bourbon Condé (Comte de Clermont), a member of the royal family. There is some doubt whether the new Grand Master tried to stop the police persecution but it seems most likely that he allowed raids against the more disreputable taverns where masonry had become a money making concern for the inn-keepers.

Some modern writers of this period of French masonic history give the impression that the new Grand Master took an active interest in French masonry, both Symbolic and high degree. The recently rediscovered *Mémoire Justificatif* of 1773, written by a prominent mid-XVIII century mason, Brest de la Chaussée, tells a different story.

> In the early days of Masonry in France, Masonry was well organised ... Tradition teaches us that, in those wonderful days of our Order, the high seats of Masonry were held by brethren who, to the lustre of their birth and rank, added the highest merit. In this way, the Grand Lodge was not only an assembly of Masters of Lodges worthy of the greatest respect from all the brethren, but they were the best from every Lodge ... This was the composition of the Grand Lodge until the death of the Duc d'Antin when the Comte de Clermont was nominated as Grand Master. This choice honoured French Masonry, but the Prince did not take an active interest in it. Soon after his nomination, the noblemen who filled the offices in the Grand Lodge abandoned their duties to their deputies. The banker, Brother Baur, whom the Grand Master had nominated as his deputy, ceased to summon the Grand Lodge. It did no further business and thus began the era of its decadence.

No doubt, de la Chaussée, writing after enduring some fifteen years of chaos and quarrelling in the Grand Lodge, was bitter on the subject and he may have overstated the negligence of the new Grand Master. As will be seen later, there is some evidence that the Comte de Clermont did take an active part in masonry—at least at intervals, particularly in the high degrees. However, even in 1743, the Grand Lodge, whilst still under the Grand Mastership of the Duc d'Antin appears to have thought that the new high degrees were a threat to Symbolic masonry. On the actual day of the election of the Comte de Clermont, 11 December, 1743, the Grand Master's personal lodge, Saint-Jean de Jérusalem, issued General Regulations, though obviously the Comte de Clermont cannot have had anything to do with their contents. One Article condemned high degree masonry.

Article 20
> As it has been learnt that recently some brethren are calling themselves *Ecossais* masters and are assuming privileges in private lodges and demanding powers of which there is no trace to be found in the ancient archives and customs of any lodges on the surface of the earth, the Gd Lodge has directed, in order to ensure the union and good harmony which must reign among FMs, that unless these *Ecossais* masters are officers of the Gd Lodge or of some private lodge, they will be considered by the

brethren like other apprentices or companions whose dress they will wear
without any sort of mark of distinction.

In June 1745, these restrictions were removed and *Ecossais* masters
were given supervisory powers:

Article 44
   The *Ecossais* will be the superintendents of the work, and will be the
first to vote. They will sit where they wish, and when they are at fault, this
can only be corrected by *Ecossais*.

In 1755, similar statutes went even further.

   The *Ecossais* masters will be the superintendents of the work, only in
correcting mistakes. They can speak when they wish, will be always armed
[i.e. wearing their swords] and covered [i.e. wearing headgear] and they
cannot be corrected, if they make a mistake, except by *Ecossais*.

It will thus be seen that the *Ecossais* masters must have had a
considerable influence on French masonry for many years. No doubt
they were carefully chosen from senior masons.
   In 1744, French exposures of masonry began to give information
about this new type of masonry as the following extracts from *The
Early French Exposures* show. *Le Secret des Francs-Maçons* by the
Abbé Perau, which appeared re-edited in *L'Ordre des Francs-Maçons
Trahi*, has in its preface:

   I am not ignoring that there is a vague rumour among the Freemasons
about a certain order that they call '*Les Ecossais*'; superior, as they
pretend, to ordinary Masons and who have their special secrets.

In the same year, *Le Parfait Maçon* stated:

   It is said among the Masons that there are still several degrees above that
of the masters ... some say that there are six in all, & others go up to
seven. Those called *Ecossais* Masons claim they form the fourth grade. As
this Masonry, different from the others in many ways, is beginning to
become known in France, the Public will not be annoyed if I relate what I
have read about it. Instead of weeping over the ruins of the Temple of
Solomon, as their brethren do, the *Ecossais* are concerned with rebuilding
it ... It is from this great event that the *Ecossais* derive the epoch of their
institution, & although they are later than the other Masons by several
centuries, they consider themselves of a superior grade.

Though it is necessary to treat all exposures with caution, the author's
remark that Scots Masonry 'is beginning to become known in France'

suggests that it was not of French invention. He then describes the degree.

> When the question arose of rebuilding the Temple of the Lord, Zerubbabel chose from the three grades of Masonry, the most capable workmen; but as the Israelites had to suffer many obstacles & reverses during the course of their labours, at the hands of the Samaritans & other neighbouring nations, the work would never have been completed, had not the Prince taken the precaution of creating a fourth grade of Masons, whose number he limited to 753, chosen from amongst the most excellent artists. ... Their work being more arduous than that of the other Masons, they were also awarded a more favourable rate of pay: & to be able to recognize them, Zerubbabel gave them a sign & particular words.

The short catechism given in this exposure included:

Q   Are you an *Ecossais* Master?
A   I was brought out of the captivity of Babylon.
Q   Who honoured you with the degree of *Ecossais*?
A   Prince Zerubbabel, of the line of David and Solomon.
Q   When?
A   Seventy years after the destruction of the holy city.
Q   In what are the *Ecossais* Masons occupied?
A   In rebuilding the Temple of God.
Q   Why do the Ecossais Masons carry the sword & buckler?
     [There is a footnote to the exposure which states that the *Ecossais* Masons all wear a wide red ribbon from which hangs a kind of shield.]
A   In memory of the order given by Nehemiah to all workmen at the time of the rebuilding of the Temple, to have swords always at their sides & their bucklers near at hand, for use in case of attack by their enemies.

The similarity of these fragments with the subsequent English Royal Arch reinforces the theory of the latter's development from the Scots Masters' degree. The same legend appears as the 15° and 16° of the A & A Rite.

La Franc-Maçonne which appeared in the same year in Brussels reproaches the Masters of the Paris Lodges for their ignorance in not knowing that masonry had seven degrees, of which four were *Ecossais*. Finally, *Les Francs-Maçons Ecrasés* of 1747, which tends to be unreliable and is anti-masonic, purports to give extracts from a ceremony of making an *Ecossais* Master. The degree is called that of the *Architect*, but it is not possible to connect it with any known degree, so it may be no more than a product of the author's imagination.

There are a number of reasons why French masons should have wanted to develop the high degrees. The somewhat aristocratic

Frenchmen who were interesting themselves in masonry from about 1730, seemed to find the simple ceremonies from England unsatisfying. This was at a time when the relations between the two countries were poor, so there was also an obvious desire to do something superior to the three English Craft degrees which, in any event, tended to put the Frenchman of high social class too much on a level with working masons. For the types referred to by the *Avocat Barbier*, the ideas stemming from an oration written by the Chevalier Ramsay would have had an immediate appeal. Ramsay was a Scot who had spent most of his life in France, and had come into prominence by acting as tutor to the children of people of influence. For a while, he was a keen mason and became Grand Orator of the Grand Lodge of France. In 1736, he wrote an oration which received much attention. The original version was given in a lodge at Epernay in December 1737. A second version was prepared for the Grand Lodge meeting for March the next year but was never delivered. This version and a third were however printed. The following extract gives the important element of their theme.

> The Kings, princes and lords returned from Palestine to their own lands and there established divers lodges. At the time of the last Crusades many lodges were already erected in Germany, Italy, Spain, France and from thence, in Scotland because of the close alliance between the French and the Scots. James, Lord Steward of Scotland, was Grand Master of a Lodge established at Kilwinning in the West of Scotland 1286, shortly after the death of Alexander III, King of Scotland, and one year before John Baliol mounted the throne. This lord received as Freemasons into his Lodge, the Earls of Gloucester and Ulster, the one English; the other Irish.
>
> By degrees, our Lodges and Rites were neglected in most places. That is why, of so many historians, only those of Great Britain speak of our Order. Nevertheless, it preserved its splendour among those Scotsmen to whom the Kings of France confided during many centuries the safeguard of their royal person.

This completely fictitious story which joined Christian knighthood with masonry caught the imagination of many French masons. The high degrees appealed not only to the upper classes, but also to those just below this strata of society who could now use masonic titles and wear costumes of masonic knighthood, and so feel equality, if only in lodge, with their social superiors. It has been suggested that Ramsay invented some or all of the high degrees, but this is not the case—he stimulated their spread. As will be seen from Appendix II, some form of *Ecossism* preceded his oration by several years.

Ramsay ensured that his Oration had the maximum publicity. In a letter now in the Bodleian Library at Oxford dated 2 August 1737 to a Jacobite named Carle, he wrote; 'I have sent the Oration which I did for the meeting, at different times, to eight dukes or peers and two hundred officers of the highest rank, and to his most noble highness, his Grace, the Duke of Ormonde'. (Ms Carle, No 226 folio 398.)

There is no doubt also that the supporters of the Stuart Pretenders gave encouragement to the high degrees. As has been explained, when masonry first came to France in the 1720s, the Scottish exiles took a full share in the work of the few lodges. When masonry sank in social status, particularly in Paris where the inn-keepers started to organise proprietory lodges for profit with warrants making themselves Masters for life, the Scottish exiles were no longer at home. In the high degrees, they would find Frenchmen of their own class, often sympathisers with the Stuart cause. Naudon, who has made a study of this question, includes influence by the Jesuits.

> Nothing is more certain than that the Stuarts and the Jesuits, who were their best supporters, used the *Ecossais* Masonic lodges whose respect for tradition and for Catholicism served their cause: and that the high degrees favoured this action.

On balance, it seems likely that the Stuart supporters were involved with the high degrees in their early days and this may have been one of the reasons for the word *Ecossais* but, after the failure of the 1745 attack on England, the Stuarts had no influence on masonry either in France or England.

Some modern writers consider that one of the basic reasons for the development of the high degrees in France was the desire by the best type of French mason to restore order in freemasonry. There is evidence to support this theory. French contemporary exposures give much information about behaviour in French lodges, particularly in the Paris lodges with permanent masters.

> ... considerable number of brethren who dishonour it by their low character and unpleasant aims.
> (Preface to *L'Ordre des Francs-Maçons Trahi*)
> ... wrong motives, thoughtless zeal and even less excusable reasons have admitted carelessly, and without selection, a number of people who dishonour Masonry, until one fears that it will pass away, like Rome, not of its greatest, but of its excessive growth.
> (*Le Sceau Rompu*)

To quote Naudon again, who is himself quoting other writers:

> In fact, the creation and development of the high degrees had a double

objective; on the one hand, the desire to rebuild the Order, invaded in the three degrees of Apprentice, Fellow-Craft and Master by a crowd of disorderly brethren, far busier with the petty distractions and with banqueting; with songs and gallantries, rather than with the duties of brethren who have been initiated; on the other, the ceaselessly growing interest, at this period, in all mystical and occult doctrines—a natural reaction to the materialism of the century.

There is no doubt that the early degrees of *Ecossais* masonry were designed in France to ensure a process of elimination of the undesirable, both social and masonic. There is even a suggestion of this in the little that we know of the contemporary English ceremonies, as they seem to have been restricted to Master Masons when this was, by no means, an automatically obtained degree. In France, only masons who were knowledgeable were admitted, usually after a strict examination and then, as we shall see, they were given powers of inspection over the symbolic lodges, and had some disciplinary authority. This authority, however, was not always recognised, certainly never in Britain.

It is perhaps wise not to go too far with the second half of Naudon's suggestion. Some French writers persist that English masonry owes much to the Rosicrucianism of the XVII century and Waite agrees with them. As a result of comparatively recent research into the life of Elias Ashmole, this is questionable. However, it is indisputable that the mystical parts of many of the high degrees of the XVIII century were fertilised by knowledge of the Kabbala, Rosicrucianism and even the mystical parts of the Book of Revelation. (See the author's paper in *AQC* 97 for the effects of Rosicrucianism on Freemasonry).

There may be doubts about the reason for the emergence of the high degrees. Whatever the reasons were, they had a remarkable effect in producing from about 1735 onwards, a flood of new degrees and rites which gradually transformed Continental masonry.

In conclusion, it must be stressed that Scotland had no real connection with any kind of high degree masonry in spite of the way in which the terms Scots or *Ecossais* were used during this period. As late as 1757, Dr Thomas Manningham, Deputy Grand Master of England was consulted by the Grand Lodge at The Hague about 'Scottish' masonry, and he replied:

> Lord Aberdour & all the Scotch Masons (or rather Scotch gentlemen that I have conversed with & I have made it my business to consult many) are entirely unacquainted with the Forms and Titles you mention.

In spite of this remark, it is clear that Dr Manningham was himself aware of the existence of high degrees, as he continued.

Amongst some of our lowest Brethren, I have met with, & frequently heard of such Irregularities. ... Three foreign Gentlemen and Masons lately visited the Lodge I belonged to & were introduc'd by me to the Grand Lodge & the Grand East; by discoursing with these Gentlemen I find <u>Germany</u>, <u>Holland</u> & <u>Switzerland</u> in some places have Orders of Masons unknown to me, viz., <u>Knights</u> of the Sword, of the Eagle, of the Holy Land, with a long train of et ceteras. ... I shall be glad of your Assistance & the Assistance of the Brethren in <u>Holland</u> to settle these intricate & confus'd Points & wish to know (especially from the Brethren who distinguish themselves by the Denomination of Scotch Masons) from whence they received their constitution, the Grand Master for <u>Scotland</u>, who I presume they acknowledge Head of their Society, being <u>entirely</u> unacquainted with their Order.

This letter has the double value of showing, not only that there was no official connection between the Grand Lodge of Scotland and high degrees, but also that the senior members of the premier Grand Lodge in England knew practically nothing about them in 1757.

However, *Ecossais* Masonry of some sort was still functioning in a small way as Manningham, in a previous letter, dated Dec. 1756, turns down a Dutch request to hold Scotch lodges, but writes:

'Of late some fertile Genius's here, have attempted considerable Innovations & their manner of working in Lodge, they term sometimes Irish, another Scotch Masonry, why, or wherefore they themselves best know; this I am certain off, all Innovations in our Society must lead to confusion. ...'

It is possible that he was referring to some of the lodges of Frenchmen then working in London, rather to the few lodges in the north-east of England who probably worked Harodim degrees of which he would have probably been unaware.

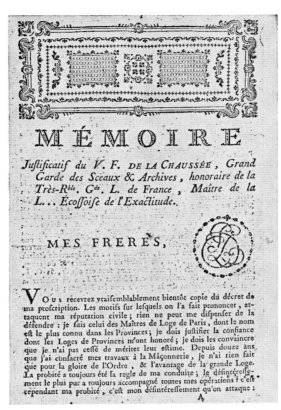

Facsimile of the cover page of de la Chaussée's pamphlet dated March 1773.

2

THE EARLY DEGREES OF ECOSSAIS MASONRY

MANY MANUSCRIPTS of high degrees exist in museums and private collections but few are earlier than about 1750. No printed ceremony before 1760 has been found.

In 1962, however, an article appeared in the Transactions of the Quatuor Coronati Lodge of Research No 2076 (*Ars Quatuor Coronatorum* Vol 75) by Eric Ward. This referred in detail to a ritual which he dated earlier:

> In the archives of the Pilgrim Lodge, there is a ritual in German, undated but apparently printed in the late eighteenth century. ... It is almost certainly translated or based upon a French version of an adapted English craft ritual, but the whole is so simple and free from elaboration as to suggest an origin not far removed from 1740.

There can have been no direct association with the Pilgrim Lodge which was not warranted until 1779. It must also be realised that all early high degrees followed the same style as the English Craft rituals, i.e. an opening, a making ceremony, an instructional catechism and a formal closing. However, as this ritual is definitely of an early date, and because it has been referred to in other books on the Rite, it is briefly described below:

In the preamble, it is stated that the lodge is hung with green cloth and that the brethren wear aprons lined with the same colour. The floor cloth is similar to that of the Third Degree, except for the addition of the word JEHOVA and an eight-pointed star. In the four corners are representations of a lion, a fox, an ape and a sparrow-hawk. These animals, implying virtues such as courage, cunning, etc. indicate an early date. Similar animals appear in the garbled ritual, referred to earlier in the French exposure, *Les Francs-Maçons Ecrasés* of 1747. Animals are also in the armorial device of the Grand Lodge of the Antients and appear in the Royal Arch ceremonies. The Lodge is then called to order:

... then immediately follows the question to the S.W. 'What time is it?'
The answer: 'It is high noon'. The J.W. is asked the duties of the S.W. and
replies that he has 'to see the doors closed, the Profane excluded and all in
order.' The S.W. in reply to the question, 'What is your name?' replies
'NOTUMA'. The W.M. after asking whether it is the correct hour,
declares the Scots Lodge open, laying his sword upon the book.

Ward suggests that 'NOTUMA' is an anagram of Aumont. The latter
was the mythical successor to de Molay, the last Grand Master of the
Knights Templar who was executed by the King of France in 1314. In
one of the legends associating Scotland with the high degrees,
Aumont is named as escaping to that country and keeping the Order
alive. However, a Duc d'Aumont was the first important initiate of the
King's Head Lodge in Paris in 1732, and the Lodge later took his
name as its title. The Aumont family was one of the hereditary
dukedoms of France and the name appears regularly in masonic
history, so there are too many alternatives to draw safe conclusions
about the anagram.

The candidate is announced as a Master who has asked to be made
a Scots Master:

> ... after his sword and hat have been taken from the candidate, he kneels
> on a stool between the two wardens' pedestals, with the brethren standing
> round him, pointing their swords. The candidate is then told that he must
> account for his actions and, having been tried and found guilty, must
> expect to suffer for his misdeeds. The J.W. is instructed to seize the
> candidate, turn him round, make him sit reversed on the stool, bind his
> hands together behind his back and place a rope round his neck. The
> W.M. then announces that he is the ruffian who has slain our Master [i.e.
> Hiram] and ought to be punished, but because of his knowledge, the Order
> will show mercy. He is therefore released and the W.M. reads the Oath.

The candidate took a simple obligation to preserve the secrets of the
Scots Masters' degree and to carry out his duty as a Scots Master. He
is entrusted with a sign and word 'Jehova', clothed with a leather
apron, given a grip and his sword and hat returned. The return of the
hat is significant as the privilege of wearing a hat in a lodge was once
claimed by all Scots Masters. Normally at this period, this privilege
was reserved for a Master of a Lodge.

The ceremony was continued with a retrospect of all previous
symbols, and he was instructed that there were no more than those he
had just received.

> ... They are closely related to the previous ones. As a Master, you left the
> slain Hiram in the grave. ... Here you find him dead no longer, his grave
> surrounded by palms, he has awakened.

The ceremony continues with some explanations and a catechism which starts with the question: 'Are you a Scots Master?' with the reply 'I was initiated in the Scottish Isles'. He is told that the colour of a Scots Master is 'Fire'. This colour, which appears in the French as *ponceau* or poppy-coloured, constantly recurs in the high degrees. When he is asked where he has previously worked, he has to reply 'At the rebuilding of the Temple under Ezra'. The Lodge closes at 'High Midnight, in the name of the Most High and through the Holy Number'. No explanation is given of this last phrase.

The degree is a curious mixture, as it includes parts of the Third Degree of Craft masonry, a Templar element and, with the reference to Ezra, a suggestion of the rebuilding of the Temple. This would indicate that it must have been produced early in the development of the high degrees, but its closer dating can only be a matter of speculation.

The first manuscript ritual of a high degree that can be dated precisely is that of an *Ecossais* Masters' Lodge but it has no similarity with the degree just described. A document, in three parts, ritual, lodge regulations and catechism, and dated 1751, has recently been found in private hands. However, signatures verifying the document show that it is a copy of one not later than April 1748. Copies of the document, dated about 1750 and in the *Bibliothèque Nationale* in Paris, are almost identical.

It is clear, from the *Bibliothèque Nationale* document, that the *Ecossais* Masters' degree was already part of a series of degrees which had been formed during the 1740/50 period. These degrees were

1°, 2°, 3°	— Symbolic Masonry.
1st Great Degree	— Perfect Master.
2nd –do–	— Perfect Illustrious Irish Master, Judge of the Workmen.
3rd –do–	— English Master.
4th –do–	— *Ecossais* Great Architect.
5th –do–	— Kt. of the East.
6th –do–	— Kt. of the Sun.

Possibly a little later than 1750

The 1748 ritual of the *Ecossais* Master (almost identical with the 4th Great Degree above) has certain similarities with the Royal Arch degree being used in parts of Britain at this time. These similarities have led some modern French Masonic historians to question whether the *Ecossais* degree was a French invention or a development from the British Royal Arch. There is not enough evidence to decide about such an interesting idea, but the following brief description of the French degree shows the chief likenesses.

There are three presiding officers, Solomon, the Most Excellent; Hiram, King of Tyre; and Mahanon, 'one of Solomon's favourites who succeeded the son of the widow whose fate we have mourned'.

The lodge is opened with 27 × 3 knocks and the words 'Submission', 'Union' and 'Gomez' are repeated in turn by the Most Excellent and his two Wardens. 'Gomez', a word which appears often in later high degree Masonry, means 'Beauty' and is traditionally the first word spoken by the first man when he saw what God had made out of nothing.

The candidate, dressed as an English Master, enters after he has proved himself, in an anteroom, in the three degrees of Symbolic Masonry. Before being presented to the Most Excellent, lustration of his face, hands and feet is carried out from what appears to be a representation of the Brazen Sea of the Temple. When he has taken his Obligation on the Bible, some drops of water are sprinkled on his head symbolizing his rebirth.

He is invested with a red collar to show that he should be prepared to shed his blood, as did HAB, rather than betray the secrets of the degree. Red, or flame-colour, is the colour of the degree, and used for hangings, robes and regalia. The investiture includes a grip given with the F.P.O.F. accompanied by the three words used at the opening of the degree. The sign of distress in the 1748 ritual is the one still used by Masons 'on the Continent of Europe' but in the *Bibliothèque Nationale* edition this is changed, presumably because of its use in other degrees.

The degree closes with a catechism of 44 Questions and Answers. These start with references to the Old Testament history but move forward to a Christian form as the following examples show:

Q   Where were you made an *Ecossais* Mason?
A   In the Lodge of St John.
Q   Where did St John hold his Lodge?
A   On the banks of the Jordan where the son of Jehovah was baptised.
Q   What do the 12 beasts signify? [On the Brazen Sea]
A   In the Old Law, they signify the 12 tribes: in the New, they designate the 12 Apostles.
Q   What does the red ribbon that you wear mean?
A   It symbolizes the Blood which the Saviour shed for the human race.

Many of the questions in the Catechism appear in high degree rituals in later degrees.

The first printed book to give ritual of the high degrees is *Les Plus Secrets Mystères des Hauts Grades de la Maçonnerie, dévoilés ou le Vrai Rose-Croix, Traduit de l'Anglois, suivi du Noachit, Traduit de l'Allemand A Jérusalem MDCCLXVII par* M. de Bérage. This book is not particularly rare and can be found in many masonic libraries. It was printed in Berlin, not, of course, Jerusalem, and was probably compiled by French masons, and edited by de Bérage. The degrees were certainly not translated from English—a claim added to suggest authenticity.

A facsimile edition was published in Paris in 1981. It contains interesting notes. All students of high degrees should read this book.

The following degrees are given in detail. As they all appear later in a more developed form in the A & A Rite, under different numbers, these are shown for comparison:

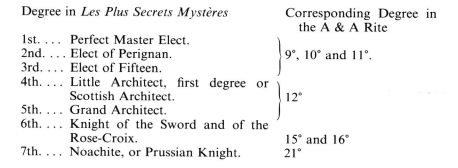

Degree in *Les Plus Secrets Mystères*	Corresponding Degree in the A & A Rite
1st. . . . Perfect Master Elect.	
2nd. . . . Elect of Perignan.	9°, 10° and 11°.
3rd. . . . Elect of Fifteen.	
4th. . . . Little Architect, first degree or Scottish Architect.	12°
5th. . . . Grand Architect.	
6th. . . . Knight of the Sword and of the Rose-Croix.	15° and 16°
7th. . . . Noachite, or Prussian Knight.	21°

With the exception of the Noachite or Prussian Knight degree, all these degrees are known to be of very early origin and are based on legends associated with the building or the rebuilding of the Temple at Jerusalem. The degree of Knight of the Sword and of the Rose-Croix tells the story of the release from captivity of the Jews under Zerubbabel by Cyrus King of Persia. As stated in Chapter 1, this legend is mentioned in 1744 in the exposure. *Le Parfait Maçon.* The inclusion of the 7°, Noachite or Prussian Knight is curious and seems quite out of place. One may assume that it was included in a book printed in Berlin because it was a German degree. Its eventual survival in the A & A Rite must be due to the references to the King of Prussia. All these degrees, as well as the other degrees of the Rite, are commented on in Appendix III. It will be noted that the Red Cross referred to above has no relationship with the Rose-Croix 18°.

The next printed book is the *Recueil Précieux de la Maçonnerie Adonhiramite* 'containing the three points of Scottish masonry, the Knight of the East & the true Rose-Croix, which has never been printed, preceded by the three Elect and followed by the Noachite, or the Prussian Knight, translated from the German'. This was the second volume of the same name and was published in 1785. The first volume, published some years earlier, contained the three degrees of Adonhiramite Symbolic Masonry and the Perfect Masters' Degree 4°. The *Recueil Précieux* is a copy of *Les Plus Secrets Mystères* with the important difference that a condensed form of the Rose-Croix degree, as we know it, follows the degree of Knight of the Sword. This seems to be the first time that a version of the modern Rose-Croix theme appears in print.

One more printed book, apparently written about 1769, though not appearing until about 1781, is important as giving the first ritual of the Kadosh or Knights Templar degree. It is known under the title of '*G.I.G.E.* [Grand Inspector General Ecossais] *Chevalier Kados, connu sous les titres de Chevalier élu, du Chevalier de l'aigle noir.*'

In addition to these few early printed books describing degrees, there are many collections of manuscripts which show that hundreds of degrees existed — a friend of the author can list over a thousand — though many were never used, and there were at least a score of different rites. In the second half of the XVIII century, the proliferation of degrees was remarkable. For example, the Rite of Strict Observance of 1754 had 7 degrees; the Clerks of Relaxed Observance of 1767 had about 12; the Primitive Scottish Rite of 1770 had 33; while, of the many later rites, that of Mizraim had nearly 100. Mackey's *Encyclopaedia of Masonry*, to be found in many masonic libraries, lists most of these degrees and rites. Manuscript books are comparatively common. One book, which will be referred to frequently under the title of the *London French Ms* is in the library of the Supreme Council in London. It has been dated as 'before 1790' and contains some thirty early degrees which are in an undeveloped form and certainly much earlier than 1790. None is the same as any degree of the A & A Rite but many are similar. Two other collections of manuscript degrees are also in the Library of the Supreme Council. Both were written by Henry Francken, dated 1771 and 1783, and will be referred to later.

It is possible to divide the early high degrees by types, though there is some overlapping; with some fitting into more than one group.

(a) Those dealing with the replacement of Hiram and the completion of King Solomon's Temple. They seem designed to teach the symbolical lesson that every man must make his own spiritual temple. Degrees, now in the A & A Rite, which come into this group are 4° to 8°, 12° and 13°.

(b) The 'vengeance group' concerned with elaborating that part of the story in the Traditional History of the Third Degree which deals with the finding and punishment of the assassins, and the rewarding of their captors. The titles of this group often include the word *Elu* (Elect). It requires considerable imagination to invoke anything but a negative symbolism from these degrees, though Albert Pike who rewrote many for the Supreme Council of the Southern Jurisdiction, USA, has tried to soften their somewhat sordid theme. The A & A Rite degrees with similar legends are the 9° to 11°.

(c) The rebuilding of the Temple by Zerubbabel and the search for lost secrets in the foundations of the old building. They seem to symbolise man's search for his personal divinity. These degrees have a variety of names but often refer to vaults and arches. The 14° to the 16° of the A & A Rite are in this group which also includes the various modern Royal Arch ceremonies (including the Babylonish Pass, not practised in England) and Cryptic Masonry.

(d) Degrees conferring powers of inspection and discipline. These usually start, as one would expect, with the candidate having to show his proficiency in the degrees which he will be expected to supervise in the future. The most important early degrees of this type were the Scots Master *ad vitam* and the Prince of Jerusalem. Appendix II gives regulations which conferred powers on the holders of these two degrees. About 1765, a rite of 25° was formed (see Chapter 5) with the degree of Sublime Prince of the Royal Secret conferring the highest powers on its holders. It first appeared as the 25°, but was moved to the 32° when the rite was expanded into the A & R Rite, about 1800. In the A & R Rite, the 30° to the 32° theoretically confer powers on their holders but, in England and Wales, these are now exercised entirely by the Supreme Council 33°.

(e) The Philosophical, Templar and Christian degrees. Known degrees in these categories number hundreds, but many are unimportant and little more than the whim of their inventor. Degrees of this type, as will be seen in Appendix III, fill all the gaps in the A & A Rite. The most important, to members of the rite controlled by the Supreme Council for England and Wales, is the 18°, which is referred to in the next Chapter. In many of the degrees of this group, it is possible to find the prototypes of those now worked in other rites in the United Kingdom and USA i.e. the Templar degrees, the Red Cross of Palestine, the Red Cross of Constantine, the Knight of the Holy Sepulchre, the Allied Degrees, etc.

3

THE 18°—ROSE-CROIX

THE 18° ROSE-CROIX is the only degree worked in full by Chapters of the Supreme Council for England and Wales. It is therefore best known to members of the Ancient and Accepted Rite, so much so that many of those upon whom it has been conferred do not appreciate that it is merely one degree in a Rite of thirty-three degrees. It is not unusual to hear brethren talking of 'joining the Rose-Croix' when they are actually joining the A & A Rite by having the 18° of the Rite conferred upon them in full, after having had the Intermediate Degrees given by name.

The degree is of particular interest to many masons, including those on the Supreme Councils of England and Wales, Ireland and Scotland, as it is probably their first experience of Christian masonry. It will be appreciated, however, that in certain foreign Supreme Councils the A & A Rite is now theist in character, but the interest in the 18° remains as it contains certain elements not found in other degrees in the Rite. It is strange, in these circumstances, that it has been accepted, by most English and American writers on masonry, without any attempt being made to discover its origin. Early writers unfortunately accepted quite uncritically that the degree began with a document known as the *Charter of Arras*. The story is that the degree was first given to Jacobite masons in a charter from the Stuart Pretenders about 1745 at a meeting of a Chapter held at the town of Arras in France. There are a number of variations of the story and the original document has never been found. In some versions, the event is put before the 1745 rebellion and in others after it. Unfortunately all are equally mythical. In one version, the Young Pretender is supposed to have referred to himself—somewhat ingenuously—as 'the Pretender to the English Crown': in another as 'King of England'. Actually, the Charter first made its appearance at least 15 years later and there is no evidence that there was a Chapter at Arras until about 1765 or that any of the Stuarts ever visited the town. Mackey in his *History* accepts the story but, in its supplement, the well-known masonic historian, W. J. Hughan, comments:

Seal of Rose-Croix Chapter of Arras dated 1745 to support the story of the forged Charter of Arras. The Chapter was actually started in 1765 or later.

At p 280, Dr Mackey cites the *Charter of Arras* (Rose-Croix) said to have been granted by Charles Edward Stuart. Now is it likely, is it even possible, that in his father's lifetime, he would describe himself as 'We Charles Edward, King of England, France, Scotland and Ireland?' Surely, in the face of such a declaration, there is no authority to say as to the authenticity of this Warrant 'There appears to be no doubt'? It could not be authentic if the documents contained such a title.

The modern Rose-Croix degree seems to have originated from one that was mainly of German origin and associated with the Rite of Strict Observance which, in its turn, was influenced by Rosicrucianism. The correspondence of the masons at Lyons of this period is in the archives of that city, and has been studied by Madame Alice Joly who subsequently wrote *Un Mystique Lyonnais et les Secrets de la Franc-Maçonnerie, 1730—1824*, in 1938. Her researches show that the Rose-Croix degree was developed by a Frenchman, Jean-Baptiste Willermoz, a leading local mason. He was the moving force behind a group of Lyons masons forming a new rite of 25 degrees about 1761, the last of which was Knight of the Eagle, of the Pelican, Knight of St

Andrew or Mason of Heredom. Most of these degrees were little more than names until Willermoz developed them. In 1761, he was corresponding with a Master of one of the Metz lodges, an important mason named Meunier de Précourt, who was in touch with a number of nearby German lodges. De Précourt knew little about the Rose-Croix degree, except that it existed in some form in Germany, and it is not known where he got his information.

A plausible theory is that the influence in passing the information came from the Baron de Tschoudy who wrote the book about the Kadosh degree, referred to in Chapter 2. De Tschoudy lived in Metz from 1756 to 1765, presumably busy at writing his book, *L'Etoile Flamboyante*, which was published in 1766. This book covers masonry generally but includes much material about the high degrees. On account of his nationality, he had many Central European contacts and would be able to compare the various rites. He shows his approval of the new Rose-Croix degree by printing in *L'Etoile Flamboyante* a long and critical letter from 'an old masonic friend':

> I make out a similar case [of approval] for the Rose-Croix, not that of the inextinguishable lamp [presumably some earlier degree of the same name] but the Rose-Croix properly called 'or Mason of Heredom' though in truth it is no more than a new type of Masonry or the Catholic religion put in a degree.

Whatever the contacts were, de Précourt wrote to Willermoz in 1762 that the German Rosicrucians knew of the 'Order of the Temple' and that they were in possession of 'a thousand marvellous secrets'. These secrets, he apparently passed to Willermoz, and Naudon's suggestion is that they were the basis upon which Willermoz completed the ritual of the Rose-Croix about 1765. Willermoz's degree, if he was in fact the author, did not come entirely from German sources. A degree of Knight of the Eagle is also thought to have been in existence at least as early as 1761, with recipients using the title of Sovereign Prince Rose-Croix. The degree may have been a name only but it is possible that Willermoz knew about it and included extracts in those parts of his degree which dealt with the Knight of the Eagle.

A curious feature of these events is that, within months of Willermoz completing his degree, the printed book of ceremonies, *Les Plus Secrets Mystères*, was published and this had a degree 'The Knights of the Sword and of the Rose-Croix' which was totally unlike Willermoz's version. The latter became popular very quickly though the following letter suggests that, for a short while at least, there were attempts to restrict it to selected Masons. The letter, written in January 1767, is from the Comte de Clermont the Grand Master, to the Marquis de Gages the Provincial Grand Master of the Nether-lands. The letter is specially curious as it directly contradicts the views of the contemporary writer, Brest de la Chaussée (given in Chapter 1), who said that the Comte de Clermont took no interest in masonry. In his letter, the Comte de Clermont wrote:

> I have always tried to hold [my people] tightly through the beauty and purity of our work, so I have only allowed a small and limited number the sublime Rose-Croix degree in all its perfection, only including the seven Grand Masters. [He may have meant Provincial Grand Masters or Masters of Lodges]. It is true also as said Zambaut [Secretary-General of the Grand Lodge of France] that those who know it are admitted with honours into my Royal Lodge. [Is this the inner circle of the Council of Knights of the East?] But, although the number is very large, owing to the indiscretion of my people, those who know everything is limited to thirty-three.

In spite of the Comte de Clermont's hopes, there was a body founded in Paris in 1768, calling itself the First Sovereign Chapter Rose Croix. It issued Statutes and Regulations in June 1769 and the first two Articles show its claims and status:

'The knights of Rose Croix are called knights of the Eagle, of the Pelican, Sovereigns of Rose Croix, perfect Prince Masons free of Heredon.

The name of Heredon is added to the other qualities because of the place where the knights took their origin which is so called.

At Heredon, there is an old castle on a mountain, situated between the west and the north of Scotland, 60 miles from Edinburgh, seat of the G.M. of Ecossais masons which very often is also at Heredon though he normally lives in the latter town. The one and the other are only visited annually.

It is at Heredon that the S.G.M. of the R.C. has his seat, as does the Chapter, although the castle has lost much of its splendour. It is here that the degree was held for the first time and where is kept the exact register of all the regularly constituted knights. . . .

This chapter being more important than the Mother Lodge of England, is the reason why it has been given the powers and privileges referred to in the following articles.

Art. 2

The knights of the Rose Croix have the right to take the gavel in all lodges when they are polite enough to give it to them. But when one is refused, to displace no one, he has the right to place himself beside the master of the Lodge, before the officers, if he does not through humility place himself last in the apprentices' column'.

Whether it obtained the privileges it claimed is not known. As will be seen, similar claims had been made in the statutes issued to the lodges of the Grand Lodge of France in 1755.

This Sovereign Chapter started with seven members who would have received their Rose-Croix degrees in any of the many high degree chapters that were starting to practice the Rose-Croix degree about which the Comte de Clermont had written and which probably were starting to use the Willermoz ritual. The Chapter seems to have faded out about 1791 by which time it had initiated or affiliated some 600 knights. It is almost certain that it was from members of this Chapter or other high degree organizations in France that the 18° spread to Britain where, like in France, it claimed to be the most important or *ne plus ultra* degree, as is shown in Chapter 11.

A ritual of the degree came into Naudon's possession in 1956, and he dates it about 1765. It appears in full in his book, *Histoire, Rituels et Tuileur des Hauts Grades Maçonniques*, 1984. Another version, with wording very similar, though slightly less developed, is in the *London French Ms* and must be of approximately the same date. The text in the *Francken Mss* of 1771 and 1783 closely resemble these earlier versions and show that little amendment took place in the first 20 years of the degree's existence. All subsequent texts show surprising similarity with the 1765 original, and there seems to be far less alteration in this degree, than in any other of the Rite, in the two centuries since it was first produced.

The Naudon and the *London French Ms* have almost similar long prefaces which explain the names of the degree. These, slightly shortened, are as follows:

It is called **Knight of the Eagle,** one of the oldest names for the Son of Man who came to earth to redeem the human race. His power, independent of the Father, is symbolised by the eagle as the first name of the degree.

It is also called **Knight of the Pelican** because the pelican is compared with Our Saviour who shed His blood to redeem us, as the pelican shed his blood to feed his young.

It is also called **Rose-Croix** because the Masters of the early Scottish lodges struck medals with the design of a Cross, thus symbolizing the Passion of the Saviour on the Cross. Some of these medals later came into the hands of ignorant brethren, who did not realise the significance of the symbol and called themselves Knights of the Rose-Croix.

It is called **of Heredom** because the first lodges of the degree were held in a mountain of that name, between the East and North of Scotland.

It is then called **Knight of St Andrew.** The early Scottish lodges took different names, but there was one nameless lodge which met on the feast of St Andrew, patron saint of Scotland; and they were called St Andrew's Masons. When Masonry was revived, some of the jewels of this lodge came into the possession of German Masons, who thought that the cross of St Andrew was the cross of Masonry.

Finally, it is called the **Perfect Mason,** because it is the 7th and last degree of Masonry, to which only Christians can belong as they have submitted to the New Covenant; the former six degrees belonging to all believers in other religions.

It is possible to note certain useful facts in the development of the high degrees from the wording of these prefaces:

(a) They provide convincing proof of the persistent hold that totally imaginary legends about Scottish masonry had on Continental masons, and confirm why the high degrees were called *Ecossais*. The deliberately vague definition of the word 'Heredom' also confirms its mythical character. It seems to have first been seen in print in France in *Les Plus Secrets Mystères*, but may have been much earlier, as it was in England, in manuscript.

(b) These prefaces are the bases for some of the unexplained parts of our modern ritual. Members of the 18° will recognise phrases which have moved from the early prefaces into the body of our modern ceremonies. The title Knight of St Andrew, has moved to the 29° though it does not seem to have taken any part of the degree with it, except perhaps some of its mysticism.

(c) The mention of the 7th and last degree refers to the early high degree rite used by *Ecossais* masons in Paris and elsewhere. This is dealt with in the next Chapter. One may assume that the 'royal lodge' referred to by the Comte de Clermont was part of this rite. The uncertain dating of the prefaces makes it impossible to be sure when the French high degrees were, in fact, limited to seven degrees. The Modern French Rite of seven degrees only started about 1786.

Until recently, any suggestion that the Rose-Croix degree might have owed part of its development to Rosicrucianism would have been unpopular. Fortunately, a more balanced view is now taken and no longer is everything connected with mysticism dismissed as bogus. The three documents telling the story of the life of Christian Rosenkreutz deal with a mythical being who never existed. The legend is of a man who, in fact, practised the same principles as those which form the fundamentals of the 18°. Alchemy and occultism have no part in the real story. They came afterwards. Nevertheless, a school grew up of men who either claimed to be Rosicrucians or to follow the Rosicrucian doctrines. They invented a mystical symbolism which had an important effect on mystical thought from about 1610—when the documents started to appear—until the end of the XVIII century. We now know that there was a strong element of the Rosicrucian mysticism in Germany and some of it found its way into the Rite of

Strict Observance in the middle of the century. With the influence that this Rite seems to have had on the developers of the ritual of the Rose-Croix, it was inevitable that the symbolism followed. The symbolic association is stressed by Waite in his *Brotherhood of the Rosy Cross*.

> I am personally convinced that the whole arrangement of the Rose-Croix Grade, its clothing, its jewel, its entire *mise-en-scène*, the chambers in which it is worked, are reminiscent of the older order. The three points are in crude correspondence with the Hermetic working in Alchemy—blackness, death and finally resurrection into the red or perfect state. . . . I could carry these intimations much further . . . exhibiting parallels drawn from Rosicrucian and Hermetic texts on the Cubic Stone, the seven mystical circles, the Rose of Sharon, the Lily of the Valley, the Eagle. . . . The bond of kinship lies upon the surface and those that have eyes can scarcely fail to see it.

Nevertheless, having read this quotation, it is essential not to forget that the 18° is a Christian degree which has used some Rosicrucian symbolism to illustrate its Christian message.

As is pointed out by the author of this book in his pamphlets, *The Scripture References to the Rose-Croix Ritual* of 1970 and *A Commentary on the Rose-Croix Ritual*, 1983, the setting of the degree covers the last three days of Holy Week (three o'clock on the afternoon of Good Friday to about six o'clock on the morning of Easter Sunday). While it would be inappropriate to expand this statement here, it will be obvious that the Christian element is as plain as the Rosicrucian symbolism. Tschoudy was mistaken when he referred to the degree as 'the Catholic religion put into a degree'. He was equally in error to suggest that the last part of the ceremony was no more than a celebration of the Mass. This is a religious service of thanksgiving. The final part of the 18° may correctly be compared with the αγαπη (agape) or love feast which, in the early Christian Church, followed the weekly meeting. This had no religious significance and was no more than 'a feast of fraternal affection'—as it is to-day in the 18°—before the meeting dispersed. Another, and equally suitable simile, is that of the loving or stirrup-cup given to the knight before he starts his travels.

The source of the present ritual used in this degree is discussed in Chapter 18.

4

THE DEVELOPMENT OF ECOSSAIS MASONRY IN FRANCE

IN 1761, a French mason, a creole named Etienne Morin, was sent to the Western Hemisphere to organise its expanding masonry. The events that led up to his departure are complicated, and made more difficult by there being at least two schools of thought among modern masonic writers about this period in the development of the high degrees. What might be called the 'Bordeaux' theory, whose supporters include R. S. Lindsay in his *Scottish Rite for Scotland*, recently reprinted and available from the Supreme Council, Grand Lodge for Scotland; Alain Bernheim in the Transactions of the Lodge Villard de Honnecourt in 1974; and J. Fairbairn-Smith in the *Rise of the Ecossais Degrees*, suggest that high degree masonry had its French beginnings at Bordeaux, while the 'Paris' theory is that this is little more than a myth. It is a fact that Morin did go to the West Indies from Bordeaux, as will be recounted later, and it is an important link in the chain of the development of the A & A Rite. The two opinions about the events that led to his departure are not hard to reconcile.

The Bordeaux story starts with the foundation of a lodge there in 1732 by Englishmen principally engaged in the wine trade. It took the name of *Loge L'Anglaise*, though it originally had no connection with the London Grand Lodge, but it probably worked an English ceremony in English for some years. It submitted, many years later, for reasons quite unrelated to the present story, to the Modern Grand Lodge and received the number 204. It still exists as No 2 in the jurisdiction of the *Grande Loge Nationale Française* as *La Loge Anglaise 204*. Soon after the Lodge had founded itself, it warranted another lodge, *Loge la Française*, presumably composed of Frenchmen. *Loge L'Anglaise* refused, all through its history, to have anything to do with high degrees, but *La Française* seems to have welcomed them and started an *Ecossais* lodge sometime after 1740. It is not known how this started but there is a persistent story of an

English 'Admiral Mathews' communicating high degrees, though where this happened is not stated. There is also a suggestion that Morin brought high degrees to Bordeaux, having got them from the British governor of the Leeward Islands. There was a civilian who was an English Provincial Grand Master from 1738 onwards and his full title was 'Willm Matthews Esq, Captain-General & Governor in Chief of his Majesties Leward, Caribe Islands & and Vice-Admiral and Chancellor of the same.' The result was an Admiral, General and Civil Servant in the same person. This would explain why he appears in documents as both Admiral and General.

Matthews seems to have been Governor from at least 1720, and whether he visited England during this period is not known, No Grand Lodge records exists, except his appointment as P.G.M.

How he could have communicated high degrees to Frenchmen at this period is a mystery. It will be appreciated that the basis of the Bordeaux high degree masonry and the R.A. legend have many similarities; enough perhaps to interest French masons. This suggestion is the only answer at present to four mentions in French documents of the Matthews story dating from 1746 to 1763.

There is, however, no doubt that Bordeaux was a centre of elementary high degree masonry from about as early as 1740. The evidence that supports the theory that Bordeaux was the birthplace of high degree masonry in France comes from two main sources.

(a) Documents produced by a Russian refugee, Nicholas Choumitsky, for the *Saint-Claudius* Lodge of Research of the *Grande Loge Nationale Française* in 1927. The documents are reputed to have been preserved in the Ukraine during the French Revolution but this story is highly unlikely. Their main interest is that they include letters written by Morin from the West Indies. Unfortunately, Morin is usually referring to events which took place many years before the letters were written and his dating is often incorrect. A number are reviewed in 'Some Mid-Eighteenth Century French Manuscripts' in *AQC* 40, by N. S. H. Sitwell and 'Some Early Elu Manuscripts' in *AQC* 44 by Lionel Vibert. (Morin's masonic career is given later in this Chapter.)
(b) A collection of some 130 manuscripts from Bordeaux, known as the 'Sharp Collection', now in the archives of the Supreme Council of the Northern Masonic Jurisdiction USA. Sitwell knew of these manuscripts and mentions them in his papers.
(These, and copies of the 'Sharp Collection', are all in the UGL Library.)

These documents have suggested to Fairbairn Smith and other protagonists of the 'Bordeaux school' that there was a *Mère Loge Ecossaise* (Mother high degree lodge) at Bordeaux which controlled high degree masonry in France from about 1740. Its actions are shown to have included the following:

(a) It warranted, through a Bro Lamolère de Feuillard, a Lodge of *Parfaits Elus* in Paris in 1747.

(b) It warranted, or recognised, some seven *Ecossais* lodges in the Western Hemisphere between 1748 and 1757.

(c) It issued 'Rules and Regulations' to 'all Ecossais lodges'.

(d) It was consulted by the *Ecossais* lodges at Toulouse, Marseilles and other masonic centres about internal disputes, acting as an arbitrator.

(e) It received a request to form an *Ecossais* lodge from masons in New Orleans in 1763. This was later granted and one was founded in 1763, thus ante-dating by four years the Lodge at Albany, hitherto thought to be the earliest high degree lodge on the American mainland.

(f) It appointed Lamolère de Feuillard as a Deputy Inspector in 1752, nearly a decade before Morin received his patent from Paris.

The evidence to support these claims is too strong to be dismissed as a myth. However, in order to get the position of Bordeaux into a proper perspective, the organisation of masonry in France must be considered. The Grand Lodge in Paris, and its high degree offshoots, had little control outside the city. The Grand Master, the Comte de Clermont, even though respected as a royal prince, had no more than a theoretical, titular authority in the provinces. The Paris Grand Lodge had a very restricted membership of the Masters of the Paris Lodges, some lodge delegates and a number of senior masons; in the early days, usually of the nobility or personal appointments of the Grand Master or other senior masons of the Grand Lodge. The senior Grand Officers were represented by unimportant deputies who could command no authority in the French provinces. As a result, there were semi-autonomous masonic centres, usually including the high degrees, in most large cities such as Marseilles, Lyons, Narbonne, Metz, Le Havre and Bordeaux. The mother lodge in these centres warranted other lodges in their own areas and exercised some control over them. Submission to the Grand Lodge in Paris by one of the mother lodges could only have been voluntary. Submission by an individual lodge to its mother lodge was also, in practice, voluntary; and cases of insubordination were not infrequent in French masonic history. The mother lodges worked the Craft degrees and, when the word '*Ecossais*' was in their title, it did not necessarily imply that high degrees were worked. In practice, however, most did so.

From the earlier days of *Ecossism* in France, there were conflicting rites, each with their own degrees. Sitwell in a paper now in the library of the Quatuor Coronati Lodge, which may have been read to the St

Claudius Lodge in Paris, but which was not used by the Quatuor Coronati Lodge, suggested that there were two forms of *Ecossism* which he calls the 'false' and the 'true', the latter being the high degrees worked by the Bordeaux groups.

> (a) The 'false' system was the Vengeance School i.e. the assassins' punishment and the rewards for those who captured them. This developed into the *Elu* (Elect) degrees of the A & A Rite (9° to 11°) and was later expanded to include the Templar or Kadosh degrees which call for vengeance against those who killed the Grand Master of the Templars, Jacques de Molay, and the other knights of the Order of the Temple. Nevertheless, it is odd that it seems to have been this system which first developed masonry towards Christian themes based on the *New Testament.*
> (b) The 'true' system was the Judicial school and provided the legends necessary to stop the confusion caused by the death of Hiram and the steps taken by Solomon to restore order and progress in the rebuilding of the Temple. The system developed, in due course, into the 4° to the 8° and the 12° to the 14°.

Sitwell's theory is probably too rigid as there seem to have been several rites in being in France from the 1740s onwards, each considering itself the genuine *Ecossism*. Extracts from a letter from Paris to Bordeaux, dated 1750, make this clear:

> I was initiated by him [Stephen Morin] into the mysteries of *Ecossais* perfection, as it was called, in 1744. . . . I have at last disentangled the varieties of *Ecossism* from the chaos in which they were buried; in very truth there are no mysteries because there was hardly any sense in them. But now it is all clear; what we called our *Ecossism* is nothing else than the Old Mastership which was changed at the death of H and which was confided by Solomon to a very small number of *Elus Parfaits* [Perfect Elect] whom we represent. . . . I have only one remark to make and that is, to become a Knight of the East, one must be *Elu Parfait*, and to be *Parfait* [that is a member of the high degrees] one must have passed the 9 degrees of Freemasonry. . . . There is a Council of Knights of the East at Paris, but in addition to not having our *Ecossism*, they are in error as regards their Knights of the East.

Bordeaux's claim to consideration is that it was the principal, though not the only, masonic centre which was warranting lodges overseas. Whether it was also the first high degree centre is not known. The matter is not really important as the period was the start of intense activity in the invention of high degrees and rites throughout France.

Little is known about what was actually taking place in the Paris area in the development of high degrees from about 1740 to 1754. The fact that the Bordeaux organisation was able to warrant a high degree lodge in Paris about 1747 may merely reflect a lack of interest in the self-centred Paris lodges, many of them controlled by tavern-owners who used the lodges to increase their trade and were quite satisfied with the existing masonry. The claims of Paris as a centre for early high degrees are proved by the statutes of *Loge Saint-Jean de Jérusalem*, the Grand Master's lodge referred to in Chapter 1, which laid down their times of meeting *viz.*:

> *Article XXXX* The ordinary Masters will assemble with the Perfect and Irish Masters three months after St John's day: the Elect Masters six months after: the Scottish nine months after and those with higher degrees when they consider it suitable.

These statutes were issued in the name of the Grand Master, and one must assume with his approval, in spite of the anti-high degree regulations two years before. This suggests reasonable continuity of high degree working in the Paris area during the same period that the lodges at Bordeaux were claiming superiority.

From about 1755, events are difficult to follow. There is no doubt that masonry was in a disturbed state, though possibly it was not as serious as stated by Brest de la Chaussée, himself a member of the Grand Lodge:

> Our mysteries and our warrants became pure merchantize; anarchy was at its height with three Masters of lodges able to constitute another. One soon saw taverns [*cabarets*] with indecent orgies in our lodges, and candidates and our secrets were defiled by the lowest type of tradesmen, artisans, workmen, common labourers or even servants.

About 1758, a dancing master, Jacques Lacorne, a Master of one of the Paris lodges, who had met the Grand Master in connection with his profession, announced that he had been appointed *Substitut Particulier* (a deputy with limited powers) by the Comte de Clermont. This was apparently accepted and, for a short while, he brought some order into the proceedings of the Paris Grand Lodge. Unfortunately further quarrelling broke out which resulted in the Grand Lodge splitting into two parties. The revolt against Lacorne came from some of the Masters of Paris lodges who were led by a feather merchant, Martin Pény. Pény's supporters elected him as their president. He then issued regulations which attempted a reorganization with the object of influencing the election of grand officers. About this time, the Grand Master appointed a Paris magistrate, Antoine Chaillon de Jonville, to be his *Substitut General* (deputy with full powers).

Chaillon de Jonville, helped by Lacorne managed to have peace for a while.

Lacorne died in 1762 and his death was probably responsible for a temporary continuation of the peaceful situation. However, in September, the Pény 'Grand Lodge' sent a delegation to the Grand Master to try to undermine Chaillon de Jonville's authority: this failed and, in December 1762, Pény requested a truce with each side naming seven commissioners to draw up statutes for a new body. The result was the document known as the 'Statutes and Regulations of the Grand Lodge of France'. This was agreed and adopted about April 1763. When the new Grand Lodge met in 1763, all the major offices went to supporters of Chaillon de Jonville.

Through this period, the position had been made more difficult when de Jonville temporarily became interested in a new high degree, Kadosh; while Pény, who had previously had nothing to do with high degrees, was made a member of a newly formed body (sometime between June 1761 and December 1762) calling itself 'Emperors of the East'. This new order had been formed by a Brother Pirlet, Master of one of the Paris lodges. There can be no doubt as to the date of the start of this new Order. A manuscript written by Pirlet states that he formed the degree of Grand Emperor of the East on 22 July 1762 as superior to the Knight of the East.

When the new Grand Lodge was formed, Pirlet also only got a junior office with the result that, a few months later, members of the new Council of the Emperors tried to get rid of de Jonville, but were again unsuccessful. In 1765, new elections of officers for the Grand Lodge were held but they brought no improvement in the respective positions of Pirlet and Pény. The quarrelling continued.

In 1766, the Grand Lodge, tired (according to Brest de la Chaussée) of the many complaints addressed to it by the symbolic lodges in the provinces about the behaviour of the colleges of high degrees, issued a decree on August 14, curtailing the powers of high degree colleges in respect of symbolic lodges in their area. The decree, however, stressed the deference due by members of symbolic lodges towards members of the high degrees.

The Paris Council of Knights of the East gave their complete support to this circular, actually reinforcing it with their own version enclosed in the same package as the Grand Lodge letter. Many of the senior officers of the Paris Grand Lodge, being also members of the Council, signed both documents.

The circular written by the Council of the Knights was specially bitter about the Kadosh degree, condemning it as follows:

'All Masons, symbolic or High Degree of any degree are forbidden to recognize, confer or accept the degree known as G.I.G.E. [Grand Inspector Grand Elect] Knight Kadosh, which we declare detestable, as much contrary to the principles and aim of Masonry, as contrary to the principles and duties of the State and to the Church.'

Two weeks after the circular, the Emperors of the East and West, as they were now calling themselves, made another attempt to seize power in the Grand Lodge. The idea was to divide it into three parts i.e. symbolic degrees; high degrees up to the Ecossais degrees; and, under the control of the Emperors, all degrees beyond this. This attempt also failed.

Just over a year later, the Government, tired of the constant quarrelling in the Grand Lodge, ordered it to close itself. It remained theoretically closed, though the high degrees continued to function quietly, until 1771 when the Comte de Clermont died. The Grand Lodge was then allowed to reopen under the direction of the Duke of Luxemburg. However, its proceedings no longer affect the development of the A & A Rite and need not be taken further.

A Rite of Perfection

During these turbulent twenty years of French masonry, three important steps were taken which materially influenced the future of the A & R Rite. First, a rite now usually, but incorrectly, known as the 'Rite of Perfection' appeared. Correctly, the Rite should be known as the 'Rite of Sublime Princes of the Royal Secret'. To avoid confusion with the 'Lodge of Perfection' (1°–14°) and because the Rite is thought to have been invented by Stephen Morin, it is referred to in this book as 'Morin's Rite'. The title 'Rite of Perfection' appears for the first time in 1786 in the Preface to the Grand Constitutions.

In its full form, Morin's Rite consisted of the following 25 degrees.

1st Class	1	Apprentice.
	2	Companion.
	3	Master.
2nd Class	4	Secret Master.
	5	Perfect Master.
	6	Intimate Secretary *or* Perfect Master by Curiosity *or* Perfect English Master.
	7	Provost & Judge *or* Irish Master.
	8	Intendant of the Building *or* Master in Israel *or* Ecossais Master of the J.J.J.
3rd Class	9	Master Elect of Nine.

	10	Illustrious Elect of Fifteen.
	11	Sublime Prince Elect, head of the Twelve Tribes.
4th Class	12	Grand Master Architect.
	13	Royal Arch of Enoch.
	14	Grand Elect, passed Perfect Master, called of Perfection.
5th Class	15	Knight of the East *or* Knight of the Sword *or* the Sword Rectified *or* Knight of the Eagle.
	16	Prince of Jerusalem.
	17	Knight of the East and West *or* Knight of the West.
	18	Knight of the Rose Cross *or* Knight of the Pelican *or* Knight of the White Eagle *or* Knight of St Andrew *or* Herodim Masonry *or* Perfect Mason.
6th Class	19	Grand Pontiff *or* Master for Life.
	20	Grand Patriarch Noachite *or* Prussian Knight.
	21	Grand Master of the Key of Masonry.
	22	Prince of Libanus *or* Knight of the Royal Axe.
7th Class	23	Sovereign Prince Adept *or* Knight of the Sun.
	24	Illustrious Knight Commander of the Black and White Eagle *or* Knight Kadosh.
	25	Sublime Prince of the Royal Secret.

The first three of these degrees were worked in Symbolic Lodges, the rest in Lodges, Chapters or Consistories of the high degrees. The degrees were developed over a period. No complete and convincing list has been found earlier than those in the Francken Manuscripts. The recently discovered Ms of 1771 gives the degrees from the 15°–24°. The second Manuscript in the possession of the Library of the Supreme Council of the Northern Masonic Jurisdiction USA is complete. It was not published until 1935.

A third Francken Ms came to light after the first edition of this book was published. It is now on loan to the Library of the United Grand Lodge. The Ms cannot be dated but a reference in the text to 1786 shows that it cannot be earlier than that date. When it was found, the pages were unbound so it is possible that some of the contents are missing. However it contains the rituals of the 4°–25°, the regulations for Lodges of Perfection, and the 'Constitutions of 1762'. The text is in the handwriting of Francken, except for the 1762 Constitutions. The contents correspond generally to that of the 1783 Ms, though there are a number of errors of transcription, and some of the degrees have slightly different names and wording and their order is changed to that later to be adopted in the 1786 Grand Constitutions.

The history of the development of the Rite is as follows:

(a) The title 'Lodge of Perfection' was in use from about 1750 in the high

degree lodges based on Bordeaux. This Lodge of Perfection would not
have included the 3rd Class, the Vengeance degrees, but certainly had the
2nd Class and probably the 4th Class in which the Word, lost by the death
of Hiram, was found once more.

(b) At the same period, the degrees in the 3rd Class, and probably others
with names which included the word '*Elu*' (Elect), but with slightly
different procedures, were being worked in other parts of France. In Paris,
degrees of this type were to be found, but there were also lodges working
the Bordeaux degrees.

(c) By 1750, both the Paris and the Bordeaux schools were in possession
of the Knight of the East 15° but with differing procedures. We learn from
de la Chaussée that he also knew of the Knight of the East and West 17°
about 1762, but did not himself belong.

(d) As has been shown in Chapter 3, the Rose-Croix 18° did not appear, in
the form approximating to that now in use, until about 1765, but it was
known, at least by name, some years earlier. In 1765, it had a long and
complicated name and was considered to be the most important of the
high degrees. Its placing as the 18° out of 25 may have been due to its value
not being understood, or it may have been the top of the list when it first
appeared, other degrees being added.

(e) Even more difficult to understand is the 25° Sublime Prince of the
Royal Secret. The degree seems to have appeared for the first time as a
ritual dated 1768 and called '*Ralliement des Princes Sublimes*' (Gathering
of the Sublime Princes). It refers to 17 degrees only. Its importance lies in
the fact that it has the first mention of the Prussian influence in 'Frederick
III [obviously a mistake for II] King of Prussia, Grand Master and
Commanding General of his army of French, English and Prussian
Sublime Princes, knights of St Andrew of Scotland and faithful guardian
of the Temple'. The degree eventually was moved to be the 25° of the Rite,
an arbitrary decision probably connected with the mention of Frederick
the Great.

(f) There is no evidence that there was any fixed rite at this period. The
Council of Knights of the East, associated with the Grand Lodge of
France, represented the 15° and 16°. As they named themselves as 'Chief
Inspectors of the work for the Rebuilding of the First and Second
Temples', it seems certain they have nothing to do with the 17°–25° and
were probably not concerned with the '*Elu*' or Vengeance degrees. The
formation of a complete rite of 25 degrees is discussed in Chapter 5.

(g) It may be assumed that most of the new degrees, 17° to 25° were no
more than names but were developed during the decade.

The Patent to Etienne Morin

The second significant action taken at this time was the issue of a
patent, in August 1761, to one *Etienne* (Stephen) Morin giving him
certain powers to promote freemasonry throughout the world. The

original document has never been found and there are only copies of copies which date from about the end of the XVIII century. The usually accepted copy is in the archives of the Supreme Council of the Southern Jurisdiction USA. The French version, from which this English translation is reputed to have been made, came from one that belonged to Jean-Baptiste de la Hogue, father-in-law of the Comte de Grasse-Tilly, two men who figure later extensively in the development of the A & A Rite. The original French version which belonged to de la Hogue has now disappeared. This was made from an English version which belonged to another mason, Hyman Isaac Long.

Another version is in the book which de Grasse-Tilly produced as his 'Golden Book' when he returned to France in 1804. The book was presumably the register referred to in Article XVI of the Constitutions of 1786 which all members of the 33° were ordered to keep (see Appendix VI). De Grasse-Tilly's book was authenticated as follows, and it is presumed that de la Hogue's was also:

> I, the undersigned Hyman Issac Long P.M. [Prince Mason] Deputy Grand Inspector General, etc. declare that the above written patent, formerly granted to the very Wor. Bro. Stephen Morin . . . of which he presented a copy to P. M. Moses Cohen, Deputy Grand Inspector General for the Island of Jamaica, who himself gave me a copy is truly translated and extracted from my official documents.
>
> In witness thereof I have signed in the presence of Illustrious Brothers de la Hogue, de Grasse, Saint-Paul, Croze-Magnan and Robin as witnesses to this signature.

The authentication by Moses Cohen, Deputy Inspector of Jamaica, raises doubts. The name may have been common in the Island which had a large Jewish population but the only Inspector of this name in Voorhis' list in his *Story of the Scottish Rite* was not created a Deputy Grand Inspector until 1794, some 23 years after Morin's death. Nevertheless, there is no doubt whatever that a patent of some sort was issued. As will be seen in Appendix IV, it was issued in the name of the Comte de Clermont, Grand Master of the Grand Lodge of France, though there is no reason to imagine that he was directly concerned.

The signatories were all members of the Chaillon de Jonville group of the Grand Lodge and most held high degree rank as well.

The first signature is naturally that of de Jonville and the next is that of Lacorne who was the leader of the Council of Knights of the East. There is ample evidence that Lacorne actually signed the patent as all copies show his signature, though the other names vary in some of the copies. Lacorne's name proves that it was issued in 1761—it is actually dated 27 August—as he died shortly afterwards. It also proves that the rival new body, the Emperors of the East (whose title did not include 'and the West' for several years) though it may have been in existence at that date, could have had nothing to do with it.

The statement, made so often by masonic historians, that the Emperors of the East and West were responsible for the chain of events that led to the formation of the A A.S. Rite must be accepted as totally incorrect.

The patent is an important document in the story of the development of the A & A Rite and it is therefore given in full in Appendix IV. De la Hogue's copy, however, is a turgid and flamboyant document which can be summarised as follows:

(a) The full Council of the Grand and Sovereign Lodge of *St Jean de Jérusalem* and of the Grand Lodge, acting on a petition from Lacorne, decided to bestow letters patent upon Etienne Morin before his departure from France.
(b) Accordingly full powers are granted to Morin to form a lodge to expand Masonry in all the Perfect and Sublime Degrees in accordance with the present regulations. This Lodge of *St Jean de Jérusalem* will be called La *Parfaite Harmonie* and will be situated wherever Morin decides to make his residence.
(c) He is appointed 'our Grand Inspector in all parts of the New World' giving him power to establish Perfect and Sublime Masonry in all parts of the world.
(d) He is given power to appoint Inspectors in all places where high degrees do not exist and all brethren are ordered to obey him.

The signatories of the Patent had ample power to give Morin authority over the high degrees as well as over the Symbolic lodges in the New World, but it is not certain that the original patent did so. Morin wrote in a letter dated 1765 to the French Grand Lodge:

By virtue of the powers which your Grand and Sovereign Lodge had granted to me, dated the second month of the Masonic year 5760, and following the ordinary style, August 27th, 1761, signed by Very Worshipful Brother Chaillon de Jonville, substitute Grand Master, De La Corne etc. which powers constitute me as an Inspector of all the Lodges of America under French domination, and perpetual Wor Master of a Symbolic Lodge the *Parfaite Harmonie* with the liberty of keeping it in the place where I shall make my residence.

It will be seen that he makes no claim to authority over French high degree bodies overseas and never alludes to this in any of his other letters. Nevertheless, by 1765, he was in fact taking control of all high degree bodies in the French West Indies that would submit to him and, as we shall see in Chapter 6, over those in the British West Indies and America as well.

The de la Hogue version of the Patent, given in Appendix IV must therefore be treated with suspicion and there are other reasons as well:

(a) As stated, it gives Morin powers over the high degrees. This cannot be proved.

(b) In one of his letters, Morin gives a list of the signatories of his Patent. Research has shown that his list is far more likely to be correct than that in the de la Hogue document, which includes a number of distinguished masons who had no reason to be concerned in the matter.

(c) The high degree titles, after the signatures in the de la Hogue document, claim for their owners the possession of degrees which did not exist in 1761.

It is quite likely that Morin amended his Patent to improve his position. This cannot be proved, but there is little doubt that de la Hogue and his son-in-law amended whatever version of the Patent that they had, to give Morin's work complete legality and to give the A & A Rite a more distinguished background. We shall come on this unfortunate and unnecessary behaviour, on the part of these two men, when the Constitutions of 1762 and 1786 are considered.

There is some doubt as to who this Etienne Morin was. He is usually referred to as Stephen Morin though he normally spelt his name in the old-fashioned way as '*Estienne*'.

Until about 1927, Morin's name had only appeared in connection with this patent and little seems to have been known about him. As has been explained, between 1927 and 1931, documents about him were published by the Saint-Claudius Lodge of Research and *AQC*. Some of these documents were linked together and embellished by Alain Bernheim in 1974 in the Transactions of the *Villard de Honnecourt* Lodge of Research of the G.L.N.F.

The usually accepted theory is that he was born in New York in 1693 of French parents who had come from La Rochelle to America in 1691. It is suggested that his family were Huguenots, but that he was converted to Roman Catholicism when he moved later in life to San Domingo in the French West Indies. There is some confirmation of this story applying to a Morin in the archives of the Northern Masonic Jurisdiction, USA. However, that he was the Morin in question is contradicted by a letter written in 1757 by a mason in Martinique (French West Indies) calling Morin 'a creole born in this Island'. The correct definition of a creole, certainly at that date, means a man born in the colonies of purely European parents. Sitwell agrees that he was a creole and then makes the not unusual mistake of confusing that with a person of African blood, and drawing erroneous conclusions. Oxford says he was a Jew, but gives no reasons. Seal-Coon, who had access to Jamaican archives, and was responsible for the interesting facts about Morin's death and burial, agrees that his identity is a mystery. He quotes Gustave Bord's *History of French Masonry before 1815* as saying that there were no less than thirteen contemporary masons with the name 'Etienne Morin', and of course both names are comparatively common in France.

It is also suggested that he was the 'Mr Morin' who appears in the Register of the English Grand Lodge of 1730 as being a member of the Prince Eugene's Head Coffee House French Lodge, but there is nothing to confirm this. There is also a story which is much more probable that he may have visited one of the Bristol lodges, and actually by request carried out a ceremony on a French initiate.

There is no way of proving this as all Bristol records were destroyed by bombing in World War II. He refers to himself as a merchant (*négociant*) and this would be the reason for his travels between the West Indies and Europe. It would also explain his easy contacts in England when his ship was captured a few months after he had received his patent.

Fortunately the Morin with whom we are concerned had a very distinctive signature, and when his name is attached to a document, he can be identified with certainty. However, with so many possible Morins, 'our' Morin has been identified with certainty by Seal-Coon as dying in Jamaica on 17 Nov 1771 and being buried in the Protestant cemetery at Kingston.

Morin's early masonic career is equally uncertain. His initiation is not known but a recently discovered French document of 1763 asserts that he received an *Ecossais* degree from an 'Admiral Matthews'. This can only be the Matthews referred to earlier as Governor of the Leeward Islands though, as has already been stated, the latter's association with high degrees is a mystery. That Morin possessed high degrees at this time is proved by a letter from a French brother, writing to his mother lodge in Bordeaux in 1750, stating that Morin had initiated him into the mysteries of *Ecossais* Perfection in 1744.

Signature of Stephen Morin 1763.

Morin's first appearance in France is documented in the minute book of *Loge L'Anglais* of Bordeaux where he is recorded as a visitor on 3 March 1746, though in a letter that he wrote some seventeen years later he claims that he had founded an *Ecossais* lodge in that town in 1745. In July 1746, he was one of the signatories of the regulations of the *Parfaite Loge d'Ecosse* in Bordeaux and the next year he was Master of the *Parfaite Harmonie* Lodge. He then returned to the West Indies where he founded an *Ecossais* lodge at Le Cap in San Domingo. We can trace him again in France in 1750 at Paris, Bordeaux and Abbéville and, in the following years, in Martinique and San Domingo. All the available evidence is that he was doing good work in developing and spreading masonry, particularly the high degrees.

However, for some unexplained reason in 1752, the mother lodge at Bordeaux appointed a Deputy, Lamolère de Feuillard, who besides being an important mason, held a prominent official position in the French islands. Morin, as a trader, had no such position, though his masonic rank was the same as de Feuillard's and, when he tried to establish a high degree lodge at Port-au-Prince, he was rebuffed by Bordeaux who refused to recognize it 'until it had been recognized by our Deputy Feuillard'. This must have angered Morin and, from then on, he began to shift his allegiance from Bordeaux to Paris.

Various letters written about this time show that sometimes he was 'worshipped as a protecting god' with others strongly critical of him for 'innovations he was introducing' into *Ecossais* masonry. 'We are grieved that Bro. Morin has changed so greatly and regret it' wrote one of the local Masters and another of the lodges complained 'He and others are not true Masons'. These documents give the impression that the confusion was caused by differences in ritual between Paris and Bordeaux.

Morin returned to France about 1759–60 and became affiliated to the Lodge *La Trinité* in Paris, of which Lacorne was the Master. It was through his association with Lacorne that he received the Patent which gave him his powers in the West Indies. It may have been that the Paris masons wanted to have their own representative in the key positions overseas, as there was rivalry between the Grand Lodge and Council of Knights of the East in Paris and the provincial masonic centres, of which Bordeaux was probably the most important. Whatever the motive for the issue of the Patent, Morin was able to use it to overcome much of the opposition in the West Indies until the Grand Lodge began to receive complaints about his behaviour and allowed his appointment to lapse.

Seal of Rose-Croix Chapter, *L'Union Parfaite Orient de la Rochelle* with symbols clearly visible in the centre.

5
THE CONSTITUTIONS OF 1762

The third important event was the compiling of Statutes and Regulations for the Grand Lodge of France. Chaillon de Jonville, assisted by Lacorne until his death in 1762, managed to get the two sides together. Seven commissioners were appointed by each side to draw up rules both for the Grand Lodge and for regular lodges throughout the kingdom. The Statutes and Regulations came into force in April 1763 and were promulgated. Morin, as an Inspector of the Grand Lodge, would naturally have been one of the recipients. As he had left France soon after receiving his patent, the documents had to be sent after him. However his ship was captured by the British and he did not reach the West Indies until 1763. Later he wrote:

> '... Immediately on my arrival at San Domingo, I made use of my powers. I visited and inspected the established lodges, telling V Wor Bro Chaillon de Jonville, our Substitute Grand Master, by special letter dated 21 July 1763. The Wor Bro sent me in return the new statutes and regulations made by the 15 commissioners on the 25th November, 1762'

It has always been assumed that these documents included the Constitutions of 1762. No original of the Constitutions has ever been found and, until recently, all that existed were 'copies' written very much later. There is no evidence that any constitutions were ever sent from France and the discovery of a manuscript book in the Library of the Supreme Council for England and Wales, in circumstances recorded in *AQC* 89, has an important bearing on the subject.

One of Morin's first acts on his arrival in the West Indies had been to appoint a Dutchman, Henry Andrew Francken, as a Deputy Grand Inspector General. For the next eight years, Francken collaborated with Morin in his masonic work and, in 1771, he produced this manuscript book. Its authenticity is not in doubt as it is in Francken's known handwriting and is signed by him.

The first part of the book gives the rituals of the 15°–24°. A ritual of the 25° was originally in the book but has been removed by an unknown. The rituals in the 1771 book are similar to the complete set in the 1783 book, referred to earlier. This suggests that they were all available by this date.

There is a note at the end of the rituals about the Kadosh or 24°. This reads as follows:

'The Grand Inspector Stephen Morin, Founder of the Lodge of Perfection, etc. in a Consistory of Princes of the Royal Secret held at Kingston in Jamaica In the year of Masonry 7769, advertised the Princes Masons, that lately a commotion had been at Paris, and the Enquiry had been made, whether those Masons who stiled themselves kn^{ts} of *Kadoch* were not in Reality knights Templars.

It was therefore Resolved in the grand communication of Berlin & Paris, that the said Degree should be stiled kn^{ts} of the white and black Eagle and the Jewel of the Order should be a black Eagle &c. as mentioned in the 24th degree.'

The Kadosh degree had caused trouble since 1761. It was basically a Templar degree but Morin would have known about it when he was in Paris. In 1760, it was condemned, as we have seen, by the Grand Lodge of France and the Sovereign Council of Knights of the East. (see page 37). This was the commotion to which Morin refers, but it did not stop him from including the degree in his rite. His reference to the 'grand communication of Berlin and Paris' must be considered almost certainly as mythical.

The 1771 book also contains a copy of the constitutions of the Lodge of Perfection of Albany, New York, founded by Francken, on Morin's behalf in 1767. It is believed that the original still exists in the U.S. masonic archives (see page 60). There was also a 'Masonic Tree' giving all the degrees of the rite. The most important parts however are copies of what purports to be the Constitutions of 1762, dated 7 Sept, and Regulations for the Government of all Regular Lodges of Perfection, dated 25th day, 8th month, year 7762.

Until the finding of this 1771 copy of the 1762 Constitutions, all known copies were of many years later date. These later copies, where they vary from the 1771 one, must therefore be considered incorrect.

Up to now, it has been assumed by masonic writers that the 1762 Constitutions were sent to Morin from France, though there is no evidence of this nor is there any evidence of the association that he mentions between any high degree organization in France and a similar body in Berlin. The only high degree rite in Germany seems to have been the Rite of Strict Observance but its rituals and degrees were entirely different from those in the Francken Ms. In the Constitutions, there are references to 'the sovereign of sovereigns'. This can only be the start of the traditional association with Frederick the Great, King of Prussia. There is actually no evidence of any encouragement for masonry at this time from Frederick. He had lost all interest in it—and had said so—and he was, in fact, engaged in a struggle for survival; and was only saved from defeat by the unexpected death of the Empress of Russia. There is equally no evidence that the Constitutions were written in Paris, Berlin or Bordeaux—places mentioned in the various prefaces—or by any joint meeting of commissioners representing high degree organizations in Europe.

These cumulative objections to the authorship of the 1762 Constitutions being anywhere in Europe suggests that their production was in the West Indies and that Stephen Morin was responsible. Bro. Alain Bernheim of the United Grand Lodge of Germany's Lodge of Research No 808 and of the French Lodge of research, Villard de Honnecourt, was responsible for the work which makes this suggestion almost certain.

It has been explained above how the schism in the Grand Lodge of France was healed and that Statutes and Regulation were written in 1763. (These are given in full in *Francs-Maçons et Atéliers Parisiens de la G.D. de France*, 1973 by Alain de Bihan.) Morin received them as a Grand Inspector. These Statutes were in two parts, the first dealing with the Grand Lodge and the second with private lodges.

In his 1771 manuscript book, Francken deals with the same two subjects but puts the second part first. However, if we take them in the proper order, we find Francken's Grand Constitutions of 1762 (which are given in full in Appendix V) start as follows:

'The Great Statutes and Regulations made in Prussia and France, Sepr 7th 7762, Resolved by the Nine Commissioners named by the Great Council of the Sublime Princes of the Royal Secret, at the Grand East of France. Consequently by the deliberations dated as above, to be observed by the aforesaid Grand Council of the Sublime Princes of France and Prussia, and by all the particular & regular Councils spread over the two hemispheres.'

The Statutes and Regulations for the Grand Lodge of France start as follows:

'Statutes and Regulations decided upon by the fourteen Commissioners nominated as a result of consultations on the 3rd day of the 3rd week of the 2nd month of the masonic year 5763 to be observed and ratified by the G.L. of F. and all the particular lodges spread over the kingdom'.

Both the above are translations from the French. The first either by Morin or Francken and the second by the author. Their form is remarkably similar. Any differences that do occur are due to one referring to a Council and the other to a Grand Lodge, and differences in titles etc. In addition, some of the later articles in the Constitutions deal with high degrees and have no counterpart with the G.L. of France document. Nevertheless, it would seem, without doubt, that the Constitutions of 1762 are based on the Statutes and Regulations of the Grand Lodge of France of 1763; and many of the clauses in the former are copies of those in the latter. (Some examples are given in Appendix V.)

The Statutes and Regulations in the Francken Ms for individual lodges of Perfection start as follows:

'*Acquando Perfecit*. Regulations for the Government of all Regular Lodges of Perfection as transmitted from the Royal Council of the Sub^me Princes of the Royal Secret at Berlin and Paris (and observed by all Lodges of Perfection) to our Most Respectable Brother Stephen Morin Gnd Inspector of all Lodges, etc. in the New World and to his lawful Deputies.'

The contents of these regulations are clearly based on the 'Statutes and Regulations for the government of particular Lodges in France and their regulations with the Grand Lodge' of 1763. Some are word for word similar to those issued by the Grand Lodge but the difference between the work of lodges and high degree chapters is so wide that the comparisons cannot be taken too far.

Of special interest is Article 7 which shows that members of a Lodge of Perfection (Morin's 1°–14°) had to promise submission to the following senior degrees:

Knight of the East
Prince of Jerusalem
Knight of the East and West
Knight of the White Eagle and Rose-Croix
Patriarch of the Royal Axe
The Grand Pontiff
Chief of the Masonic Key
Knight and Princes Adept
Knight of the White and Black Eagle
Sublime & Sovereign Prince of the Royal Secret and the Gd Inspector & his Deputies.

Some of these degrees, in a document dated '1762', could have been no more than names, even if they existed. An additional proof that the date is impossible is in the name of the White and Black Eagle, only adopted by Morin in 1769 as a result of the 'commotion' in Paris in 1766.

Following these regulations and constitutions is a 'Masonic Tree'; one of those fanciful documents popular at this period. It gives the number of years service necessary in each degree before promotion to the next. Its main interest lies in the names of the degrees which vary from those given in other parts of the Francken Ms, thus showing how undeveloped was the new rite.

It is necessary to consider if there were any bodies in Europe who could have provided Francken with all this information. The most important high degree organization was the Council of *Knights of the East, Sovereign Prince Masons*. As already explained, this was the high degree council working with the Grand Lodge of France. It apparently controlled the Knights of the East (Morin's 15°) and the 'very illustrious and very valiant' Princes of Jerusalem (Morin's 16°). This Council would certainly not have produced the '1762 Constitutions' in rivalry to itself and, if it made rules about high degrees, neither Berlin or Bordeaux would have featured.

Superficially, the *Emperors of the East and West* was the sort of body to have invented the '1762 Constitutions' if only to annoy their rivals in the Grand Lodge. However, Morin never claims to have had any association with the Emperors and he was in amity with the Grand Lodge until 1765. It is not possible, moreover, to understand why the Emperors would have wanted to form an imaginery body, more important than themselves and based in Berlin and Paris, or how, if they did, Morin got hold of all their statutes and regulations.

It is difficult to suggest any person or body in Europe who would have gained by writing these Constitutions. When Morin left France, he sailed from Bordeaux, one of the high degree centres where he had been influential. He had quarrelled with the local hierarchy but he would still have had many local friends. They might have helped him but it was not until a year after he had sailed that the material upon which these Constitutions were based became available.

The date of the '1762 Constitutions' is an obvious invention as they could not have been written until after the Grand Lodge material of 1763 was available. If Morin wrote the Constitutions, he would not have needed to use them until about 1767 when Francken formed a Lodge of Perfection and a Grand Council of Princes of Jerusalem in America. Even then, only the second part, the Statutes and Regulations for Lodges of Perfection, was essential. However, the following year when Morin set up a Grand Consistory of Princes of the Royal Secret in Jamaica, one may be sure that he would produce all the documents, including the '1762 Constitutions' as authority.

The 25 degrees in Morin's rite were probably known, at least by name, when he left France in 1761. It may be assumed that he had access to the rituals up to about his 16° and in addition one or two of the others. He would thus have had no difficulty with the Lodge of Perfection (his 1°–14°) or the Princes of Jerusalem (his 15°–16°) used in America. He could easily have kept up to date with the later degrees as they developed in France. There was constant traffic between France and the West Indies, and we have mentioned his Bordeaux friends. The only doubtful degree is the last, the Sublime Prince of the Royal Secret and its origin is not known.

With the information at our disposal, it is hard to see who else than Morin could have produced the '1762 Constitutions' and invented what masonic writers—though never Morin himself—call the Rite of Perfection. No traces of anything resembling the Francken documents have been found in France, as one might expect, in such collections as the Sharp-Bordeaux papers or in the *Bibliothèque Nationale*. If there had been a rite of 25 degrees in Paris from about 1762, how would it have fitted in with the Sovereign Chapter of Princes Rose-Croix, founded in 1769, with the Rose-Croix degree as its climax? There is much extant correspondence about this latter body but nothing about what would have been its most serious rival. A further important point is that the high degrees were spreading to England (see Chapter 11) and Morin's rite and its later degrees do not appear. The *ne plus ultra* of high degree masonry in Britain was the Rose-Croix and remained so until the Ancient and Accepted Rite came from the USA in the next century.

In the Western Hemisphere, there were no competing bodies to challenge the start of a new high degree rite. As a result, the Constitutions and the other documents in the Francken Mss were all that were required as authority for Morin in Kingston. It is appreciated that high degree centres in France, such as Bordeaux, Marseilles and Paris continued to warrant high degree chapters in the Western Hemisphere, and Morin's Rite might have had little lasting effect if it had not been kept alive by Francken and the inspectors that Morin and he appointed. Its real growth started, as we shall see, when it was later exploited in Charleston.

Whether Morin wrote his rite for glory—the glory of being the supreme head of a masonic body—whether he was genuinely keen to spread high degree masonry or whether, as Choumitzky suggests in his paper to Lodge St Claudius in Paris in 1928, for gain, we shall never know. Morin died, possibly suddenly, in 1771, without any real power and penniless. We may not approve his methods but he seems to have been the true founder of the Ancient and Accepted Rite. For that, all members of the Rite will thank him.

It is not known whether Morin or Francken made the translations from the French in the 1771 book. Both were foreigners and their English is understandable but frequently much too literal a translation. Appendix V gives the Constitutions as Francken wrote them with the minimum correction in punctuation. As an original document published for the first time, it is better given as he wrote it. It can then be compared with the later 'editions' which it proves had alterations and additions.

Generally, the 'Constitutions of 1762' seem carelessly written, specially from Article 29 onwards for which there are no examples in the 1763 Grand Lodge document. The high degrees mentioned are incomplete and their names differ from those in other parts of the book.

The first four articles lay down the composition and dates of the meetings of the ruling body; the dates being the same as the meetings of the Grand Lodge in Paris. The ruling body, which is called the 'Sovereign Council of Princes of the Royal Secret' is presided over by the 'Sovereign of Sovereigns' or his Substitute General. The Sovereign of Sovereigns is sometimes called the 'Prince President'. This Council is composed of all the Presidents of Councils in the cities of Berlin and Paris. This seems to have been the start of the unknown superiors which led Morin or his successors to choose Frederick the Great.

There is much detail about the appointment and powers of the officers. The Articles, copied from the French document, read as if the intention was to give little power to any one person for fear that he might misuse it. In the turbulent and quarrelling assemblies of the Grand Lodge of France, this was a wise decision. Brest de la Chaussée in his *Mémoire Justificatif* shows how, as Keeper of the Seals, he was able to stop irregularities by refusing to authenticate documents. All this would have been unnecessary in a royal council, as envisaged by the Constitutions that Morin wrote.

Articles 22 and 23 deal with the usual disciplinary measures for offences, such as being 'heated with liquor' at the meeting of the Sovereign Grand Council. For certain offences, the Sovereign of Sovereigns had power to expel and reappoint someone in the offender's place. The impression is of a bourgeois assembly, hardly a supreme council presided over by royalty.

Articles 24 and 25 were important to the spread of Morin's rite as they give his powers. Overseas, an Inspector or his Deputy is given authority more or less to do anything i.e. 'erect, constitute, forbid, repeal or exclude according to his Prudence'. With his letter of appointment at the front of the Regulations for Lodges of Perfection, Morin gave himself absolute power.

Unfortunately, the conditions of the 1771 version of the '1762

Constitutions' appeared inadequate to those expanding the Rite after Morin's death and there are many amendments to later copies. No version appears to have been published until 1832, when the Supreme Council for France issued one. Two earlier copies, however, are in the archives of the Supreme Council for the Southern Jurisdiction USA. One copy dates from about 1798 and belonged to J. B. de la Hogue, and is certified as correct by his son-in-law, Comte de Grasse-Tilly. The other was made the previous year at Port-au-Prince in San Domingo from a copy certified by an American, Hyman Isaac Long, and four Frenchmen, including de la Hogue and de Grasse-Tilly. These two do not even agree. The former states that the Constitutions were issued in Paris and Berlin, as does the Francken 1771 text, while the other gives Bordeaux as the place of origin.

Previous books on the development of the A & A Rite have dealt in detail with the argument about the validity of the later versions of these Constitutions. The discovery of the 1771 copy now makes this unnecessary. All that is required is to point out how they were altered to fit in with the later expansion of the Rite.

(a) One of the certified copies of the Constitutions refers to them as having been sent out to the West Indies to de Grasse-Tilly. This remark, presumably to increase his importance, is ridiculous as he was not born until three years later.

(b) In the same copy, many of the signatories have '33°' after their names. The 33° did not appear until much later. This alteration of the original is an obvious attempt to justify de Grasse-Tilly's own 33° and to lay a foundation for its permanent inclusion in the Rite.

(c) In some copies, including de Grasse-Tilly's, the preface is far more elaborate than the original 1771.

... The present secret Constitutions emanate from the Grand Easts of Paris, York and Berlin, and from our well-beloved and illustrious Brother Frederick of Prussia, the 2nd Grand Master, Sovereign Commander-in-Chief of the Army of the Sovereign Princes and Knights of the White and Black Eagles, therein including the Prussian, English and French; also the Knights Adept of the Sun; of Libanus; of the Royal Axe; Rose-Croix of St Andrew; Knight of the East and West; Princes of Jerusalem; Grand Perfect Elect; Royal Arch; Mark Masons; P.Ms etc. Every Sovereign Grand Inspector General of the 33° exercises the same rights as the Grand East; he ensures that these Regulations are respected; is responsible for their execution so that the Instructions of the Holy Empire are effective for ever.

The anachronisms and impossibilities are obvious. As stated earlier, the 33° had not been invented. The reference to York must be imagination and possibly inserted to please American masons who worked the 'York Rite'. It might also help the spread of the Rite in the British West Indies. In fact, England and France were at war in 1762 so any masonic collaboration would have been unlikely. They were also at war from 1793 to 1815, except at short intervals and this was the period when the 'certified copies' were being produced. The reference to Frederick as the '2nd Grand Master' suggests a return to the legend of the Young Pretender having started high degree masonry. It could have been no one else, as the Comte de Clermont was still alive.

There are so many discrepancies in the versions of the 1762 Constitutions that it would seem they were first written for a comparatively small number of high degree Masons in the West Indies and the small part of North America that was then occupied. The branch of Masonry which Morin developed and for which these Constitutions were intended was elaborated as we shall see in Chapters 7 and 8, in Charleston. The Rite had to include or squeeze out the high degrees which had proliferated in the quarter century after Morin's death.

Naudon puts the curious story of the start of the Rite into its proper perspective.

> True legitimacy is not a matter of administrative instructions which create and organise the rituals and ceremonies. Such disappear in the course of time. The sources of legitimacy are traditions, and their tangible manifestations remain in the contents of the rituals and the use that is made of them.

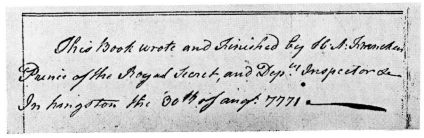

Facsimile of the ending of the 1762 Constitutions.

6

THE HIGH DEGREES IN THE WESTERN HEMISPHERE

As SOON AS Morin's ship left Bordeaux at the end of 1761, it was captured by a British warship and taken to England. As a civilian, he was not treated as a prisoner-of-war. Some masonic writers have suggested that this was due to his being considered as a man of consequence. This is not the case. He was of no particular standing as far as his captors were concerned, though he probably tried to use is position as a mason to his own advantage. It was then the normal custom for enemy civilians to be allowed complete freedom, and this continued for another forty years until Napoleon unexpectedly interned many hundreds of British civilians who, up to then, had been living in France without restraint. Morin could therefore go where he wished. The suggestion that he went to Edinburgh to look at the conditions of French prisoners-of-war there seems to be pure speculation. During the Seven Years War, there were few prisoners in Scotland, and Edinburgh was not a 'parole town' where officers could live in comparative freedom.

Morin describes his stay in Britain in letters which he wrote after he had reached the West Indies.

> At the beginning of 1762, I was seized on the seas and taken as prisoner by the enemy of the State to London where I received all the consolations and kindnesses and advantages that a mason could hope for in a like situation especially being also well recommended by you [presumably Chaillon de Jonville, Substitut Général in Paris] I had the pleasure of travelling often with the Very Respectable Bro the Earl of Ferrest [Ferrers] Viscount of Tamworth, Grand Master and protector of all the Lodges under English domination. I gave him in open lodge the patents you were so kind to grant me, to which he added his approval, congratulating me and favouring me with the title of honoured member of all the Lodges of England and Jamaica, where I received with this title all the services which I needed up to my departure for St. Domingo.

In his letter of 3 May, 1764, Morin also wrote:

Count Ferrest, Grand Master of all the Lodges under English domination, named me Inspector of its dominion in that part of the New World and decorated me with sublime degrees giving me a certificate that I am the only one constituted for the Lodges of the Grand Elect, Knight and Scotch Prince Mason.

The Lord Ferrers referred to had a curious history. He was born in 1722 as Washington Shirley, second son of the 3rd Earl Ferrers. He was an officer in the Navy for some years, serving with distinction in command of a ship in the Quiberon Bay expedition, but left owing to his interest in astronomy. In 1761, he was elected a Fellow of the Royal Society, as a compliment for a series of very accurate observations on the transit of Venus, and the following year became Grand Master of the Premier Grand Lodge. In the meanwhile, his older brother, the 4th Earl, after a trial in the House of Lords, was convicted of murdering his land steward. In spite of a plea of 'occasional insanity of mind', he was hanged at Tyburn in 1760, to which he was driven in his own coach, pulled by six horses.

According to Preston, in his *Illustrations of Masonry*, Lord Ferrers neglected his duties as Grand Master. This would have been hardly surprising considering that he had the complication of trying to regain the family estates, sequestered for his brother's crime. Actually, he attended four meetings of Grand Lodge out of the nine during his two year term of office. He was also WM of the Horn Lodge in 1762 so Preston's verdict seems not justified.

At this time, there were already six Provincial Grand Masters of the Moderns in the British West Indies and North America and it seems most odd that any Grand Master would give authority over them to an unknown Frenchman. Even Thomas Dunckerley, an extremely well-known English mason and Master of the Lodge in HMS *Vanguard* about 1760, was only given, according to Henry Sadler in his *Thomas Dunckerley, His Life, Labours and Letters*, 'authority to regulate Masonic affairs ... in any other part of the globe he might visit, where no Provincial Grand Master had been appointed.' Masonic records, including the Minutes of Grand Lodge, are very incomplete for this period. It is possible that Morin may have met Lord Ferrers, who might have been gracious and endorsed his patent, as was the custom with visitors to a Lodge, but this certainly conferred no powers. In any case, the Grand Master did not have the power to make him an honorary member of all lodges, if that is what Morin meant.

Sitwell states in *AQC* 40 that it was the rule, about this time in French Masonry, that travelling masons had to report to all Lodges they came across and have their certificates endorsed. It may be that Morin's claim that he had had his certificate endorsed was merely to show that he had obeyed this custom.

In 1762, there may have been a vestige of high degree masonry among some of the Frenchmen practising masonry in England, though there is no evidence to this effect. It is quite possible that Morin visited one of the very early Royal Arch Chapters which did exist at the time. If this is so, with the legend of the period not unlike that used in the 12° to 16° of Morin's Rite, he may have assumed that he was seeing 'sublime degrees'. While Morin was in Britain, high degree masonry was totally against the policy of the premier Grand Lodge, as is shown in the letter written by Dr Thomas Manningham and mentioned in Chapter 1.

Morin's patent as an Inspector gave him extensive powers over the Symbolic Lodges in the French West Indies. Whether he was actually given powers over the high degrees is debatable and depends on whether one accepts the copy of his patent produced by de la Hogue at the end of the century. We now know that, whether he had such powers or not, Morin intended to exercise them. What, however, is quite certain is that it gave him no powers over any form of English masonry unless it had the English endorsement which he claims was given to him by Lord Ferrers. On balance, it seems likely that Morin embroidered the stories of his travels to give himself authority in British territories where his French patent was worthless. If this is so, his scheme worked so well that he had no opposition from English or American masons, including one of the Jamaican Provincial Grand Masters. To put the matter in its proper perspective, it must be appreciated that only a very few of the masons in the English speaking parts of the Western Hemisphere were interested in the high degrees. At this period, the majority regarded them as the playthings of a few foreigners and some local eccentrics. The most important masonic question in North America and the British West Indies, and which deeply concerned the lodges, was the struggle for power between the Premier and Antient Grand Lodges of England.

When Morin arrived eventually in the West Indies in 1763, the position was that masonry was firmly established with lodges in most of the islands, but that the high degrees were confined to the French possessions, except for one lodge at New Orleans which was starting. The French high degree lodges were offshoots of the various mother *Ecossais* lodges in France and, though the mother lodge at Bordeaux was particularly active in San Domingo, others were also concerned. Many of the lodges had been founded by travellers, soldiers and sailors, and often had only a short life.

Morin's work in the West Indies has been studied by F. W. Seal Coon in his *An Historical Account of Jamaican Freemasonry* (1976) and the following paragraphs rely heavily, with his permission, on his local research.

Either on his journey from England to Port-au-Prince, or soon after his arrival there, Morin visited Kingston (Jamaica) where he appointed Henry Andrew Francken as his 'Deputy Inspector-General of all the Superior Degrees of Free and Accepted Masons in the West Indies'. The use of the words 'Free and Accepted' may be noted. The expression was not used as regularly in French Masonry as it was in British but it was to persist until it appeared many years later in the official title of the new A & A Rite. Morin probably used it as a link between the French and British masons in the West Indies. After his arrival in San Domingo, he appointed two more deputies to assist him there, and he also opened a lodge at Port-au-Prince, which he called *La Parfaite Harmonie*, as he had been instructed to do. This was his personal Lodge meeting, in theory, wherever he resided.

Information of Morin's movements is naturally vague, but it is clear that he was active in inspecting the lodges in the French possessions. Sensibly, he does not seem to have tried to do this in British lodges even though he was now calling himself 'Inspector and Deputy of the Grand and Sublime Lodges of France and England'. Many French masons also had never heard of the masonic bodies from which he claimed his powers, and felt that they owed no allegiance to him. There is no doubt that he tried to force his ideas and powers on everyone, and there grew up the allegation that he was feathering his own nest by selling high degrees. It is not surprising that he gradually became unpopular and complaints about his behaviour were made to Paris by some of the San Domingo brethren. On 17 July 1766, the Grand Lodge of France appointed a Bro. Martin in his place, i.e. 'gave him a patent as Inspector of the lodges in America and revoked the similar powers previously given to Bro Maurin [sic Morin] because the latter had responded badly to the confidence of the G.L.'

Morin could hardly have ignored his dismissal as his replacement arrived the same year and stayed until 1771. This and the known hostility of some of the local brethren may have been the cause of his move to Jamaica at once. Here he must have taken control of the high degree organization that he was setting up. This could have entailed writing the Constitutions of 1762 and the other documents in the 1771 Francken Ms. Soon after Francken returned from a visit to the American Colonies, Morin set up 'A Grand Chapter of Princes of the Royal Secret or Ne Plus Ultra' in Jamaica. The Warrant, a copy of which is in the 1783 Francken Ms is dated 30 April 1770 and appoints William Winter, the Provincial Grand Master of the Moderns in Jamaica, to be 'President and Grand Commander of all Grand Chapters, Grand Councils and Consistories'. The authority for the warrant is the 'Statutes, rules and regulations of the nine Commissioners named by the Grand Chapter of Sublime Princes of the R.S. at the Grand East of France & Prussia, consequent on the deliberations dated the 7th Dec 1762.' The Consistory's authority covered all lodges etc. from the Secret Master to the Royal Secret and there was no appeal from its rulings.

The document concludes regally:

'To which we Stephen Morin have hereunto subscribed our name and affixed our seal at arms and also the Grand Seal of Princes of Masonry in the place where the greatest of treasures are deposited, the beholding of which fills us with joy comfort and all thats good and great near the BB in Kingston the day and year above written.
S. Morin G. Insp. G.
S.P. of My etc. etc. etc.

Morin died and was buried on 17 November 1771 and Francken took over his leading role.

Morin certainly had much to do with the spread of the high degrees in the West Indies before, as well as after, he had received his patent from France in 1761. The present author is of the opinion that, in the past, masonic historians have been inclined to forget that he was only one of a band of pioneers in this field and that others, such as Lamolère de Feuillard and Francken, possibly deserve almost equal credit. There is no doubt, however, that Morin was a flamboyant personality and, owing to the many letters which he wrote still surviving, a well known one. Unquestionably, he was a keen mason, but he must have been a very difficult man to deal with, particularly in the last twenty years of his life, when he exploited his masonic authority and made many enemies. There is not enough information to show what financial advantages Morin got by conferring high degrees. It was the custom of the period that degrees had to be paid for—perhaps he overdid it.

A letter, written three years before Morin's death, by the Master of one of the San Domingo lodges, may be unkind but probably shows the contemporary feeling about him.

There is, from time to time in this colony, Br. Morin whom we recognize indeed as Master of the Lodge 'Harmony', as he is carried in the table of

Regular Lodges, but he wishes, under the titles which undoubtedly deceived the Grand Lodge, to pass as Inspector of the Lodges of San Domingo and we flatly refuse to recognize him as such, not being carried at all on the general table, where there is only Bro. Martin who resides at the Cap and not Bro. Morin who wanders here from Jamaica and from here to Jamaica. . . . Consequently, would he not be a Bro. who made a trade or lived on Masonry? He is very intelligent and has things at his finger tips . . . but he would not be my man. . . . He upsets all the lodges of Port-au-Prince, of Cayes, and of Saint-Marc with the titles of which he is the bearer, both from Jamaica and from France. All the Brs of these three Easts respect him as a protecting God.

Choumitzky sums him up.

(a) Before his powers, he was an active and zealous Mason, sincerely devoted to Freemasonry.
(b) Morin, Inspector: he whom the letters made known to us, if he lied, he only lied a little. One already felt, however, that he was a dealer in degrees.
(c) The Jamaica Mason, inventor of degrees and imaginary powers.

Francken was a Dutchman who arrived in Jamaica in 1757 and was naturalised a year later. He started by holding minor posts in the local Admiralty Court. He must already have been a mason when Morin met him and appointed him to high rank in his rite, but it is not known where he was initiated. Until 1766, when Morin moved to Jamaica, Francken was his permanent representative and probably looked after him during his visits. In 1767, Francken took leave from his civil duties and went to America. In December of that year, he authorised, on Morin's behalf, a Lodge of Perfection at Albany. In the Lodge of Perfection warrant, which still exists, Morin claims authority over the 4° to the 29°. This may anticipate what he hoped to achieve but, by that date, nothing higher than the 25° existed and his pretensions are absurd. According to Mackey, Francken left a copy at Albany of the Rules and Regulations for the Conduct of Lodges of Perfection, dated 25 November, 1762. This document, which still exists, has often been mistaken for the 1762 Constitutions.

On Morin's death, Francken took over the complete production or revision of the rituals, and his work is in the three manuscripts already referred to. There was no need to invent, only to improve and translate, as many of the degrees in question were being developed in France simultaneously. Visiting masons would certainly have helped Francken keep the degrees up to date. One can be sure also that Francken, on his return to Jamaica, took an active part in the high degree bodies in the Island, particularly in the Consistory of Princes of the Royal Secret. He is known to have continued Morin's practice of issuing patents as Deputy Inspector General both in the West Indies and the Americas. One of interest is that to Colonel (afterwards Major-General) Augustine Prevost of the 60th (North American) Regiment. When this happened is uncertain as there were several battalions of the 60th Regiment passing through Jamaica, with a number of their officers being named Prevost. One of the Prevosts, not the Colonel but possibly his nephew, also became a Deputy Inspector General and one of his appointments as a Deputy Inspector General was Major Charles Shirreff who was an important figure subsequently in the development of the Rite in England. (See Chapter 10.)

Francken had serious financial worries at times. Deaths, sickness and the bad hurricanes of 1784 and 1785 forced him to sell his property. It may have been the nadir as he was then given a series of appointments which made the end of his life more comfortable. Not long before he died, the Lieutenant-Governor, who was also Provincial Grand Master of the Moderns, appointed Francken to high judicial office. This suggests that he was also active in Symbolic masonry in Jamaica. He died in 1795.

Francken seems to have been of quite different character from Morin, though both had the same interests in the high degrees and both contributed to their spread throughout the Western Hemisphere. Morin made enemies, while Francken made friends who valued his friendship and worth sufficiently for the Jamaican Assembly, when he was in serious financial difficulties, to vote him substantial sums of money in 'recognition of his services to the public'. As the writer of the ritual in English of the degrees from the 4° to the 25°, he deserves the gratitude of all members of the A & A Rite.

NOTE.

No book on the A & A Rite would be complete without a reference to two documents which were discovered in the Golden Book (the book every member of the 33° was supposed to keep) of Dr Charles Morison, the founder of the Supreme Council for Scotland, who career is referred to later. He acquired his Golden Book in 1827 in Paris and about 1835 he copied two documents from the records of a Henri Dupont Franklin 33°, a member of the Supreme Council for various Spanish possessions in the New World and their representative in Paris. The source of these documents is lost as they were burnt some years later. Dr Morison actually copied three documents, the first being a late copy of the 1762 Constitutions. The other two appear for the first time. The titles are Dr Morison's translation.

(a) 'Institutes, Statutes and General Regulations of High Masonry as observed by our Very Illustrious and Very Puissant Brethren Sublime Elect of Scotland, Sweden, France, Germany and our own [sic] By our Very Illustrious and Very Puissant Grand President and Brother His

Majesty King Frederick II of Prussia, and approved by him on the 25th day of the 2nd month (Jiar) 5763.' The document is signed 'Frederic' and lower down 'De Prinzen'.

This document is discussed in a report by the Grand Secretary General for the Supreme Council for Scotland, R. S. Lindsay 33°, dated 5th August 1948, whose book, *The Scottish Rite for Scotland*, 1957, shows that he was a very knowledgeable mason and an able researcher. He did not, however, have the information now available, when he was writing, and he draws conclusions which in a number of important instances cannot now be accepted.

He quite rightly dismisses the signature of Frederick as impossible and attributes the authorship to Morin but his suggestion of the Grand Consistory at Kingston being dated 1764 when the warrant, now discovered, shows 1768 is an example where he unavoidably errs. Though so few copies have survived, it is impossible to dismiss the document completely because it stresses the Frederick connection, which does not appear directly in the 1762 Constitutions. That the Frederick connection existed as early as 1776 is proved by the letters written by Charles Shirreff (see Chapter 10). Morin must therefore have elaborated the idea from being no more than a suggestion in the Constitutions of 1762 (written about 1765–68) into making him the titular head of the Rite by before 1776.

How he did this is not known. These Institutes may have been issued on a limited scale but what seems more probable was that his position arose from the completion of the development of the degree of Sublime Prince of the Royal Secret. The first ritual is dated 1765 and has a West Indian background. The ritual of the Noachite or Prussian Knight also appeared for the first time in 1766. Both stress the position of Frederick.

It will be appreciated that this document had no effect on the development of the A & A Rite.

(b) 33 Articles entitled 'Secret Instructions for Grand Inspectors General and Princes of the Royal Secret'. The document is undated and unsigned but follows immediately after (a) in Dr Morison's book.

It is quite possible that Morin and his successors issued instructions to those who received patents as Inspectors or Deputy Inspectors General or to Princes of the Royal Secret; and that only this copy survived. It may have been a later elaboration of verbal instructions. The document, even if it is genuine is not an important step in the development of the Rite as it was superceded by the Constitutions of 1786. However, like (b) above, it cannot be rejected completely as bogus. Article 12 lays down a limit of 25 leagues as the territorial limit for each I.G. or D.I.G. where there is no Grand Consistory. That there seems to have been some such limitation explains the territorial instructions given by Captain Prevost in 1776, and Charles Shirreff's letter of 14 Nov. 1785. There are, of course, no such limits in the Constitutions of 1786.

Seal of Lodge *Union Parfaite*, showing early Rose-Croix jewel.

7

THE SUPREME COUNCIL AT CHARLESTON

The history of the A & A Rite from the death of Morin in 1771 until the formation of the Supreme Council in about 1800 in Charleston is a difficult period for modern masonic writers. Under the Constitutions of 1786, discussed in the next chapter, all who received the 33° were expected to keep 'A Register of his actions. . . . The Grand Constitutions, the Statutes and General Regulations of the sublime Art of Freemasonry will be inserted in this Register'. Such registers were known as 'Golden Books'.

Golden Books seem to have been one of the bases of the history of the Rite written by Albert Pike in 1872 and they have been quoted by many masonic writers since that date as evidence of what happened between 1771 and 1801. About six of the Golden Books are quoted and they date from about 1795. The first and most important—because others quote from it—was that of a Hyman Isaac Long. It is mentioned by Pike but he does not appear to have seen it and it is reputed to have been destroyed by fire early in the 19th century.

Entries in the Golden Books are certified as correct by other members of the 33°. As the numbers of those signing was restricted to a small number whose names appear constantly and as they were mutually signing each others' books, it must regretfully be accepted that they afford no real corroboration of actual events or documents.

Recent research has shown that the versions of some of the documents in these Golden Books are not true copies of originals, but are much embellished. The alterations are, in some cases, of importance and are clearly designed to confirm and justify events taking place much later. This inevitably casts the gravest doubts on the genuineness of the other entries in these books.

As little information, other than these Golden Books, is available, they cannot be dismissed entirely by writers dealing with the period but their contents must be treated with extreme caution. The two chapters following record what the author considers almost certainly happened. In deciding what facts to accept from the books, he has used material that seems reasonable while dismissing facts known to be incorrect or improbable. The result, unsatisfactory as it must be until his views are confirmed or disproved by further research, give what it is hoped was the probable trend of events leading up to the formation of the Supreme Council at Charleston. After its formation, material from responsible Americans may be accepted as historically correct.

With the death of Morin in 1771 and the comparative inaction of Francken after 1780, the growth of Morin's Rite lost its central direction. Its development fell into the hands of Deputy Inspectors General who had been appointed by Morin or Francken, and those they appointed in their turn. Voorhis names about fifty of this rank before 1800, the majority being on the American mainland, though not as far south as the Charleston area. These Deputies were quite independent of any central control during the last quarter of the century, and they seem to have welcomed the flood of new degrees and rites which were being invented in France at this time. With the American War of Independence and its aftermath lasting for nearly a decade, communication between the West Indies and North America was difficult. Morin's Rite began to lose its original form and the system of high degrees in the Western Hemisphere became chaotic.

In 1793, two Frenchmen arrived at Charleston. They were Alexandre Francois, Comte de Grasse Rouville, Marquis de Tilly and his father-in-law, Jean Baptiste Noel Marie de la Hogue. To these two must be attributed most of the credit for the early spread of the Ancient and Accepted Rite. How much they were responsible for its start at Charleston will be discussed later but separately or together, they were involved in the erection of Supreme Councils in the French West Indies, Jamaica, France, Italy, Spain and Belgium. As will be seen, their methods can sometimes be criticized as improper, but it must be remembered that the period in which they worked was one of constant war, and that they did produce, out of chaos, something that has continued, unchanged in principle, for almost two centuries.

Comte de Grasse-Tilly, as he was usually called, was born at Versailles in 1765, the son of the Admiral de Grasse who had contributed to the defeat of the British at Yorktown in 1782 but who was defeated and captured by the British Admiral Rodney later in the same year. Admiral de Grasse was presumably exchanged as he was in Paris in 1784 where he was court-martialled, but acquitted. He died early in 1788, but just previously, he was awarded an American decoration. This was a curious Order as it was presented by a society of officers of the Revolutionary Army for the purpose of cherishing the memory of the events through which they had passed. French

Signatures of de Grasse-Tilly and his father-in-law, de la Hogue.

officers who had served in the American army were eligible to become members of the society and to wear the badge. The Order of the Cincinnati, as it was called, was hereditary. There is a letter in the US Archives at Washington from the young de Grasse-Tilly to President Washington thanking him for the decoration and for '*quatre pièces de canon*' (four pieces of artillery) captured at Yorktown. The letter of thanks also asked permission to wear his father's decoration. This, of course, was unnecessary. Writers have suggested that de Grasse-Tilly was awarded the Order of the Cincinnati by President Washington for his service with the US Army some years later at Charleston. This is not the case as he inherited the honour. There can be little doubt that membership of this distinguished society must have greatly assisted de Grasse-Tilly in his subsequent dealings with the Americans.

The young de Grasse-Tilly began his career as a sous-lieutenant in the 1st battalion of the Regiment of the King. While serving in Paris, he was initiated in the *Mère Loge Ecossais du Contrat Social*. In 1789, he left the Army and went to San Domingo to manage the sugar estates which he had inherited from his father. He married in 1792 the daughter of a local notary who was also of noble family and connected with the seigneurs of Chateau de la Hogue in Normandie. His father-in-law became his associate in his masonic ventures.

De la Hogue had been initiated in the *Loge La Parfaite Union* at Port-au-Prince in 1774 and had become Master of the *Loge La Vérité* at Cape Francis the same year. From that date until 1796 when he was appointed Master of the Lodge, *La Candeur* in Charleston, his name appears in no masonic list.

In 1791, the first Negro Rebellion started in San Domingo. As an officer, de Grasse-Tilly fought first as a volunteer and then as a regular. By 1793, the situation had deteriorated so much that the French started to evacuate the Island. De Grasse-Tilly, with his wife and four of his sisters and de la Hogue with his family went to Charleston as refugees. They remained here until 1802, though de Grasse-Tilly paid a short visit to San Domingo about 1797. Most histories state that de Grasse-Tilly was employed for some time as an engineer in the new US Army but the official records have no trace of this appointment. It cannot have been an easy time for the families. Amongst other work, the Comte taught fencing and he also took classes in a school which de la Hogue opened in 1800.

De Grasse-Tilly's character must be borne in mind when his various masonic activities are considered. He started with the advantage of being the son of a distinguished admiral and having a title of Bourbon nobility. He would have been brought up in comfortable prosperity but, in due course, the loss of his estates as a result of the Negro Rebellion ruined him and, for the rest of his life, he was in financial difficulties. This would account for the fact that he had to accept comparatively junior appointments in the United States and in the French Army. It probably was also one of the reasons why he manoeuvred himself, aided by his father-in-law, into becoming one of the most important members of the A & A Rite in Charleston and the West Indies. His 'Golden Book' shows the tariff that he charged for conferring degrees and, by any standards, this was high. Later in life, while under 40 when he returned to France, as we shall see in Chapter 14, he was able to assume immediately virtual control of all *Ecossais* lodges as the personal representative of the Grand Master, a younger brother of the Emperor Napoleon.

In this Supreme Council, among the officers were veteran marshals of the Army and older and senior members of the nobility who appeared to accept his authority. However, in the following years he was so short of money that he charged the comparatively insignificant sum of two francs for sealing any document. Soon after, he rejoined the Army, whether from patriotism or because he needed employment, is not known. Later, on his return to Paris, there is no doubt that his masonic career was hindered when he got into debt. In spite of all this, his knowledge and enthusiasm for masonry, particularly the high degrees, may not be questioned. Much of the result of his work is still with us and, for that, the present members of the Rite owe him a debt of gratitude.

One feels that Comte de Grasse-Tilly must have had great charm, personality and presence but his dealings with men much richer than himself must have soured him. It also seems likely that, when his father-in-law died, he lost a guiding hand as, from that period, his judgement became less sure. He lasted a few years longer but, in the end, he was undoubtedly badly treated and, about 1818, faded into masonic obscurity at the comparatively early age of 50.

Before they left San Domingo, neither de Grasse-Tilly nor de la Hogue appear to have had any special high degree rank—in fact the latter had taken little interest in masonry for many years. However, in Charleston, with other refugees, they founded the Roman Catholic lodge of *La Candeur* and de Grasse-Tilly became Grand Marshal of the Grand Lodge of South Carolina in 1801. There is no doubt that they began to have a considerable interest in the high degrees. A Lodge of Perfection had been established in Charleston in 1783 by an American Deputy Inspector General, Isaac da Costa, and in 1788, a Council of Princes of Jerusalem was also founded.

According to documents written by de Grasse-Tilly or de la Hogue, on Nov. 12 1796, an American Hyman Long, who had received the rank of Deputy Inspector General in Jamaica, raised seven French refugees in the Charleston area, including de Grasse-Tilly and de la Hogue, to the rank of Deputy Inspector General. The Frenchmen immediately set up a Consistory of the 25° or Princes of the Royal Secret. This was done in January 1797 and caused much annoyance to the existing Consistory in Jamaica, which only confirmed the Charleston body after giving it a sharp reprimand and receiving an acknowledgement of Jamaica's supremacy. It is hard to see what the Jamaica Consistory had to complain about as de Grasse-Tilly and his compatriots acted within their powers. The only body that could have taken exception to their action was the mythical Sovereign Council of Sublime Princes in Europe.

A possible reaction by the local inhabitants to a party of Frenchmen setting up an independent high degree masonic body, senior to the local ones, is more interesting. If it had any impact at all, it cannot have been favourable, either at the behaviour of foreigners on US territory or to Jamaica masons trying to dictate to a masonic body in America. So soon after the American War of Independence, there were strong nationalistic feelings. It is possible that the new body was the impetus which caused the local high degree American masons to think about organizing their own high degrees so as to make them impervious to outside interference.

Masonic writers have suggested that de Grasse-Tilly's masonic ambitions were still unsatisfied and that he immediately started to issue patents of the 33° to his father-in-law and other Frenchmen but there is no real evidence, either of this or of his forming the Supreme Council of the French West Indies at this date. In fact, there is no record of high degree activities except in their own Consistory by de

Grasse-Tilly or de la Hogue from 1798 until May 1801. Whether the Americans, who were to found the new Supreme Council, used these two Frenchmen is not known. Subsequent events suggest that the Charleston masons intended to produce a high degree body in which the two Frenchmen were to have no part. There is no reason why de Grasse-Tilly or de la Hogue should have objected to have been used in this way as, when they left America, it was for what they thought was to be their permanent home in San Domingo.

These are, of course, no more than speculations, but the records are so contradictory that it is hard to discover the exact sequence of events. In December 1802, the new Supreme Council issued a long circular giving the history of the Ancient and Accepted Scottish Rite. The authenticity of this document is not in doubt as it was sent to most masonic bodies in the world. The interested reader will find a copy in Mackey's *History of Freemasonry*, Volume VII. Unfortunately the early part of the Circular is not factually reliable as it is based on 'amended copies' of Morin's patent and the Constitutions of 1762. However, it is hard to believe that the later events, occurring just before it was was written, leading up to the formation of the Supreme Council, are not correct, even though there are some omissions.

It is suggested that, on the 25th May 1801, a meeting was held at Charleston of members of the 33° but the names of only a few of those present are known. A large number of documents dealing with this meeting exist but there must be doubt as to whether they were written at the time or later. As an example, the patent conferring the 33° on Dr Frederick Dalcho, who was to be the first Lieutenant Grand Commander of the new Supreme Council, is signed by John Mitchell, the Sovereign Grand Commander designate; most of the new members, all entitling themselves 33°; and de Grasse-Tilly and de la Hogue who sign respectively as Sovereign Grand Commander and Lieutenant Grand Commander of the Supreme Council 33° of the French West Indies. It is, of course, possible that the two Frenchmen were among those who had conferred upon them or who conferred upon themselves the rank of 33°. However, another document shows that the American Supreme Council gave letters of credence of this degree rather later and, in fact, appointed de Grasse-Tilly as Sovereign Grand Commander of the Supreme Council of the French West Indies, with de la Hogue as his Lieutenant Grand Commander, on 21st February 1802.

The matter is of academic interest only as, on 31st May 1801, the new Council was opened. Thus was founded at Charleston the American Supreme Council of the Scottish Rite. The Supreme Council of the Southern Jurisdiction USA, in its booklet celebrating

The birthplace of the Charleston Supreme Council showing the house at the corner of Church and Broad streets, Charleston, South Carolina. This oil painting hangs in the House of the Temple at Washington DC. The figures in the foreground are, *left to right*, Dr Isaac Auld, Rev Abraham Alexander, Colonel John Mitchell, Dr Frederick Dalcho and Dr James Moultrie.

the bicentenary of the USA, states that both de Grasse-Tilly and de la Hogue were present as founding members. This is not unlikely, but there is no direct evidence to support the statement as all the documents concerned have anti-dated signatures.

It is not difficult to suggest why a Supreme Council was formed at this date. The conjecture that the Americans, in their newly won independence, might dislike foreign interference has already been made. It is also to be noted that the masonic situation in Charleston was confused. According to a 'Register' still extant, there were in 1802, in addition to the Craft lodges, who were still divided into Antients and Moderns, three different groups.

(a) The 'new' system divided into three sections, that is
    A lodge of Perfection 4°–14°.
    A Council of Princes of Jerusalem 15°–16°.
    A supreme Council of Grand Inspectors General ruling the 17°–33°.
(b) An 'old' system of Morin's Rite, controlled by a Grand Consistory of Princes of the Royal Secret.
(c) A Sovereign Chapter of Rose-Croix of Heroden.

Except for the Lodge of Perfection, all were under Mitchell as President. One may assume that in due course all three were welded into the A & A S Rite.

De Grasse-Tilly, and possibly de la Hogue, left Charleston in 1802 and returned to San Domingo where de Grasse-Tilly hoped to recover his estates. However, the rebellion started again. Even so, it is probable that it was during this brief period that de Grasse-Tilly actually erected his Supreme Council for the French West Indies. It could not have lasted long as de Grasse-Tilly was captured once more, but using his US nationality, he was moved to Jamaica in 1803 by the British. It is not known whether de la Hogue was with him and, if he was, how he escaped.

It seems certain that, during the few weeks that he was in Jamaica, de Grasse-Tilly raised the local Consistory to a Supreme Council. Naudon suggests that there may have been a Supreme Council in Jamaica even before the arrival there of de Grasse-Tilly. The evidence is slight and depends on documents of which only copies still exist. However the letters of Glock d'Obernay (see *AQC* 94) written in 1820 make it clear that, when he visited Jamaica, the members of the Jamaica Supreme Council considered that it had been formed by de Grasse-Tilly in 1803 when he was there on parole.

The new rite had thirty-three degrees, thereby equalling in number some of the other rites in Europe at this time. The authority for the increase in degrees in Morin's Rite from twenty-five to thirty-three and the manner in which this was done were the Grand Constitutions of 1786, which are considered in the next Chapter. It will be noted that the preface to the Latin version of these Constitutions refers to Morin's Rite as the Rite of Perfection, a term taken up subsequently by many masonic writers and used incorrectly ever since.

Part of the preface to the 'Latin' version of the 1786 Grand

Constitutions lays down the method of expansion of the Rite. As will be explained in the next chapter, this Latin version did not appear until about 1834 and the original members of the Supreme Council would probably have known nothing about the reorganization that it laid down. However the degrees in this preface agree with those which had been adopted about 1801, though their order varies from that in certain patents and letters of credence still extant. The reference to the Primitive Rite in the Latin version preface is almost certainly incorrect as the only known rite of that name did not start until 1818.

> All the degrees from the first to the eighteenth, will be classed as the degrees of the Rite of Perfection in their respective order and, because of their connection and similarity, they will form the first eighteen degrees of the ANCIENT AND ACCEPTED SCOTTISH RITE; the nineteenth Degree and the twenty-third Degree of the Primitive Rite will form the twentieth degree of the Order. The twentieth and twenty-third Degrees of the Rite of Perfection, that is the sixteenth and twenty-fourth Degrees of the Primitive Rite, will form the twenty-first and twenty-eighth of the ORDER. THE PRINCES OF THE ROYAL SECRET will take the thirty-second Degree, immediately below the SOVEREIGN GRAND INSPECTORS GENERAL, whose degree will be the thirty-third and last Degree of the ORDER. The thirty-first Degree will be that of Sovereigns Inquisitor Commander. The Grand Commander, Grand Elect of Knights Kadosh will become the thirtieth Degree. The Chiefs of the Tabernacle, the Princes of the Tabernacle, the Knights of the Brazen Serpent, the Princes of Mercy, the Grand Commanders of the Temple and the Grand Scottish Knights of St Andrew will compose respectively the twenty-third, twenty-fourth, twenty-fifth, twenty-sixth, twenty-seventh and twenty-ninth Degrees.

There is agreement that the final reorganization of the degrees took place in Charleston from about 1800 onwards, but the rituals of some of them were not completed for several years after the foundation of the American Supreme Council. The additional degrees, except for the 33°, and possibly the 31°, came from rites that had been working in France. The reference in the Preface to the Constitutions to the Primitive Rite may be wrong but another source of importance could have been an organization stemming from the de Grasse-Tilly's mother lodge, *Contrat Social*. This was the *Mère Loge Ecossaise de France* and, after the disappearance of the Emperors of the East and West, it controlled most of the high degrees. From about 1781, it was forming lodges overseas and many of their members would have been acquaintances of de Grasse-Tilly and the other Charleston Frenchmen. This Mother Lodge had also made itself responsible for collecting and organizing the degrees of other rites. According to Baynard, who says that he compared and searched through hundreds of degrees, the 23° to 26° of the new American Supreme Council came from the Philosophical Rite, as did the 31° where it is called Inspector Commander. Naudon gives their origin as the Lyons Chapter du *Globe de la Sainte Trinité.* There is no reason why both these channels should not have been correct with the *Mère Loge Ecossaise* being the source from which they came to America. All this suggests that de Grasse-Tilly and other Frenchmen may have been advising the founders of the Supreme Council about the degrees of the new Rite.

The subsequent history of the Ancient and Accepted Rite in the United States is outside the scope of this book. The interested reader will find good accounts in the *History of the Scottish Rite of Freemasonry, Supreme Council 33°* by S. H. Baynard Jr, 1938; *The Rise of the Ecossais Degrees* by J. Fairbairn-Smith, 1965; or *The Story of the Scottish Rite of Freemasonry,* by Harold V. B. Voorhis, 1965.

To make later dealings, between the high degree organisations in America and those formed later in Europe, easy to understand, the following short *resumé* is given.

The life of the Supreme Council for the 33° for the United States of America, which was formed in the manner just described, under its original title, was short as, in 1813, it set up a Supreme Council for the Northern Jurisdiction of the United States, awarding it certain territorial rights in 1827. It then took the title of Supreme Council for the Southern Jurisdiction. For the first fifty years of its existence, it made comparatively little progress but all this was changed when Albert Pike became Sovereign Grand Commander. It is now an important body with many thousands of members. Its headquarters are at Washington.

Events in the northern part of the United States were more complicated and there was considerable confusion from about 1807 onwards when several illegal bodies appeared and began to issue high degrees. In 1813, one of the representatives of the Supreme Council from Charleston was authorised to open a Supreme Council for the Northern Jurisdiction of the United States. Unfortunately, some of the illegal bodies persisted in their work and it was not until about 1867 that all the independent bodies united. It is now also an important masonic body based on Lexington, Mass. USA.

Both the American Supreme Councils have set up other Supreme Councils throughout the world and, later in this book, we shall see how this affected the Supreme Councils in Great Britain and Ireland.

Seal of the Supreme Council of Charleston, USA, dated 1802, with signatures of officials of the Council.

8

THE CONSTITUTIONS OF 1786

THE NEW Supreme Council only announced itself some 18 months after 25 May 1801 by a Manifesto which it circulated to most of the masonic bodies in the world. In this Manifesto and in Orations given in 1801 and 1803 by Dr Frederick Dalcho, the first Lieutenant Grand Commander, the authority given was the Grand Constitutions of 1786 issued under the signature of Frederick II of Prussia.

Complete copies of these Grand Constitutions did not appear until 1832, when a version in French was published in Paris, and another in Latin appeared in America. Up to these dates, only fragments have been found.

The Orations given by Dr Dalcho, in which he describes the formation of the new Rite and in which he defends it against the accusation that it is connected with Illuminism, were published in Dublin in 1808 by the College of Knights of K.H. and the Original Chapter of Prince Masons of Ireland. The pamphlet includes an Appendix in which some four articles are referred to. An undated version of these extracts is extant and may even be earlier. Dr Dalcho shows that he had no doubt that the Constitutions were produced by authority of Frederick the Great and that they were immutable. The fact that he was a Prussian by birth and that his father had served in Frederick's Army would have influenced him:

> 'All the sublime degrees of Masonry were established before the year 1776 ... Only one has been established since, on 1st May 1786. By the constitutions of the Order, which were ratified on the 25th October, 1762, the King of Prussia was proclaimed as Chief of the Eminent Degrees with the rank of Sovereign Grand Inspector General and Grand Master.' [He was not] ... 'The Sublime Degrees are the same at this moment as they were at the time of their first formation. Not the *smallest* alteration or edition has been made to them. The same principles and the same ceremonies are everywhere observed; and as we know from our archives, they have existed for many hundreds of years in their original state.'

The first high degree was possibly some sixty years old and, as far as alterations were concerned, there is every reason to consider that the

33°, for example, had not even been written. Dr Dalcho's ignorance is understandable as it was to establish order out of chaos the Supreme Council was formed. It was not only Dr Dalcho who was muddled by the plethora of rites in existence at this time. His own 'letters of credence' appointing him to the 33°, dated 25 May 1801, and signed by most of the members of the new Council, give his last degree as 'KH, Knight of the White and Black Eagle, Prince of the Royal Secret, Grand Inspector and a member of the 33°', thus omitting the 32°. In addition, the new degrees which its preface shows to have been authorized by the Grand Constitutions are not in the correct order. The document is also signed by de Grasse-Tilly as 'KH PRS Insp 33 Gd Comd of the Sup Council of the West Indies' and similarly by de la Hogue as his Lieutenant Grand Commander. There is thus a strong suggestion of confusion in addition to the fact that some of the signatures must have been added months, if not years, later. However, these latter additions do not alter the conclusion that there was uncertainty, in the early days of the Supreme Council, about the contents of their own founding document.

An undated manuscript, written by de la Hogue in French, but stated to be a translation from the English, gives similar extracts to Dalcho's. Finally, in America, we get similar parts of the Constitutions in a Manifesto issued by Emmanuel de la Motta, another of the original members of the Charleston Supreme Council, in New York in 1813.

In 1813, the 1786 Constitutions were referred to at an assembly of the French Supreme Council in Paris. This Supreme Council had been set up in 1804 by de Grasse-Tilly when he returned to France from the West Indies. The information about the Constitutions was announced by the Grand Secretary General of the Council, Pyron, and in the following year he published a pamphlet '*Abridged History of the Organisation of France of the Thirty-Three Degrees of the Ancient and Accepted Scottish Rite.*' In the previous year, he had mentioned Frederick the Great but, in the pamphlet, he was more explicit:

The new Statutes and general Regulations (of 1762) and the division of the twenty-five degrees into their proper seven classes has been scrupulously carried out in both hemispheres until 1786, the year when the A & A S Rite was raised to thirty-three degrees by Frederick II, in his capacity of Sovereign of Sovereigns and of Grand Master of the Order of Masonry. . . . In 1786, Frederick II, King of Prussia, Sovereign of Sovereigns of the A & A S Rite and Grand Master, the successor of the Kings of Scotland and England, anticipating that his days were short, wished to consolidate the A & A S Rite for ever, as he had a particular affection for it. He wished to give it, where possible, the powers needed in every State or Empire so that it could free itself from the bonds of that senseless ignorance which destroys everything, or from the ambitious claims of other systems; and finally, by its overwhelming pre-eminence, to prove once more those principles of universal equality and mutual tolerance which must make the various Masonic systems into one union coming from the same throne. As a result, Frederick II, presiding in person on the 1st May 1786 over the Supreme Council [of Presidents of all the Consistories of Princes of the Royal Secret, presumably in accordance with Article 1 of the Constitutions of 1762] with whose assistance he organized and directed the Order, raised to thirty-three degrees the system of twenty-five degrees perpetuated by the Grand Constitutions of 1762. . . .

However, only in 1832 was a complete copy of the Constitutions, as given by de Grasse-Tilly, published in the *Recueil des Actes du Supreme Conseil de France* and this has become known as the 'French version'. Its contents would have been known earlier, as it is the same as one given by de Grasse-Tilly to the Supreme Council of Belgium when he founded it in 1817.

In 1834, there appeared a similar document which is now known as the 'Latin version'. The text is little different from the 'French version', but there is a long preface and other additions which are described later in this chapter. The document was produced in Paris about 1834 by a somewhat flamboyant South American who called himself, amongst other titles, Count de Saint-Laurent. According to Voorhis, he was born in 1774 near Bogata and his career included the command of a flotilla of the Mexican navy. His masonic life is something of a mystery but he must have been involved in high degrees in Central and South America as, by 1814, he was a member of the Supreme Council for the French West Indies, in Paris. He also claimed to be Sovereign Grand Commander for the Supreme Council for New Spain, Mexico, etc.

Saint-Laurent visited New York in 1832, where he met the Cerneau high degree group, and suggested an amalgamation between it and his own moribund Supreme Council. This appears to have been effected under the name of the 'United Supreme Council for the Western Hemisphere'. Saint-Laurent claimed that he left his original copy of the 1786 Grand Constitutions which he had got from a former Viceroy of Mexico who, by this time, was conveniently dead, in the archives of this new Supreme Council. Shortly afterwards, these archives were, equally conveniently, destroyed by fire.

In 1832, Saint-Laurent returned to Paris and was made an honorary member of the Supreme Council for France. In 1834, he was a full member. At this time, a masonic treaty was signed between the Supreme Councils for France, Belgium and Saint-Laurent's Council for the Western Hemisphere. Soon after the treaty was signed, Saint-Laurent wrote to the Supreme Council for Belgium a letter which is still extant and which, as translated by Lindsay, contains the following:

> "You will find at the end of the treaty now ratified by the Ill:. and P:. Bro Duc de Choisel, Grand Commander of the Council of France, and by the Council itself, a translation made of the original Latin in the genuine Grand Constitutions of 1786. This original . . . was in my hands since 1795 in my capacity as G:.C:. of the S:.C:. of New Spain etc. I communicated it to the Prince Cambacérès, to Bros:. de Lacépède [an important figure in French masonry c. 1815–22] de Grasse &c. &c. but I was never agreeable to copies being made of it. I have deposited it in the archives of the United Supreme Council of the Western Hemisphere as stipulated by the treaty of 1832, and of it, I had the honour of sending you a facsimile to Brussels in 1833. It is from the copy of this precious document, officially inserted in my Golden Book that the convention has had printed the translation which you will receive with the treaty you have just signed.'

The origin and validity of the 1762 Constitutions have been discussed in Chapter 5. The validity of the 1786 Constitutions has also been argued at length by masonic writers. No masonic body in France could have produced them. The Knights of the East joined the Emperors of the East and West in 1770, but both disintegrated with the start of the French Revolution. During the Revolution, masonry was at a very low ebb, and a document like the Constitutions of 1786 was far beyond the capabilities of the little rites which were just managing to survive the Terror. As far as Germany was concerned, the high degrees in that country were of quite a different type, and under the control of the Rite of Strict Observance since about 1764. There seem therefore to be two points at issue. Did Frederick II (the Great) of Prussia have anything to do with these Constitutions? If not, where did they come from?

Masonic students, interested in the details of the arguments, are advised to consult Naudon or Lindsay, who reject the Frederick story, or the writings of Albert Pike and some other American authors who uphold it. Modern writers now favour a total rejection of the Frederick story, so some of their main reasons are given below:

> (a) One doubts that an autocrat, even an 'enlightened despot' as Frederick was called, would write 'Liberty of opinion is the first and most sacred of all the liberties.' These are liberal sentiments, typically the product of the American War of Independence or the French Revolution. The freedom of speech, so often referred to in connection with Frederick's court, was in fact almost entirely restricted to Frederick himself. He never

had any leanings towards 'universal equality and mutual tolerance' which Pyron attributes to him in 1813.

(b) There are many anachronisms in the Constitutions. In one place, for example, Frederick is referred to in the past tense. In another, it is laid down that the fees be paid in *Louis anciens* (*veterum Ludovicorum*) when, in reality, the gold Louis was still in circulation in 1786.

(c) It will be seen that Article V lays down that 'each Supreme Council is to be composed of nine Inspectors-General, of which five must profess the Christian faith', i.e. must not be Jewish. As four of the founder members of the first Supreme Council in America were of the Jewish faith, this regulation, supposedly made fifteen years earlier, is remarkably farsighted. Perhaps as important is that the admission of Jews into controlling positions in masonry in Prussia in 1786 would have been almost unthinkable; even in France it would have been unusual until after the Revolution.

(d) It is laid down that there will be only one Supreme Council in each country in Europe, etc. but two in North America. In 1786, the area now the USA was no more than a small string of settlements on the East Coast of America. Why should they get this extraordinary preferential treatment? France, with several competing rites; Great Britain with four Grand Lodges and even Frederick's own Prussia, of great masonic importance, are only allotted one Council.

(e) There are grave doubts about the validity of the signatories of the Constitutions. Lindsay analyses these in detail and rejects them, as do several other writers.

(f) Finally, as regards Frederick himself. This has naturally been the subject of intense research for more than a century, even by the members of his own Berlin Lodge who, in 1861, issued a statement rejecting the possibility of Frederick having signed the document, or being involved with it in any way. This appears as an Appendix to Findel's *History of Freemasonry*, 1866 and has never been refuted. Nevertheless, as Albert Pike, later a Sovereign Grand Commander of the Supreme Council of the Southern Jurisdiction USA, proved there was nothing wrong medically with him which would have prevented the signing of documents. Even in the last moments of his life, he was conducting affairs of state from his bed and was fully in possession of all his mental faculties. Why should he have bothered about the A & A S Rite? As the *Encyclopaedia Britannica* states, 'In the loneliness of his old age, his inclination to cynical mockery and the hardening of his character became increasingly marked.' Is this the man who, not having taken any interest in masonry for twenty years and referring to it as 'valueless and playwork', would suddenly start to take a paternal and benevolent concern in high degree rites which affected neither himself nor his country?

If it cannot be accepted that the Constitutions of 1786 were issued under the authority of Frederick II of Prussia or in France, the reasonable alternative is that they were produced in the Western

Hemisphere in the years before or during the formation of the Supreme Council at Charleston. The claim by Saint-Laurent that he received the Latin version in 1795 is unsupported. If it is genuine, they obviously must have been written some time before that date but the story that he got them from a dead Viceroy of Mexico can be dismissed as fiction. However, the production of the Constitutions at any time after 1795 makes the many phrases, which would be anachronistic for a 1786 document, fall easily into place; as do the liberal views attributed to Frederick.

As regards the authors, it is hard to believe that de Grasse-Tilly and his compatriots in Charleston were not involved. Not only have we seen, and shall see again in later chapters, that he was not overscrupulous in gaining his masonic ambitions, but he was one of the few brethren in Charleston who had the necessary knowledge of both Continental and American high degree masonry, and their background. This knowledge would have been acquired after his arrival in Charleston and probably after January 1797 when he and his French friends founded a Consistory of Princes of the Royal Secret. It will be remembered that he was also active in local masonry, becoming in due course an officer of the South Carolina Grand Lodge.

The most acceptable solution is that the organization of the Supreme Council and the rules to govern it were a joint Franco-American affair planned in order to sort out the confusion into which the high degrees in the Western Hemisphere had lapsed. The 1786 Constitutions may well have started as a few simple rules and enough extra degrees to produce a body larger than any other and so able to control the existing bodies. The fact that only extracts of the Constitutions were known until some years later suggests that they took form gradually.

The inclusion of the name of Frederick was not a new idea. The Frederick tradition had started with Morin's Rite some thirty years before and was known to all high degree masons. All that may have been done was to expand the degrees in his name so as to give the new Council authority and to form a Council of Sovereign Grand Inspectors General. If this is what happened, there can be no suggestion that men of integrity, such as Mitchell and the other members of the new Supreme Council, were concerned in a fraud, however well-intentioned. Such a suggestion is reinforced by the obvious ignorance about high degrees shown by Dr Dalcho in his Orations.

It is not clear when the 1786 Constitutions started to take their final form, but the document must have been completed by the end of 1803 when de Grasse-Tilly left for France. It is possible that he knew enough of the conditions to form the Supreme Council in Jamaica earlier in the year. It is known that he gave a copy to Belgium when he formed a Supreme Council there, and he may have given copies to Italy and Spain even earlier. This 'French' version seems to have been little more than a simple text of eighteen articles adequate to constitute a new Supreme Council.

The Latin version which appeared two years later was a much more elaborate document. There was a long preface in the name of Frederick (see pp 84) with the origins of the new degrees (see p 72), a slightly altered version of the eighteen articles and an Appendix describing the ensign of the Order, the regalia of a Sovereign Grand Inspector General and the Great Seal (see Appendix VI).

Whether this text was an embellishment of the French version by Saint-Laurent or whether he picked it up in New York must remain a matter for speculation. All that one can say is that his statement that it came from Mexico can be rejected and that there is a convenient story that the original was burnt in America.

The 1786 Constitutions have seldom been published, so the majority of the members of the Ancient and Accepted Rite in England and Wales are unaware of their provisions. These are important as they are the guiding rules which all Supreme Councils throughout the world acknowledge. They start with a long preface which includes the reorganisation of the degrees of Morin's Rite and which was given in the last Chapter. Other parts of the preface are given later. Many of the Articles are purely administrative and might appear in any set of masonic regulations. A complete copy of the Articles from the Latin version of the Constitutions is given in Appendix VI, but the following is a summary of the important and unusual instructions.

Article II.

The 33° confers on masons the titles, privileges and authority of Sovereign Grand Inspectors. As such, their special duty is to instruct and enlighten their brethren; to teach them Charity, Unity and Fraternal Love; to maintain correctness in the work of each degree and to ensure that this is observed by all the Brethren; to make respected and, in all cases, to respect and defend the Tenets, Doctrines, Constitutions, Statutes and Regulations of the Order; and to apply themselves to the task of Peace and Mercy.

Admission of a candidate to the Supreme Council must be by the unanimous choice of the existing members.

Article III.

If a Sovereign Grand Commander dies or resigns, he is automatically replaced by the Lieutenant Grand Commander who will choose his own successor from among the other members of the Supreme Council. The replacement for the Council is then elected.

Article V.

Every Supreme Council will consist of nine SGIGs, of which at least four shall profess the dominant religion of the country. [In the 'French version', the wording is 'of which five must profess the Christian faith'.]

In each great Nation, Kingdom or European Empire, there be only one Supreme Council. In the States and Provinces which make up North America, there shall be two Councils as far away from each other as possible. In the States and Provinces which make up South America, either on the mainland or in the Islands, there shall be two Councils as far as possible from each other. There shall be only one Council in each Empire, Sovereign State or Kingdom of Africa, Asia, etc. [In the 'French version' there were also the Supreme Councils for the French and for the British West Indies.]

Article VII.

Every Mason above the rank of 16° has the right of personal appeal to the Supreme Council.

Article XI.

The degree of Knight Kadosh 30°, as well as the 31° and 32°, can only be conferred on those considered worthy, in the presence of at least three Sovereign Grand Inspectors General.

Article XIII.

Any Supreme Council can form another in any country where none exists [as in Art V.] The manuscript rituals of the Sublime Degrees [30° and above] will only be given to the two senior officers of each Council, or to a brother charged with the duty of forming one.

Article XVII.

Where a Supreme Council already exists, its decisions shall be by a majority vote.

Those who drew up the 1786 Constitutions may be assumed to have done so because they were needed for the proper administration of the Rite. As explained, the authors were possibly Frenchmen, Americans or masons of both nations working together. The result is epitomised in sensible words from members of the newly formed Supreme Council for Mexico in 1860:

We obey the Constitutions of 1786, not because they were made by any special person, but because at the time of our foundation, we have accepted them as the fundamental law of the Ancient and Accepted Rite of 33°. . . . Besides, if these Constitutions were not authentic when they were promulgated in the name of Frederick II, they have become so by the orders, wishes and unanimous approval of all regular Scottish bodies.

Here we find a firm acceptance of the legend of the Rite. It was not invented by the men who compiled the Constitutions of 1786. They only took the story which had been current since at least 1762 and added slightly to it. As shown in Chapter 5, Frederick the Great was already the 'patron' of the Rite. He was known as such to Francken in 1771 and, as we shall see in Chapter 10, he was being acknowledged as early as 1785 as its head, by Major Charles Shirreff.

As masons have found since the earliest days, a figurehead is essential. The operative masons used the St Johns as their patrons while the speculative masons turned to the Old Testament. The traditional leaders of the Craft or Royal Arch degrees, such as Moses, King Solomon or Prince Zerubbabel who formed the Sacred, Holy and Royal Lodges, would have been unsuitable in a chivalric rite with many Christian references of much more recent foundation. The Crusaders, drawn into masonry by the Chevalier Ramsay and the old Scottish legends, produced no great names and the unwarranted venom shown in the Kadosh degrees made any Knight Templar hero completely undesirable. France and England, fighting in a war for survival, could nominate no name acceptable to both nations. The United States did not exist.

For the masons of the middle of the XVIII century, Frederick the Great of Prussia was an obvious choice. He was a known patron of masonry, whose increasing lack of interest had not yet become common knowledge. By his successes in battle, he had become the hero of Europe while his tolerance in an intolerant age had made his name command respect and authority throughout the XVIII-century world. It is a choice that one can easily understand. The glamour of his name may now have diminished, but it had enormous appeal at the time that Morin's Rite was being launched by the Constitutions of 1762.

Surely, for too long, members of the Rite have disputed whether history can prove if Frederick did take an active part in its organisation? In some Supreme Councils it is almost a convention not to discuss the subject for fear of discord. Has not the moment come when we can agree that this is no more than of academic interest? In the same way that Solomon of Israel, Hiram of Tyre and Hiram Abiff are the traditional founders of Craft Masonry, so Frederick the Great must be acknowledged to be the traditional founder of the Ancient and Accepted Rite. In his name, our predecessors brought order out of the chaos of the XVIII-century rites and degrees. Why should we not be grateful to them and welcome with pride the legend of our Rite?

The story of the Ancient and Accepted Rite lies in the Preface to the 1786 Constitutions. This is the real legend!

WE, Frederick, by the Grace of God, King of Prussia, Margrave of Brandenburg, etc etc etc.

Sovereign Grand Protector, Grand Commander, Grand Master and Protector throughout the world of the very ancient and very respectable Society of Ancient Freemasons, or united Architects, otherwise known as the ORDER of the Royal and Military Free Art of Stonemasons or Freemasonry.

To all the Illustrious and Well-Beloved brethren

Tolerance   Unity   Prosperity

It is clear and undisputable that, faithful to the important obligations imposed upon US in accepting the office of Protector of the very ancient and very respectable Institutions, known in our time under the name of the Society of the Liberal Art of Stonemasons or ORDER OF ANCIENT AND UNITED FREEMASONS, we have dedicated ourselves, as all will know, to cherishing it with our special care.

*   *   *

New and pressing representations have been addressed to US from every side, and have convinced US of the need to impose a powerful obstacle in the way of the spirit of intolerance, sectarianism, schism and anarchy which innovators now seek to introduce among the brethren. Their schemes are nearly ready. They are either imprudent or wrong; presented under false colours; their aims in altering the free art of Freemasonry tend to distract it from its objective and must inevitably cause the disintegration and ruin of the Order. In view of all that is happening in neighbouring kingdoms, we realise that intervention on OUR part has become inevitable.

These reasons, and other causes no less serious, force on US the duty of assembling and uniting all the RITES of SCOTTISH Masonry whose doctrines are, as we know, nearly the same as those of the ancient Institutions which have the same objects and which, being but branches of one and the same tree, only differ in a few words, easy to reconcile.

These RITES are those known by the names of the Ancient Rite, of Heredom or of Hairdom, of The East of Kilwinning, of St Andrew, of The Emperors of the East and West, of the Princes of the Royal Secret or of Perfection, of the Philosophical Rite and finally of The Primitive Rite, the latest of all.

Adopting, therefore, as the foundation of our beneficial reforms, the title of the first of these Rites and the number of degrees in the last, WE now DECLARE them now and for ever united in single ORDER which, professing the Beliefs and pure Doctrines of ancient Freemasonry, includes all the systems of the SCOTTISH ANCIENT AND ACCEPTED RITE.

*   *   *

And so that the present decree can be faithfully and permanently executed, WE order our Beloved, Valiant and Sublime Knights and Prince Masons to watch that it is carried out.

Given at Our Palace, at Berlin, on the day of the Calends, first of May, the year of Grace 1786, and of our reign the 47th.

Frederick.

PART TWO
How the High Degrees came to England

9

THE REVIVAL OF 1770

IN THE EARLY part of the XVIII century, there were some authenticated cases of high degrees being worked in England. These are referred to in Chapter 1 and detailed in Appendix I. Unfortunately, little is known about what took place. There had always been ample opportunities for masons travelling between England and France to carry information of degrees with titles like 'Scots Master' or '*Grand Ecossais*' but, as has been explained, there is no proof whether such high degrees originated in England or France.

In England, as opposed to France, the meetings of lodges which practised such degrees were isolated occasions which were not looked upon with favour by the rulers of the Craft, as is shown by the caustic remarks of the Deputy Grand Master, Dr Manningham, in 1757. It now seems impossible to trace these few English lodges which, after working high degrees from about 1735 to 1750, either stopped doing so or disappeared. Many lodges at that period tended to be ephemeral; others probably got involved in the newly developing Royal Arch and may have been responsible for its spread. A few, almost entirely in the North East of England, practising a type of high degree which has no claim to be a predecessor of the A & A Rite, survived until about the Union of 1813. The story of this last group has recently been told in *AQC* 91 by the Rev N. Barker Cryer in 'A Fresh Look at the Herodim'. No one can prove that the lodges which had practised the high degrees in other parts of England all died out about 1750. Lodges, particularly in country districts, were both isolated and often independent and could have practised any ceremonies that they fancied. It is possible that some lodges working high degrees did survive, and the remarkable way that the degrees spread in England from about 1770 may have been a revival, rather than a new development. Nevertheless, it is clear that, during the period from about 1750 to 1770, except for the specialised Harodim in the North-East, the high degrees were moribund, if not dead.

At the same period, they were extremely popular in France and expanding rapidly. About 1770, this popularity spilled over in a variety of ways, so it was from France direct or through Ireland or even America that this type of masonry returned to England. There is not enough evidence to tell a simple, connected story of how this happened. The available information is only a collection of fragments which eventually coalesce into a high degree organisation that becomes recognisable about the Union of 1813, but which was not stabilised until after the death of the Duke of Sussex in 1843. An outline of what happened may make the following pages easier to understand.

For a decade or so after 1770, when the high degrees again appear in England, they continued to be worked by any body of masons which wanted to do so. This was the story of the Antients until the Union. They considered their lodge warrants as adequate authority and they were actively encouraged to work the Royal Arch. We also know that many of their lodges were working the Knights Templar degrees towards the end of the century and, though there is little evidence, the Rose-Croix as well. For example, in the Union No 1 Lodge of Jersey, a Modern lodge which actually worked Antient procedures, some of the certificates are marked with high degree symbols after the signatures. What the Antient lodges did at the Union is not clear. They must have stopped working the high degrees or separated them from the Symbolic degrees to form an independent body. This probably happened reasonably quickly in England, but there is evidence of lodges in the West Indies working the Royal Arch, Knights Templar and Rose-Croix under their Antient warrants as late as 1821. This may have happened elsewhere, even in England.

With the normal Modern lodges, the position is better understood. About 1791, Thomas Dunckerley, a prominent mason of the period, organised many of the Modern masons who were working high degrees in independent lodges or chapters into a Grand Conclave of Knights Templar, and this continued to function, with varying degrees of efficiency, until it became properly organised about 1846 as the prototype of what is now the Great Priory of the United Religious, Military and Masonic Orders of the Temple and of St John of Jerusalem, Palestine, Rhodes and Malta in England and Wales and its Provinces overseas.

From 1770, there is ample evidence of a variety of high degrees being worked in England and Wales. Towards the end of the XVIII century, the predominant degree was that of the Knights Templar and it was worked by Modern masons, in bodies usually calling themselves Encampments. In the Encampments, a number of other high degrees were usually also worked. One of these, almost always, was the Rose-Croix or *Ne Plus Ultra*. It is not clear how the Knight Templar degree got its leading position. It seems likely that the degree came to

England from Ireland. How it originally got to Ireland is also obscure, but it almost certainly went there from France, and immediately became very popular. In the various rites that later came direct to England from France, the Templar degree, usually with some name that included the word 'Kadosh', was only one of a series of high degrees, the others being unconnected with Templarism. The Knight Templar degree was not the most important in France. Until about 1762, these had been the Scottish Master, Prince of Jerusalem and Grand Master *ad vitam* and they had conferred powers and privileges on their holders.

After this date, there were various rites, including that of the Emperors of the East and West; the First Sovereign Chapter Rose-Croix, which worked from 1769–1791; and others working in the French provinces and loosely connected with the Grand Orient. With many of these, the Rose-Croix degree was important and often the senior. The French story continues in Chapter 14 but, in the intervening years, high degrees were moving into British masonry through visitors, fugitives from the French Revolution and returning travellers.

In England, however, though the Rose-Croix and *Ne Plus Ultra* were the final steps, they could only be conferred on brethren who had passed through all the other high degrees which were worked by the Encampment concerned. One of these was always the Knight Templar and usually the Knight of Malta degree and the Mediterranean Pass as well. The masonic body concerned was almost always known as a 'Knight Templar Encampment' though sometimes the initials KDS (Kadosh) or HRDM (Heredom) formed part of the title.

This remained the pattern until after the death of the Duke of Sussex when, as explained in Part III, the high degrees divided to form the Supreme Council and the Great Priory.

10

OUTSIDE INFLUENCES, IRISH AND MILITARY

ONE OF THE principal ways in which the high degrees reached England and Wales was by a gradual seeping of information from Ireland, through military lodges, from retired soldiers and from Irishmen coming to England and joining Antient lodges. Unfortunately there are few facts before 1770 of what must have been a continuous trend.

As has already been stated, the Antient lodges in England considered that a craft warrant gave them the right to confer any degree of masonry. They probably got this idea from the lodges of the Grand Lodge of Ireland who were acting on this principle early in the second half of the XVIII century.

A patent in Latin is in possession of the Grand Lodge of the Netherlands. This is signed by three men with Irish names, on 26 Dec 1755 in Dublin, on behalf of 'our Grand Master, Substitute of the very illustrious and very worshipful Grand Master of Great Britain'. It states that several Irish brethren travelling abroad had received a Dutchman who called himself Grand Master W.M. of the Amsterdam lodge, *Le Bien Aimée*, and had communicated to him the 'true secrets of Ecossais and Elus'. The patent authorizes him to confer these degrees and to appoint other Masters to do so.

The Lodge *La Bien Aimée* was constituted in February 1756 and continued to work until the end of the century and two other high degrees lodges were also formed at the same time. The degrees worked were similar to those worked by the Council of Knights of the East of the French Grand Lodge.

All this suggests very early Irish working, possibly of degrees brought from France by Irishmen. The mention of the Grand Master of Great Britain has no easy explanation. It is too early to refer to the Antient Grand Lodge and may merely hint at mystical unknown superiors—a common idea at this period. However, it is clear that high degrees of some sort were being worked at a very early date i.e. between the disappearance of Scots degrees in England and the start of the Rite of Seven Degrees.

The first known record of a lodge working the Knights Templar degree is 1758 and, after this date, the degree was common, particularly among the many military lodges of the regiments on the Irish establishment. The *History of the Grand Lodge of Ireland* gives a list of members of the 'Early Grand Encampment of Ireland' at its 'revival' in 1786 and the first name in the list dates back more than two decades.

In a book dealing with the A & A Rite, we are not concerned with details of early Templar ceremonies used in Ireland. They had, however, already diverged from the French Kadosh Templarism. The interested reader will find particulars in 'The Templar Legends in Freemasonry' in *AQC* 26 by W. J. Chetwode Crawley which may be summarised as follows:

> The Anglo-American system was as emphatically British in origin and practise as that we have been discussing was Continental. The differences between the two forms was radical in matter, in manner and in doctrine. The ceremonies of the alternative system [that used in Ireland] had nothing to do with Retributive Justice, and made no pretence of awakening a dormant Order. Its prevailing characteristic seems to have been a more or less reverent adaptation of certain ecclesiastical solemnities whereby the Brethren might be reminded of the Christian inter-communion that bound together the Knights of old. Originally great stress was laid on the tests and trials which the candidate had to undergo. . . . The Brethren who were responsible for its introduction were almost to a man, adherents of the Grand Lodge of Ireland, or of the Grand Lodge of Scotland, or the Irish-born Grand Lodge of the Antients or the moribund Grand Lodge of All England at York.

The popularity of the high degrees at this time is also mentioned in the *History of the Grand Lodge of Ireland*:

> This period [the ninth decade of the century] is also notable for the fact that, while the Grand Lodge of Ireland refused to recognise any degrees, but that of the Craft, some of the best Masons in Ireland were at the same time propagating the Higher Degrees and endeavouring to persuade the Grand Lodge of Ireland to take them under its protection. The degree of Royal Arch, High Knight Templar; and Prince Mason, which was introduced in the year 1782, were all worked by good and zealous Masons, and there was hardly a Craft Lodge in Ireland which did not come to have a knowledge of the first two mentioned and appoint special nights for working them.

The Knights Templar Encampments of the Moderns in England could have started through information from members of the

Antients Grand Lodge or direct from Ireland. The later noticeable strength of the Encampments in the North-West or West country may certainly be attributed to information crossing the Irish Sea. There was also the influence of the military lodges of all constitutions which might be stationed in England and Wales. Nevertheless, the first entry of the Knights Templar degree being conferred is at the Phoenix Lodge No 257 at Portsmouth; and that was not until October 1778. It seems likely that, in any Encampment that was formed in the early days, only the Knights Templar ceremony was practised. This would slowly change. One of the reasons was that military lodges, particularly those in North America or the West Indies, would be learning about the degrees of Morin's Rite which was being increasingly promulgated there since Etienne Morin's arrival in 1763.

Information is available about some of the British Army officers in the Western Hemisphere, who received high rank in Morin's system and who must have been members of their own local military lodges. The Colonel Prevost, referred to in Chapter 6, was one of these, though there is some uncertainty, as there were several officers of this name in the 60th Regiment about this time.

Two were cousins. One of the cousins, August*ine*, succeeded a Colonel John Young as O.C. 3/60th. He saw service in Canada, America, West Indies and Europe. Eventually he became a Major-General, dying aged 63 in 1786. This is probably the Colonel Prevost who was made a 'Deputy Inspector General for the Windward Is and the British Army' about 1770, either by Morin or Francken. One may assume that he would have considered it his duty to confer the high degrees in the lodges in his area. Knowledge of the degrees must have spread during the American War of Independence, 1775–81, when the British Army was very large and the majority of units had at least one lodge.

The other Prevost was August*in*. Born about 1740, he was in the 60th Regt by 1765. He is known to have been with his Regiment in Albany in 1767/6 as a lieutenant where he received the degrees of 4° to 14° in the Albany Lodge of Perfection. In due course, he was promoted Captain-Lieutenant as Adjutant of the 3rd/60th. J. Fairbairn-Smith says that 'Prevost became tremendously interested in the Rite (sic) of Perfection and, by appointing new Deputies, made the Rite available to Scotland and England. The records of the appointments are well known. On 20 January, 1776, Captain Prevost granted a patent to Lieutenant J. P. Rochat of the 60th Regiment, appointing him a Deputy Inspector General with authority to establish the Rite in Scotland, and about the same time granted another patent, while the battalion was at St Augustine, East Florida, to Charles Shirreff. . . .

There is no record of Scotland's Deputy making any use of his patent.' However, Lindsay is inclined to think that Rochat may have passed his patent on to masons in Scotland.

After the War of Independence, the British military garrison in North America and the West Indies was drastically reduced, with thousands of officers and men returning to Europe on half-pay or discharge. Many of these would have been masons who would pass on their knowledge of the high degrees to the lodges which they joined or visited on their return. Amongst these was the Charles Shirreff referred to above.

Charles Shirreff

An account of the life of Major Charles Shirreff, by the present author, is given in 'Freemasonry in Jersey, Part I', *AQC* 86. Shirreff was an Army officer who had a mediocre military career, inevitable for any man who had neither the money or the influence to gain promotion. He was, however, a distinguished mason who was initiated about 1760 in one of the many lodges warranted in Canada after the fall of Quebec. At the end of this war, he returned to the UK and was appointed to a minor military post in Jersey. In 1765, he started the first permanent lodge in the Island, but returned to his Regiment in Ireland after three years. We can next trace him when he was Fort Adjutant at St Augustine about 1775. He was again very active in masonry, though what he did is hard to follow. There is no doubt that he was a Modern but, at St Augustine, he refers to himself as a Deputy Grand Master—presumably Provincial—though the only Provincial Grand Lodge in East Florida was Scottish. He also corresponded with a number of the senior Antient masons in London about the issue of warrants to local lodges. In 1776, he was granted his patent as a Deputy Inspector General but there is no record of his having done anything about the high degrees until his return to England on half-pay, the equivalent of retirement, in 1783, when he settled in Shropshire.

There was no masonry in the county of Shropshire at this time and Shirreff was urged to start a local lodge. He then began a correspondence with the Grand Secretary of the Moderns in London. Unfortunately, it is one-sided as only Shirreff's letters are in the Library of Grand Lodge, while the Grand Secretary's replies are missing. Extracts dealing with high degree masonry are as follows.

(*To Grand Secretary, 1 May 1785*) '... Having, after the first three degrees, full powers Invested in me by commission to act and do as I think proper, for which purpose I am a Deputy Inspr Genl & Arrived at the ne plus ultra ... I do not propose working in the Lower Degrees of Masonry any more. ...'

(*To Grand Secretary, 26 June 1785*) '... I had the pleasure of dining with Mr Ruspini (Dentist) Pall Mall who read my patent. ...'

(*To Grand Secretary, 14 November 1785*) '... my patent which gives me such extensive powers in the process of the work proceeds from His Majesty of Prussia, through one of his Deputy Grand Inspectors in North America, over all Lodges wherever held at the distance of 25 leagues from each other round the Globe, and I have the honour to be one of the D.G.Is. ...'

In spite of his unwillingness to get involved in Craft Masonry, Shirreff did start a Craft Lodge at Whitchurch, and in due course became Deputy to a 'figurehead' Provincial Grand Master who only visited Shropshire for a few weeks in every year. Shirreff never seems to have tried to use the powers of inspection and control over Craft Masonry that his high degree patent gave him. He was certainly sensible enough to appreciate that this would not have been popular in England. His Craft work delayed his efforts to start the high degrees. Nevertheless, by 1788, the Grand Secretary was starting to show an interest, and Shirreff sent some of his rituals to London. Up to 1783, the Grand Secretary had been James Heseltine but he then became Grand Treasurer, and William White took over. It would have been Heseltine who was already interested in the high degrees and who would read the manuscripts which Shirreff must have brought from America. As will be seen in Chapter 11, Heseltine had travelled to Paris, three years earlier, for a conference on high degree matters.

On 6 May 1788, Shirreff formed his converts into a Lodge of Perfection. The Charter for this, the first and only charter of its kind to be issued, was presented to the Supreme Council in 1877. It is referred to in the *Rosicrucian and Masonic Record* of 1 Oct 1877 but its provenance is not known. It is given in Appendix VIII. In addition to Heseltine (as Master) and White, its members were John Allen, Provincial Grand Master for Lancashire and Past Junior Grand Warden; James Galloway, Past Junior Grand Warden; and a George Sweetingbourg, a Past Master and Assistant to the Grand Secretary.

The next year, Shirreff was encouraging his new converts, with more enthusiasm than tact.

To Grand Secretary, 3 June 1789
'... and when I can see you and my other Brors in my Philosophical Lodge and learn the true exercises of your S—ns and twisting thro' Jacob's ladder, etc. then I doubt not you will say farewell to spurious Masonry and adhere to that which is founded on reason and truth.'

Four years later, he repeated what he had said, but he gives no reason for the long delay in going beyond the 14 degrees which he seems to have given them. He was very hard up and complains bitterly of his half-pay of one shilling and eight pence a day, so he could not afford the expensive journey to London very often, and even postage must have been a burden. Also, he was frequently ill with attacks of gout. Things thus moved very slowly, especially as he was a martinet for accuracy, and it may have been that the busy men in London with whom he was working did not take his cherished high degrees seriously enough.

To Grand Secretary, 22 September 1792
'Now that you have the whole of Symbolic Masonry genuine [4° to 14°] I hope my worthy and enlightened Brothers will practice, and the next time I have the pleasure of seeing you and them, I shall find a Brilliant Lodge for if proper attention is paid to every detail, it will plead for itself and must Convince that every other system practic'd is spurious from the 3rd and Borrows in part from the true one. . . . I shall be happy to find that you are of this opinion for it will not be in my power to proceed further with any Brother in the Superior Degrees [presumably up to 25°] that dissents from those he has already received,'

This ends the correspondence. Shirreff moved to London in 1798 and remained there until 1807 when he returned to Whitchurch and died. Gaps in the correspondence would have been due to Shirreff's visiting London; and when he lived there, letters were unnecessary. We are left to wonder what happened to his 'Brilliant Lodge' and whether he did pass on his manuscripts of the 'Superior Degrees' to Heseltine. There is no trace of them in the Library of Grand Lodge. Shirreff had interested very senior masons in the high degrees, so it seems unlikely that all his enterprises ended with his death. Yarker, unfortunately not always a reliable source, says in *AQC* 17 that Shirreff's 'Rite of Perfection' was adopted by some Templar Encampments in the South and in the North of England. Whether this is correct is now impossible to prove, but Shirreff's efforts probably did have an effect on the spread of the high degrees, if only by making a few influential masons interested: and therefore not obstructive to others who worked them. It must also be remembered that Major Charles Shirreff was only one of scores of masons, with knowledge of the high degrees, who had returned to England after the wars in North America, but who have left no trace of their activities.

11

HIGH DEGREES FROM FRANCE

The Rite of Seven Degrees

During the XVIII century, London had a large French colony, even when Britain and France were at war. From the earliest days of Grand Lodge, there were a succession of lodges working in the French language. One of these lodges, *St George de l'Unaminité* No 148, founded in 1736, may have had a very early interest in high degrees but the first definite evidence is later. In 1766, another French lodge, probably the Lodge of Integrity No 331, sold its warrant to some unattached French masons. This transaction, normal in France, came before the Committee of Charity of the Premier Grand Lodge but its illegality was condoned as both parties had acted in good faith.

The activities of the French lodges in London are difficult to follow. Whether the new lodge (by now No 270) or the *Lodge of St George de l'Unaminité* (by now No 68) got into financial difficulties is not known but seems likely. A minute book, now in the Library of the Grand Lodge in London, records a meeting in October 1777 at which the latter changed its name to *St George de l'Observance* and apparently absorbed at least the symbolic elements of the former. At this meeting, a Frenchman, Lambert de Lintot, who had been master of No 331, was present as a visitor but his involvement is clear, as at the next meeting, he was appointed as *administrateur* to sort out its financial problems. The minutes show that the new lodge was 'in union' with a chapter of Heredom, presumably the high degree elements of both Nos 68 and 270. There is no doubt from all these manoeuvres that de Lintot had been working high degrees since 1766.

In 1779, de Lintot was appointed *Vénérable* of *St George de l'Observance*, remaining so for six years. He was thus in complete control of the symbolic and high degrees of the group. When William Preston founded the Grand Lodge South of the River Trent, the records of the Lodge of Antiquity (Vol 1, p 385) show that de Lintot applied on behalf of the 'Lodge of l'Observance of Heredom in

Scotland in Union and alliance with the Lodge of St George in Great Tichfield Street, No 68, for a Constitution.' In due course, one was granted as No 1 Lodge of Perfect Observance, with de Lintot as Right Worshipful Master. He seems to have wisely split his group with the high degrees under its new name in Preston's organization but with the symbolic degrees of *St George de l'Observance* remaining under the Premier Grand Lodge.

De Lintot worked a high degree rite which he called *Le Collège Metropolitain D'Ecosse d'Hérédom des Septs et Derniers Degrés*

De Lintot's Plate for the Seven Degree Rite.

This plate was engraved by Lambert de Lintot for his Rite of Seven Degrees. The design was later used by Thomas Dunckerley for the certificates of Knights Templars. Dunckerley blocked out de Lintot's spurious claim to association with Scotland by removing from the square border the words 'Constitutions du Colege D'Ecosse' and 'Ordre Royal D'Ecosse Tenu en Francois en Faveur des Estrangers'. He also removed from the circle the words 'Herdom' and 'Kilwining'.

usually known as the Rite of Seven Degrees. His organisation lasted for a number of years and probably faded out about 1790 when Thomas Dunckerley began to take an active interest in the new masonic system. It had a second existence, however, becoming a

Knight Templar Encampment under the name of Observance of Seven Degrees.

Pierre Lambert de Lintot et de Cavirol was probably born about 1726 and became a mason in France in 1745. Nothing is known about his career until he arrived in England, presumably some time before 1765. He claimed to have been a First Lieutenant of the Volunteer Grenadiers of Normandy. His full aristocratic name seems rather improbable as he was an engraver by trade and brought a number of his plates with him. It is known that he did work for the Chevalier Ruspini for the new Masonic Girls' School and seals used by Dunckerley are also from recut plates of his design. Other examples of his work are known and are of good quality. He started his masonic career in England as Master of Lodge No 331 and continued with various offices for at least fifteen years. At intervals, he variously described himself as Administrator, Grand Conservator, Grand Administrator General, Deputy Grand Master KDS (Kadosh) and *Grand Maître particulier des Chevaliers Kados*.

The Rite of Seven Degrees is given in a combined minute book and ritual in de Lintot's handwriting which William Wonnacott in *AQC* 39 complains is in execrable French and almost illegible. On the inside cover is a list of former Masters of the Lodge of Perfection from 1764. The first name is Prince de Clermont GM (his correct titles were either Prince Louis de Bourbon-Condé or Comte de Clermont). As Grand Master in France, the Comte de Clermont was automatically the head of all such lists, even though he had little authority over masons outside Paris. The second name is that of the Duc de Chartres who succeeded the Comte de Clermont in 1771. His name can only have been included for effect as, one assumes, were the next four names of noblemen, who may have been masons, under whom de Lintot probably served in Normandy. De Lintot's name then followed as the Master in 1766, the year when the warrant was bought from Lodge No 331.

Previous writers have suggested that the Rite of Seven Degrees stemmed from the Chapter of Clermont but, as the latter is now known to have been mythical, the Rite must have been one of the many being developed in France or a mixture of degrees chosen by de Lintot and his associates. As de Lintot seems to have recognised no superior authority, the second is the more likely. Fortunately an outline of the Rite is given in a letter he wrote to the Grand Lodge of Scotland in 1782. This shows that many of his degrees were those developed in France during the 1770s, but in a different sequence to Morin's Rite or any known rite in France or America.

Comte de Clermont, Prince Louis de Bourbon-Condé, Grand Master of France, 1743–1770.

First Degree. The three Craft degrees.

Second Degree. An Elect or Vengeance group of three parts dealing with the search for the assassins, their punishment and the rewards for those who found them. They compare with the 9°–11° of Morin's Rite as written by Francken about the same period.

Third Degree. Three parts covering the steps taken by Solomon to continue the building of the Temple. They include the substance of the Secret Master 4°, Perfect Master 5° and Provost and Judge 7°, in Francken's ritual.

Fourth Degree. Another group of three parts concerned with the search for and finding of the true name of God in vaults under the Temple. This group is closer to the Francken Royal Arch of Enoch 13° and Scotch Knight of Perfection 14° than to the modern Royal Arch ceremony.

Fifth Degree. Two parts covering the return of the Jews from Babylon under Zerubbabel and the rebuilding of the Temple. The substance is that of the Knight of the East 15° and Prince of Jerusalem 16° in Morin's Rite.

Sixth Degree. The degree starts vaguely on the lines of the present Rose-Croix 18° but continues with the old legend of masons joining the Crusades and the spread of masonry throughout Europe on their return.

Seventh Degree. A group of seven parts on a purely Templar theme. Long traditional histories range from Zerubbabel to Oliver Cromwell, and cover the whole history of the Knights Templar, their destruction and dispersal but it also deals with King Athelstan and Prince Edwin, and there is hermetic influence. Perhaps it is unfair to criticize a degree from a synopsis but, from that, it makes little sense.

Wonnacott suggests that the Rite of Seven Degrees played an important part in extending the high degrees overseas, but it is now possible to say that this is unlikely. The influence of the Rite in Ireland and Bristol, particularly the Rose-Croix, is discussed later. Some military lodges in England may have learnt about the Rite before their units went overseas, but they have left no trace of their activities. Morin had been in the West Indies since 1763 and he and Francken had spread his Rite as far north as New York. However, it is known that there were other rites being worked in America at this time and one of them may have been de Lintot's. It will be remembered that a principal object of the Constitutions of 1786 was to bring order out of the chaos of high degrees in the Western Hemisphere.

There is clear evidence of the absence of any connection between the Rite of Seven Degrees and Scotland. About 1782, de Lintot, possibly irritated by the long quarrel between Preston and the Grand Lodge of the Moderns, seemed to want to change his allegiance from Preston's schismatic Grand Lodge to Scotland. A farcical correspondence, given in *AQC* 68, ensued and it is from one of its letters that we get the synopsis of the Rite which is given above. It is clear that the Scottish masons who received his letters had no idea what he was writing about. The reply from the offices of the Royal Order of Scotland asked for more information but, when they got it, they were little wiser, so they made de Lintot a member of the Royal Order and the matter was then dropped.

Some of the efforts to give the Rite status, and presumably the maximum publicity, were ludicrous. For example, in 1774, de Lintot appointed one of the King's sons, the Duke of Cumberland, Grand

Master of his Rite in place of the Young Pretender, Charles Edward. The Duke, initiated a few years earlier, and to be Grand Master of the Moderns in 1782, would never have accepted the patronage of any form of irregular masonry not approved by Grand Lodge. The removal of Prince Charles Edward from a mythical office, about which he probably knew nothing, merely suggests that de Lintot was aware of the spurious Charter of Arras. On another occasion a few years later, the Rite of Seven Degrees admitted the Prince of Brunswick and the Prince of Hesse-Cassel to be members 'on condition of paying the necessary charges'. There are no records to show that they were aware of being so honoured or whether they paid.

Nevertheless, there is no doubt that de Lintot and his Rite contributed materially to the spread of the high degrees in England and Wales. As far as is known, no lodges, except the original two, were formed by the adherents of the Rite of Seven Degrees, but a large number of masons, both English and foreign, were initiated to its various degrees. It must be accepted, however, from the information available, that his central organisation was confined, certainly in its early days, to a few Frenchmen mostly of doubtful financial stability and often a charge on the Committee of Charity. From the frequent complaints that appear in his papers of candidates who failed to pay their fees, de Lintot gives the impression that he was primarily working a degree peddling organisation. Those who failed to pay had their names struck out and the word 'Abiram' i.e. traitor added. It is only fair to say that, in its later stages, the Rite attracted a number of men of better repute.

Emmanuel Zimmerman and Pierre Laurent

In the previous Chapter, the development of the Knights Templar degree in Ireland and its influence on British high degree masonry was considered. The next phase is the start of Rose-Croix Masonry (or Prince Masonry as it is called in Ireland). This came to Ireland from Continental sources, possibly through the Rite of Seven Degrees in London.

One of the foreigners living in Dublin at this time was a Swiss language teacher, Emmanuel Zimmermann. He probably arrived in Ireland a year or so before 1775, as he was initiated into masonry in an Irish lodge at this date. Some time between then and 1782, he became a member of the high degrees up to, at least, the Rose-Croix or 6° of the Rite of Seven Degrees. When all the papers of the Rite are examined, it may be found that he received these degrees in the London lodges belonging to de Lintot's College of High Degrees. It is possible, however, that he received the high degrees on one of his visits to the Continent. About the end of 1781, he was joined in Dublin by a Frenchman, Pierre Laurent, who also must have held high degrees which included the Rose-Croix.

There were of course Knights Templar Lodges in Dublin at this time and, into one of them, the two foreigners introduced the Rose-Croix degree. At a ceremony in January 1782, a meeting was held at the Kilwinning Lodge of Dublin which opened with a Knight Templar ceremony and three brethren received the degree. Then, according to the minutes:

> Kilwining [sic] Lodge of Emergency open'd to form a Prince Mason Knt of the Red Cross Lodge. Bror Laurent in the Chair when . . . [six brn.] . . . were raised to the sublime Degree of Prince Mason, of the Red Cross & our Worshipful Bror . . . [one of the six] . . . Bror Laurent invest'd with the authority of Most Wise Sovereign Prince Mason with all accustomed honours.

Zimmermann was present, as his signature follows that of Laurent in the Minutes, and both use the Rose-Croix abbreviation after their names. The position of Laurent, and possibly also of Zimmermann, is curious. Laurent did not receive the Kadosh i.e. the French Templar degree until some months later in London. However, he was present in the Dublin lodge when the Irish Templar degree was conferred. One must assume that the Irish degree was, even then, so dissimilar from the Kadosh degree that it was not thought to be a true Kadosh degree. The incident is important as it proves the early and complete divergence between the Irish Knight Templar degree, which is the prototype of that now used by all English-speaking Knights Templar throughout the world, and the French Kadosh degree, which became the $30°$ of the present A & A Rite.

For the next four months, the two foreigners visited Zimmermann's Irish Lodge regularly but did not confer any more Rose-Croix degrees. The Kilwinning Lodge also refrained for a few months as it did not consider itself ready, but from the time that it started to do so, Prince Masonry has flourished in Ireland. It is therefore reasonable to suppose, from a knowledge of the present Irish $18°$ ritual that the ceremony conferred by Laurent was of the normal Continental type and not the curious version used in the Rite of Seven Degrees. *The Ritual History of the 32° in Ireland* states:

> We believe Ireland to be the first English-speaking country to receive the Rose-Croix. The Irish Templar Masons obtained the $18°$ directly from the hands of Pierre Laurent and Emmanuel Zimmermann in 1782, and our

earliest Rose-Croix Chapter constituted an Independent Governing Body for the Degree, of which the 'Council of Rites' the Grand Chapter of Prince Masons of Ireland is the lineal successor.

There are other claimants. In America, an Ecossais Lodge was founded about 1763 in New Orleans and it is probable that this lodge worked the Rose-Croix degrees when it was developed a few years later. There was also the Grand Chapter of Princes of the Royal Secret that Morin had set up in Jamaica in 1770. Finally, there is the Rite of Seven Degrees in London which started in the 1760s and which had a Rose-Croix degree in it. However, the Irish Chapter which worked the Rose-Croix degree in English in 1782, and which is still working, must be the oldest English-speaking Chapter with a continuous life.

In June 1782 Laurent went to London where he received the Kadosh degree from de Lintot's organisation:

> The year of our Lord, the 12th July 1782, the brother Pierre Jean Laurent has been received into the seventh and last degree K. [Kadosh] The said brother Laurent has received his diploma for the symbolic [Lodge] and paid half a guinea for the poor K——s [Kados?]

A copy of this diploma, translated from de Lintot's French is an example of the extraordinary pretentions and absurd claims of his small College of High Degrees:

> We, Grand Administrator General, Deputy Grand Master and Grand Conservator of the most Sovereign Lodge and College of Heredom of Scotland and of the Seven and last degrees, Physical, Philosophical, Moral and Encyclopaedic, Master of the Lodge of Perfect Observance No 1 under the Constitutions of the Grand Lodge of England South of the River Trent of all antiquity established at York. Certify to all Chapters spread over the surface of the Earth that we have received admitted and constituted a Knight Kadosh, our most wise brother Pierre Jean Laurent. After showing us proofs of his zeal for Faith, Hope and Charity, he has made his final obligation on the Summit of our East in front of the Great Architect of the Universe, conforming to our Statutes and Regulations, and in reward for his labours in the Seventh and last degrees of the Royal Art, we have constituted him Master of our Symbolic Lodge giving him the authority to make and receive App:: Comp:: and Masters:: Symbolic in his capacity of Kadosh throughout the world. . . .

Laurent presumably returned to France and no more is heard of him. Zimmermann remained in Dublin until the end of the century. In 1785, he proposed a brother with an Irish name into the Kadosh degree in de Lintot's College. There is also a record of his visiting a lodge in London. In *AQC* 79, it is stated that there is evidence he received a 'Constitutional Warrant' similar to the patent given to Morin, presumably from the London College of High Degrees. There is also proof that Zimmermann used these powers in Ireland. Whether it was he, or his successor who carried out the work, the Irish Rite at this period became very similar in form to the Rite of Seven Degrees.

Movement of masons with high degrees between London and Dublin was normal, and brethren living in the ports or in towns along the routes used by such travellers must have learnt about the high degrees from them. The influence of such men would have encouraged the start or revival of high degrees in the West Country, Bath and Bristol. This is one of the methods in which high degrees found their place in the many Knights Templar Encampments starting in England and Wales in the last two decades of the century.

The Influence of Other Masons

The period when the high degrees were being developed was one of easy travel for the rich as there were no present-day complications like passports or visas. Between the end of the Seven Years' War, 1763, and the outbreak of the Napoleonic Wars, 1793, Englishmen streamed abroad for pleasure, to improve their minds with the 'Grand Tour', on business or to live. Many were masons or became masons while they were overseas. We shall never know the stories of the hundreds who must have brought back information about the exciting new degrees which were spreading through Western Europe. Nevertheless, information is available about a few distinguished travellers and illustrates what must have been a normal trend.

One of the best known is General Charles Rainsford (1728–1809). He had a distinguished military career but was on half-pay for long periods when he was able to indulge his other interests. He was made a Fellow of the Royal Society in 1779 and was also a Fellow of the Society of Antiquaries. He made a large collection of documents on subjects which interested him and this is now in the British Museum. (*Additional MS 23644–80.*)

His collection does not really show whether he was a genuine inquirer or just a dabbler in anything that took his fancy. He was interested in alchemy, treating it as if it was a genuine science, and his masonic activities covered as wide a field as was possible at that period. He belonged to a number of Rites, many related to the high degrees, including:

  A Rosicrucian order which would only have been related to masonry by those of its members, like Rainsford, who had dual interests.

The Grand Orient of France, through its well-known lodge, *Les Amis Réunis*, and the *Rite des Philalethes*.

A 'Grand Lodge' at Lyons, possibly *La Loge des Maîtres Réguliers* of *c* 1761, from which was evolved the Philosophical Scottish Rite of 1771.

Two other Mother Grand Lodges, at Avignon and Strasbourg.

Various other high degrees. It is suggested that he held the 32°.

He held high rank in the Rite of Seven Degrees and among his documents are many that belonged to de Lintot, and which Rainsford acquired when de Lintot died.

Lodges and Chapters under the Modern Grand Lodge, though there is no trace of his having been a Grand Officer. He was a Grand Steward (in 1769).

The semi-masonic Order of the Mopses and a Lodge of Adoption both of which admitted women to freemasonry.

General Rainsford describes his masonic philosophy in a letter of 1786. He complains that he found it difficult to meet other masons of as high a standard as he considered himself to be:

> I have applied myself to fathom the Mysteries of Masonry and to penetrate into the most Sublime Degrees. The misfortune is that I find so few persons who are fit for this mysterious science, but I console myself with the hope of coming by degrees to the end of my researches and of establishing a Worshipful Lodge of Brethren worthy of the highest secrets.

This rather pompous letter was written to an important French mason, Savalette de Langes who, in 1773, had started the Rite of Philalethes in Paris. The Rite, whose aims were the study of masonry and its principles, was meant to be universal in character. It did not expand as fast as its founders had hoped and, nine years later, it only had about twenty lodges. One of the lodges of the Rite may have been in London as, when its leaders decided to call a convention of distinguished masons in 1785, five Englishmen attended. The names of those who went to the Paris convention from London make it clear that, if there was no actual lodge, there was a small circle of important masons in London who were interested in the high degrees. One of the names was 'Rainsford said to be an English general' so General Rainsford was there. Another was Heseltine, by now the Grand Treasurer who, a few years later, was to become a member of Major Charles Shirreff's 'Brilliant Lodge'. Two others may possibly be identified. Thomas Bousie, who figures much in Rainsford's letters, was concerned with the German lodges in London and the 'Brook' is possibly the Provincial Treasurer of Essex. He was appointed by a George Downing who succeeded Thomas Dunckerley as Provincial Grand Master of Essex on the latter's death in 1795. Downing knew Rainsford well and describe him in a letter to a clergyman friend.

General Rainsford who, tho' a peculiar man in some of his speculation is an ingenious & worthy man, wishes to establish a Masonic lodge, consisting wholly of men of literary attainments or literary propensities, for the express purpose of inquiring into the origins, etc. of the Order; he has already been at great pains in tracing it through its various Channels, and elucidating the symbolic part of it. Will you be one of the party? You must take it that it will not be a convivial thing. Let me know your mind on these two points & believe me your faithful friend, May 2nd 1797.

Geo. Downing.

It is not known if this predecessor of the Quatuor Coronati Lodge ever got started, but it does show that General Rainsford and his circle wanted to expand their interest in the high degrees, about which they must already have known much, and which were starting to spread throughout England and Wales.

Owing to the Napoleonic Wars, contact with the Continent of Europe was interrupted and one might have expected that the flow of information about the high degrees would have declined. The next section shows why this did not happen.

French Prisoners of War

An important way in which a knowledge of the high degrees circulated through the whole of the United Kingdom was through the French prisoners-of-war. The standard work on the subject is John T. Thorp's *French Prisoners' Lodges*, 1935. Thorp made a collection of the masonic certificates issued by the prisoner-of-war lodges and much of our information is based upon them.

As a result of the Seven Years' War and wars in India and Canada, there was an annual prisoner-of-war population in the United Kingdom of about 19,000, with a maximum total in one year as high as 40,000. The prisoners were held in existing prisons, in the hulks of old ships specially fitted out for the purpose and in 'parole towns'. The last were primarily for officers who were allowed limited freedom and could mix with local civilians. There were masonic lodges in the prisons and in the hulks, but it is from the lodges of the parole towns that most information comes. Lodges were known to have been formed at Basingstoke, Petersfield, Leeds and Launceston, and there were certainly others. In the parole towns, the French lodges did not always confine their activities to their own nationals and some drew candidates from the local population. There was a complaint about this from the English Lodge at Leeds.

In this first prisoner period, the high degrees were comparatively new, but it is known that some of the prisoner lodges practised them.

The Launceston Lodge, *De la Consolante Maçonne*, issued a certificate to a Frenchman which is signed by the Vénérable (Master) who put after his name the rank of '*Ch. de L'Or^{ent}.*' (Knight of the East), possibly the highest degree worked at this time. Another certificate is to an Englishman, Robert Martin, who already had some high degrees and was given more by the Lodge. His certificate reads 'A Master Mason, Perfect, Irish Elect and English Master was received by us and admitted to the degree of apprentice, fellow-craft and Scottish Master Mason, after having given the necessary proofs.' This suggests that high degrees were probably being worked, even before Lambert de Lintot's Rite of Seven Degrees had started in London, possibly in some Antient lodges under a Craft warrant. It also shows how quickly some knowledge of high degrees had arrived in London after their development in France.

All these prisoners were returned after the Treaty of Paris in 1763. During the Napoleonic Wars from about 1793 to 1815, the prisoner-of-war population was much higher. The number rose from about 25,000 in 1799 to over 100,000 between 1803 and 1814. In the last year, at least 67,000 were sent back to France. As on the previous occasion, they were kept in prisons, hulks and parole towns; the number of the last rising to over 50.

The French usually formed their own lodges, a simple matter as any lodge could be constituted by a Knight of the East, Sublime *Ecossais*, etc. under the powers shown in Appendix II. The high degrees in France were now widespread and one can assume that all officer prisoners, who were masons, were members of some high degree rite or quickly joined one. The Grand Orient of France had adopted the *Rite Moderne*, of which the 7° was Knight of the East, and, after 1804, when the Supreme Council of France was formed, there were members of the Ancient and Accepted Scottish Rite who had the power to form lodges and chapters. It is therefore surprising that the prisoners at Ashby-de-la-Zouch, Chesterfield, Leek and Northampton went to the trouble to apply to the Grand Lodge of the Moderns for warrants. They may have felt that it would give them local standing and prestige but, whatever the reason, the requests fell on sympathetic ears as the Acting Grand Master, the Earl of Moira, had been a prisoner of the French and had been released on exchange. He quickly gave the necessary authority.

The certificates collected by Thorp show that many English masons joined the high degree system worked in the prisoners' lodges. By the start of the XIX century, there were already a number of Knights Templar Encampments working in Britain and the Ancients worked the degree in Craft lodges. Thus, there were many local masons who had some high degrees and who would want to increase their knowledge.

In addition to the French rites referred to above, there were others about which we know very little and which have disappeared. One, the Adonhiramite Rite of 13 degrees seems to have been prominent in some camps as signatures of surviving certificates are supported by titles of its degrees. Many years later, three volumes of manuscript rituals of this Rite were found at Rouen. In the first two is the stamp of *De la Bonne Union of Northampton, Angleterre*. It has sometimes been suggested that the Rite never existed, except in the imagination of Louis Guillemain de Saint Victor who wrote *Le Recueil Précieux de la Maçonnerie Adonhiramite* of 1787, with a previous volume dealing with the symbolic degrees printed a few years earlier. This evidence of the Rite in England shows that it was actually worked.

Besides having their own lodges, Frenchmen were initiated or became joining members of local lodges. Thorp cites references to minutes showing this took place at Leicester, Winchester, Selkirk, Kelso, Hawick, Melrose, Redruth, Bandon (in Ireland) and other towns. There were also interchanges of visits between French and local lodges and, in places, relations were very cordial. The lodge at Chesterfield, for example, worked so happily with the locals that, at one of the banquets, the toasts of the Emperor Napoleon and the Grand Orient were followed by those of the Grand Master of the Grand Lodge of England and the Masters of all regular English lodges. If it is appreciated that, at this time, Napoleon was as unpopular in England as Hitler was in 1939–45, the power of masonry to produce a peaceful atmosphere will be realised. With many of the Frenchmen belonging to high degrees, the interest of the English brethren must have been kindled at such reunions.

Certificates still available show that there were few areas where the high degrees were not being worked by the prisoners-of-war. Under the French system, high degree clothing was worn in symbolic lodges so all English visiting brethren would be aware of the high ranks. This would have further stimulated interest as would have the arrival, in 1813 at Abergavenny, of the ex-Sovereign Grand Commander of the Supreme Council for France, the Count de Grasse-Tilly as a prisoner-of-war. At once, he started conferring high degrees and many examples of the elaborate certificates that he signed are available. Extracts from some of these prisoner-of-war certificates are given below:

(a) A Benjamin Plummer, who was a past Senior Grand Warden of the Antients Grand Lodge and also 'Superintendent Grand Commander of the Order of Knights Templar etc. for the Principality of Wales', was made a joining member of de Grasse-Tilly's Abergavenny Lodge on 20 July, 1813. This was *Des Enfants de Mars et de Neptune*. His certificate is signed by de Grasse-Tilly as 33° and by others as Grand Inquisitor 31°, Knight Kadosh 30°, a Knight of the East and West and five members of the Rose-Croix.

He was also made a member of a lodge at Wincanton, and this certificate is signed by a *Maître Elu* and a Knight of the Sun.

(b) A Craft Certificate to a local Englishman, dated 22 October, 1813, who would presumably be receiving one of the symbolic degrees of the A & A Scottish Rite, is signed by de Grasse-Tilly. Other signatures on it show abbreviated ranks of the 27°, Kadosh 30°, Grand Inquisitor 31° and Sovereign Prince Rose-Croix.

(c) A Rose-Croix certificate to a Thomas Richard Marchant of Abergavenny appointing him, on 20 February 1814, 'a Knight of the Perfect Eagle, a Free and Accepted Prince Mason under the title of the Rose-Croix of Heredom' is signed by several Frenchmen with various ranks. The last signature is that of de Grasse-Tilly who signs himself as 'The special representative of the Grand Master of the Grand East of France in his Grand Chapter and honorary Sovereign Grand Commander for life, 33°.' It is unlikely that he had any right to the first title, though he was entitled, under the Constitutions of 1786, to the second.

(d) Existing certificates show curious titles of degrees of which the majority, though not all, are degrees of the A & A Scottish Rite. For example, one from the Lodge at Ashby-de-la-Zouch, working under authority from the Earl of Moira, has signatures with the usual abbreviated titles of Knights of the East, Sovereign Prince Rose-Croix and Commander of the Temple. It also has the following which show the diversity of the Rites worked by French masons at the end of the XVIII century.

'*M. de la R.L. et S.C. de St. Jean du Désert, O. de Valenciennes*,' which is possibly '*Maître de la Respectable Loge et du Souverain Chapitre de St Jean du Désert* (St John the Baptist—Matt Chap 3, v. 1) *Orient de Valenciennes*', the last being one of the Mother Grand Lodges of high degrees which sprang up from about 1760 onwards. Another set include '*M du S.Ch. Gal France O de l'Anvers, Ir. Gard du Ch de cette L.*' possibly '*Maître du Souverain Chapitre Général de France Orient de l'Anvers* (Antwerp) *Premier Gardien de cette Loge*', another independent Mother Grand Lodge.

The French prisoners were neglected by their country and the majority, even the officers, were very poor. It may be that these certificates indicate that there was a traffic in the high degrees. Whether this is so is immaterial to the result, which was the spread of these degrees throughout the British Isles. This was extensive as, with so many certificates having survived, it is certain that hundreds were issued.

Seal of the Lodge of *Frères Unis Ecossais, Orient de Versailles.*

12

CONTROL OF THE HIGH DEGREES

The Dunckerley Period

THOMAS DUNCKERLEY, the illegitimate son of George II, was born in 1724. His royal parentage was not acknowledged until he was over forty years of age, so he was brought up in poor circumstances and served for most of his working life as a warrant officer in the Royal Navy, which he joined at the age of ten. He was initiated in 1754 and immediately became a keen mason, forming lodges in a number of ships in which he served. When his birth was recognised, he was given a pension and an apartment at Hampton Court Palace. His new style of life allowed him to extend his masonic activities and he quickly became well known and popular among English masons. His life has been written by Henry Sadler in *Thomas Dunckerley, His Life, Labours and Letters*, 1891, and by Ron Chudley in *Thomas Dunckerley, a Remarkable Freemason*, 1982. These show that he became Provincial Grand Master of several provinces and that he was particularly active in promoting the Royal Arch, in which degree he was Grand Superintendent of no less than seventeen provinces.

The start of his association with the high degrees is told in his own words:

Hampton Court Palace
March 22nd 1791.

Most Excellent and Exalted Knight Companions of the Encampment of Redemption (being No 5 of England) held at the Golden Lion Inn in the City of York.

I accept with gratitude the confidence you place in me as Grand Master by the Will of God, of the Most Noble and Exalted Religious and Military Order of Masonic Knights Templar of St John of Jerusalem. I must request that as soon as possible you send to me the Names, Ages, Professions & Residence of all the Knights of your Encampment, as I intend to have a regular Register of our Order. Being Grand Superintendent of Royal Arch Masons at Bristol, I was requested by the Knights

Templar of that City (who have had an Encampment time immemorial) to accept the Office of Grand Master, which I had no sooner comply'd with than petitions were sent to me for the same purpose from London 1, Bath 2, the first Regiment of Dragoon Guards 3, Colchester 4, York 5, Dorchester 6, and Biddeford 7. I suppose there are many more Encampments, which with God's permission I may have the happiness to revive & assist. It has already been attended with a blessing, for I have been but *two* months Grand Master & have already 8 Encampments under my care. . . . I shall form a few Statutes for regulating our Order as soon as I have appointed the Grand Encampment of All England, to be held on the 24th of June annually at London. . . .

Your Most Affectionate Compⁿ, &c.

Thos. Dunckerley.

The Statutes of the Order were produced the same year and it is likely that Dunckerley wrote them. The early statutes of the Knights Templar are given in *AQC* 89 and have no unusual features. The preamble, however, gives the Order a firm footing:

The flourishing state of Symbolic Masonry under the protection of his Royal Highness the Prince of Wales, Grand Master, and the great increase in Royal Arch Chapters, patronized by his Royal Highness the Duke of Clarence, having animated the Knights Templar of St John of Jerusalem &c with a desire to revive their antient, royal, excellent, religious, and military order, they confidently and unanimously elect their brother and knight Companion *Thomas Dunckerley* of Hampton Court Palace in the County of Middlesex, Grand Master of the confraternity under the patronage of his Royal Highness Prince Edward.

Many of the Encampments concerned in this new organisation worked other high degrees, or at least the Rose-Croix, in addition to the Templar degree. It is not possible to say how most of them got the necessary information, except by one of the methods suggested in the preceding chapters. We get no assistance in solving this problem from Dunckerley. He wrote many letters about the Order, including one giving a design for a coat and button for it, but no letter mentions the Rose-Croix or any degree, other than the Templar. His letters make it clear that he considered the Knights Templar to be the most important part of his organisation, even though in his Supreme Grand Conclave, he must have worked the Rose-Croix and possibly also the Kadosh degree. His seals, reproduced by Sadler, leave no doubt of his involvement with these degrees. A Kadosh seal, with a seven-rung ladder rising from the letter M (for Masonry) to N (for Ne Plus Ultra) and, with other high degree symbols is, quite convincingly, one of de Lintot's engravings, or based on one. The other seal, that of the

Supreme Grand Conclave, includes the inscriptions 'HRDM KOD[H], K.T., P.H.P.R., IN HOC SIGNO VINCES' and three crosses, Malta, Templar and Greek Apostolic and, to ensure that it is all-embracing, is topped with the double-headed eagle.

It is not clear from available information what the Grand and Royal Conclave was and whether it was, in fact, little more than Dunckerley himself and one or two London friends, possibly assisted by 'Your Sister D, the Lady Patroness of Knights Templar' in the clerical work and in sending out to the Encampments the various stars, crosses and books of statutes that Dunckerley had produced. There was a feast in 1791 in London on the day of St John the Baptist, when the new statutes were issued. This Grand and Royal Conclave was meant to be an annual event and, during Dunckerley's lifetime, it may have been, though there is no evidence to that effect.

The appointment of Prince Edward, afterwards Duke of Kent, to be the Patron of the Order started with a private invitation from Dunckerley but was actually the beginning of a close relationship between the Order and the Duke, which was to last for two decades. The Duke was only 24 when he was appointed as Patron and he was almost continuously on military service overseas from 1790 to 1803. While Dunckerley was alive, he kept the Duke informed about what was happening in the Order; after Dunckerley's death, there is no record that this continued.

Dunckerley died towards the end of 1795. R. M. Handfield-Jones in his *Origin and History of the United Religious and Military Orders of the Temple*, writes that, by this time, there were as many as 28 Encampments, though this number by no means represented the full extent of the high degree working in England. Dunckerley's enthusiastic leadership had established the high degrees of the Moderns in England and Wales, for the first time, on a firm basis. Unfortunately, there were still some bad times ahead.

Lord Rancliffe as Grand Master

The letter to all Encampments announcing the death of Dunckerley was signed by a William Hannam as Acting Grand Master. Hannam was the Provost Marshal of His Majesty's Guards and he was also a keen member of de Lintot's College of High Degrees, being its Grand Master in 1790. The Templar part of the College to which Dunckerley refers in his letter of 1791 as 'London 1' was now the 'Observance of Seven Degrees' with 'Time Immemorial Status.' Hannam ends his letter:

After having paid a decent attention to the loss of Our Grand Master, it behoves us to turn our attention upon whom shall be his Successor.

Permit me to Point out as the Person Most Eligible to do Honour to the Society The R^t Hon'ble Lord Rancliffe, who is a Member of the Chapter and Conclave of Observance. The more so from his being a Colonel in the Army.

If my Idea in his Lordship's favour meets your approbation, You will please to signify the same in a line to me in answer as soon as you get the sence of the Noble Knight Companions of your Chapter on the subject.

I have the Honour to be,
Dear Sir Knight

Savoy, London   Your Bro & Kt. Comp^n.
23rd November 1795   W. Hannam   Acting G^d Master.

The suggested name must have been acceptable to the Encampments, as Lord Rancliffe was installed as Grand Master on the 3 February, 1796. He renewed the appointment of William Hannam as his Acting Grand Master or Deputy. For the high degrees, Rancliffe is a shadowy, disappointing leader. He was born Thomas Boothby Parkyns in 1755 of rich parents. Before he was 30, he was a member of Parliament, first for Stockbridge and then for Leicester Borough, holding this seat until his death in 1800. Early in the Napoleonic Wars, he raised a regiment, the Prince of Wales's Fencibles and became its Colonel. In masonry, he was concerned with all branches. He was Provincial Grand Master of Nottingham (1783–1800), Derbyshire (1789–92) and Leicestershire and Rutland (1789–1800). In the Royal Arch, he was Grand Superintendent for Derbyshire (1793–1800) and for Leicestershire and Rutland (1793–1800). He was also 2nd Grand Principal from 1792 to 1793 and 1st Grand Principal from 1794 until his death. Rancliffe, as he became with his Irish peerage, had more masonic commitments than he could deal with properly. J. T. Thorp, in the *Transactions of the Leicester Lodge of Research*, wrote

> ... he does not appear to have taken the slightest personal interest in Masonry in this Province during the 11 years that he presided over it, except on one solitary occasion, namely being present at an Emergency Meeting of St John's Lodge, Leicester, on April 27th, 1791, after which he presented the set of silver jewels for the officers which are still in use.

Nothing is known about his work as Grand Master of the Knights Templar. He may have held the annual Grand Conclave when he first assumed the appointment, but a letter, referred to later, dated 23 October, 1804, states that the Grand Conclave had been dormant for 'at least six years', so he could only have called it during the first years of his appointment. Only one Encampment, at Ashton-under-Lyne,

Thomas Boothby Parkyns, 1st Lord Rancliffe, 1775–1800, Grand Master Knights Templar, 1796–1800.

was constituted during the whole period. The Duke of Kent, the Patron of the Order, was overseas.

A probable explanation of Rancliffe's inertia can be found in his involvement with the Unlawful Societies Bill. When the Bill was under discussion, there was no exemption for masonic meetings; this amendment was made during the passage of the Bill in the House of Lords and was sponsored by the Duke of Atholl for the Antients and Lord Moira for the Moderns. Lord Rancliffe was concerned with what took place. It is likely that the Knights Templar were in a difficulty over the Act when it became law in 1799. The exemption was thought to be confined only to existing Craft lodges. It had been badly drafted and, for a time, both Grand Lodges resorted to altering old warrants for new lodges instead of issuing new ones. Obviously the other masonic organisations had to be very careful and there was little authorised activity.

Lord Rancliffe died unexpectedly at the age of 45 and no one was appointed to succeed him.

The Interregnum and Waller Rodwell Wright

The Duke of Kent was overseas when Rancliffe died, and there does not seem to have been anyone with sufficient authority or inclination to assemble the Grand Conclave to choose a successor. The Duke returned to England in 1803, but he had been recalled from his post as Governor of Gibraltar because of a small mutiny in the army for which he incurred some blame. He was indignant at his treatment and too busy with his own affairs to take any action to revive the Knights Templar organisation. However, towards the end of 1804, the following letter was sent to all Encampments. There is no evidence that the Duke was personally concerned, but he must have agreed to what was being done:

> To the Knights Companions of the Encampment No:
> Brethren and Sir Knight.
> It is with infinite concern and regret that I now inform you that the Grand Conclave has been dormant for at least six years, to the great detriment of the Order and to the Bn Sir Knight Companions in general.
> I am therefore directed by the Members of the Encampment No 20 of the 'Holy Cross of Christ' under our Grand Commander the Duke of Kent (being the only encampment in London meeting at the Queen's Arms Tavern, Newgate Street), to state that it is their intention to form and congregate themselves into a general Conclave for a revival thereof, presuming it will meet your concurrence and approbation, as we hope of the other Encampments in the Country.

Waller Rodwell Wright, Grand Master of Knights Templar between 1807 and 1812. This print shows him wearing the device of the Knights Templar and HRDM.

Permit me, therefore Bro Sir Knight, to request the favour of an immediate reply on or before the Second Monday in next month, being the night of our Encampment, with your Sentiments and Support thereto.
I have the honour to subscribe myself,
Your most Obt. humble Servt.
ROBERT GILL, Esqr.
Acting Grand Commander.

It is of interest that Robert Gill was a distinguished Antient mason, having been Senior Grand Warden of the Atholl Grand Lodge in 1796 and 1798–1801. At Craft level, the relations between the two Grand Lodges were acrimonious at this period but must have been better in the high degrees. The letter was responsible for the revival of the high degrees in England. Early in the next year (20 Jan) the Duke of Kent accepted the title and office of Most Excellent and Supreme Grand Master. He also accepted the title and office of Royal Grand Patron for life. As he had been Patron of the Order almost since the start of Dunckerley's Grand Mastership, one must assume that this had also lapsed during the interregnum. In 1807, the Duke resigned the Grand Mastership and was succeeded by Waller Rodwell Wright. In theory, not much was done during the two years that the Duke was Grand Master; in practice, the Order was being revived by several men who were to be its mainstay during the next forty years.

Waller Rodwell Wright was born of comparatively undistinguished parents in 1775 but he had a meteoric legal and masonic career. His masonic life, other than his association with the high degrees, is given in *AQC* 85 by D. Caywood. Wright was initiated at the age of 19 in Bury St Edmunds, but moved to London and joined the exclusive Prince of Wales's Lodge on 18 December, 1801. He was Deputy Master of the Lodge on several occasions and, through this, he made friends with the Duke of Kent and his brother the Duke of Sussex. Wright went overseas as British Consul of the Ionian Islands in 1803 but returned to England in 1806. Two new Encampments had been formed in 1805 and seven in 1806. It is only fair to the other men responsible to make it clear that the Order was already doing very well, even before Wright was installed as Grand Master by the Duke of Kent in April 1807 when the Duke resigned.

Wright and his colleagues revised the Statutes of the Order which dated from Dunckerley's era, but they actually made few changes. Their work continued until 10 April, 1809, when a Charter of Constitution by the Duke of Kent confirmed Wright as Grand Master. Among other officers appointed were John Christian Burck-hardt as his Deputy and Robert Gill as Great Vice-Chancellor and

Registrar. These two were to hold the Order together and remained in office, Gill until his death in 1822 and Burckhardt until 1846.

Gill's career has already been mentioned. Burckhardt was a German by birth whose father had moved to Holland in 1760. He was initiated in his father's lodge at Leyden in 1790 and later left Holland, becoming a permanent resident of England. His first masonic connection in England was when he joined the Lodge of Antiquity, No 1 of the Premier Grand Lodge, in 1808; and was its Master in 1818–19. His chief interest seems to have been in the Royal Arch and high degrees where he worked closely with Waller Rodwell Wright. It is not known when he was installed as a Knight Templar, but in his own entry in the Book of Founders of the Dunovarian Encampment No 6 of Dorchester, he claimed that he had started in the Chapter of Observance of Seven Degrees to which many distinguished masons had belonged. As will be seen, Burckhardt played an important part in the high degrees when they were in comparatively difficult times. An account of Burckhardt's life is given in P. J. Dawson's article in the 1983 Transactions of the Leicester Lodge of Research No 2429.

The Charter is addressed to 'The Knights Companions of the Exalted, Religious and Military Order of the Holy Temple and Sepulchre, and of St John of Jerusalem HRDM KDSH.' but in the body of the documents, there are no references to any degree, other than that of Knights Templar. The new Statutes, issued on the same day as the Charter, were signed by Wright as Grand Master and countersigned by Gill. A copy of all these documents appeared in *AQC* 89.

Under the direction of Waller Rodwell Wright, the Order increased and, by 1810, there were 33 Encampments on the list of the Grand Conclave. There were difficulties, however, as it was found necessary to issue a letter on 11 March, 1810, signed by the Duke of Kent and countersigned by Wright, forbidding intercourse with irregular bodies or individuals. It seemed aimed at Antient lodges, still conferring high degrees under Craft warrants, and perhaps also at a few independent Encampments of Moderns which were still not ready to submit to the authority of the Grand Conclave.

In the letter, there is a reference to 'conferring the degree of Rosea Crucis'. This is almost the first reference to the Rose-Croix degree which was now being conferred, as a normal procedure after that of the Knights Templar, in many Encampments.

Wright is a very interesting character in masonic history. Besides his high degree work, he was deeply involved in the Royal Arch and was one of those who made the Union possible. In 1809, he had actually time to write a poem about the Ionian Islands, where in fact he had been badly paid and not at all happy. Nevertheless, his 'Horae Ionicae' was of enough merit for the usually critical Lord Byron to treat it kindly in his 'English Bards'

> Blest is the man who dare approach the bower,
> Where dwell the Muses in their natal hour.
> Wright, t'was thy happy lot at once to view
> Those shores of glory and to sing them too.

The Grand Mastership of the Duke of Sussex

From early 1811, there seems to have been a movement to replace Wright by the Duke of Sussex. There is no reason to think that this was not with Wright's full approval. One can speculate that he felt a royal head would help the Order, that he was so involved with other masonic work or that he knew that he was about to be sent abroad. No one now knows. The sequence of events was that a meeting of the Grand Conclave was held on 18 April, 1811, at which the Duke of Kent presided as Grand Patron. At this meeting, he appointed the Duke of Sussex as Captain-General of the Order. The Duke had been initiated into Masonry in 1798 in the Berlin Lodge, Victorious Truth. Gould states that he also received the degrees of Perfect Scots Architect, Master of Mount Heredom, of the Cross and Eagle and Elect of New Jerusalem. It is not known where he received Templar degrees, possibly in Paris.

Waller Rodwell Wright was a poor man and constantly short of money. It must have been a considerable relief when he learnt, in 1812, that he was to be appointed to the well-paid post of President of the Appeals Court at Malta. He undoubtedly owed this appointment to his influential friends. Immediately, he began to resign from his many masonic appointments, though he actually delayed his departure for Malta until the Union of the Antient and Modern Grand Lodges was arranged. The following summons shows his resignation as Grand Master of the Knights Templar Order. It will be noted that other high degrees were starting to appear in official documents. In addition, the influence of the now defunct Rite of Seven Degrees still appears to have been strong.

GRAND CONCLAVE
OF THE
Royal Order of H.R.D.M. K.D.S.H. Palestine.
1st and 2nd Columns
OF THE
Seven Degrees 3, 5, 7, 9 . . . lxxxi
NE PLUS ULTRA

Sir Knt.,—You are respectfully requested to attend the Duties of the Grand Conclave at Freemason's Tavern, on Tuesday the 5th May, 1812, at 7 o'clock in the Evening.

A.L. 5816, A.D. 1812, A.O. 694, A.C. 489.

ROBERT GILL

Grand Scribe and Registr.

No. 16, Sun Street, Bishopsgate Without.

N.B. You are desired to attend the Meeting of the Grand Conclave as above for the purpose of electing a Grand Master of the Order in the room of the Most Eminent Sir Waller Rodwell Wright, who has resigned the situation, and recommends the Duke of Sussex as his Successor.

Note: A.O. is the year when the Order was founded in 1118.
A.C. is the year when the last G.M. of the Templars,
Jacques de Molay, was executed in 1314.

The Duke of Sussex accepted the appointment and was installed as Grand Master by his predecessor on 8 August, 1812. The appointment seemed to be an admirable one, but there were difficulties. R. M. Handfield-Jones tells the story in his *History of the Order* and, with permission, it is given below:

... one year later, he [the Duke of Sussex] was installed as the first Grand Master of the United Grand Lodge of England. When in 1817 Grand Lodge and the newly formed Grand Chapter took their stand upon the first sentence of Article II—viz that Freemasonry consisted of the three degrees, with the Royal Arch, thereby repudiating the extra-craft degrees, the Duke was placed in a most embarrassing position. He could hardly show his disagreement and disapproval by resigning from the U.G.L. which he had done so much to bring about. What other alternatives had he? I think he had to choose between three lines of action. First he might resign from the Temple and sever all connection with it, but this he could not contemplate as he was devoted to the Order. Second, he might do nothing, and third, he might quietly and unostentatiously take unofficial action to keep the Temple alive until a more settled and favourable time should arise.

He chose the third course and, as a result, he has been accused of neglecting the Order. ... I imagine that he felt that he could not risk a recrudescence of the recriminations, controversies and difficulties which attended the birth of the U.G.L., nor could he risk fanning the flames of ill-feeling between the anti- and pro-extra-Craft parties. To avoid strife, he must play for time until the Grand Lodge had gained sufficiently in stability and prestige to withstand shocks both from within and without. I think that the Freemason of today does not appreciate the extent of the opposition to the extra-Craft degrees. ... To meet this situation and at the same time to keep Templarism alive, the Duke adopted a wise and diplomatic policy. While apparently taking no interest, he kept a skeleton

office in existence with John Christian Buckhardt as Deputy Grand
Master and Robert Gill as Grand Registrar, to whom he gave loyal and
tacit support. The Duke, having ostensibly surrendered all autocratic
authority, could neither summon Grand Conclave nor issue warrants, but
Burckhardt and Gill got over this by giving dispensations to hold
encampments until a formal warrant could be issued.

In 1820, Robert Gill's house in Soho Square was burnt to the ground
and all his records were lost. . . . Two years later, Gill died and for the next
24 years Burckhardt, assisted possibly by W. H. White [the Grand
Secretary] kept the Temple flag flying, confident that the Duke was behind
him. Then suddenly, in 1830 or thereabouts, the Duke threw aside the veil
and openly assumed autocratic control. Thereupon he allowed Grand
Conclave to remain in a state of coma or dormancy and broke all
precedent by issuing charters to Encampments and by appointing Provincial Grand Commanders without reference to the nearly defunct Grand
Conclave. . . .

The suggestion above, that the Duke was fond of the Order of the
Temple is completely confirmed by a letter in his own handwriting,
dated April 25, 1826, addressed to J. G. Lambton, afterwards Earl of
Durham. 'In returning home last night I found your kind note which I
hasten to answer the first thing this morning. Interested as I feel to get
on to safety the *papers connected* with the Order of the Temple, your
kind proposal is most acceptable to me, as it must be to all those who
are anxious for the welfare of the Order.'

Surely this must kill for ever the suggestion that he ever had any
intention of suppressing the Order of which he was the Grand Master.

The Duke died in 1843 and Burckhardt automatically became
Acting Grand Master.

13

SOME CHAPTERS OR ENCAMPMENTS WORKING THE HIGH DEGREES

INFORMATION ABOUT masonic bodies working the high degrees at the end of the XVIII and start of the XIX centuries is limited. Many only existed for a few years and their records have disappeared, while the fire at Robert Gill's house in 1820 must have destroyed all the records that were held at the headquarters of the Order. The following pages give accounts of three bodies about which something is known.

The Baldwyn Rite

This claims 'time immemorial status', useful for precedence but useless in fixing dates. A much quoted extract from *Felix Farley's Bristol Journal* of January 1772 is often produced as evidence of high degrees in this area:

> ... A young recruiting party, Captain Turpentine, Lieutenant Sweet, Ensign Grog, Sergeant House, Corporal Hemp and Drummer Guzzle ... then went home to spend the night under the Rose with the Knights Templar.

The words 'Knights Templar' in a newspaper satirical article do no more than show that Templarism, in some form, was common knowledge in Bristol at this date. There were ancient ties between Crusader Templarism and Bristol, as there was a former Templar Manor to which the city had to pay dues until comparatively late in the Middle Ages. Several parts of Bristol have names with the word 'Templar' in them and this may have been the reason for the newspaper satire. There is, of course, no reason why there should not have also been some form of masonic Templarism, but there is no proof. It could have been brought by Irish or French masons, or by some transient military lodge which worked the high degrees. If the last suggestion was the reason for the newspaper extract, this is hardly a connection between Bristol and high degrees at this date. On the other hand, travelling masons, such as Stephen Morin, could have passed through Bristol on their many journeys from the port, even as early as 1760. There is, however, no trace of high degree activity in the City at this time though the making of Scots Masters is recorded in the minutes of the Bear Inn at nearby Bath from 1735 to as late as 1758, and at Bristol itself in Lodge No 137 in 1740. It is of interest also that also that a Felix Farley became a member of the Bear Inn in 1733 (*AQC* 59). This is not a common combination of names and it may have been that he (or a son) was the owner of *Felix Farley's Bristol Journal*. There is no evidence that a Farley was a member of any high degree, though if there had been one, the Farley family would obviously know about it. The allusion 'under the rose' is even less helpful. It may merely imply '*sub-rosa*' or unknown, or without authority from their superior officers and suggested that the recruiting party were going to an inn. If it only refers to an inn of that name or one which had a rose painted on the ceiling of one of the rooms, we are no further: if it could be proved to be a genuine play on words hinting at a Rose-Croix degree in England by this date, it becomes of interest.

It will be seen later (Chapter 16) that Davyd Nash, in his letter to the *Freemasons' Magazine* of June 1857, claimed that the high degrees arrived from overseas but it is far more likely that they came to Bristol through de Lintot's Rite of Seven Degrees. Qualification for the Rose-Croix degree in Bristol was always membership of the Knights Templar. This was not an essential qualification in France, but it was in Ireland where the Rose-Croix had also come from de Lintot's Rite. This is confirmed by Eric Ward in his 'Impartial Survey of the Baldwyn Rite', *AQC* 71 where he suggests the Rite was developed in Bristol with the help of William Hannam who is shown, in Chapter 12, as recommending Lord Rancliffe as Dunckerley's successor. Hannam was a keen member of the Encampment of Observance of Seven Degrees, and, as Ward says, 'he appears to have done for Bristol Knights Templary more or less what Laurent and Zimmermann . . . did for Dublin KTs.'

The Rite was changed about 1813 after the Union. In this year a prominent Bristol Mason visited Paris and it is known that he was presented by the Grand Orient with Ms copies of their rituals which had been approved in 1786. These contained the ceremonies of the Craft and the four degrees of *Elu, Ecossais*, Kt. of the East and Rose-Croix. Their similarity with the series used at Bristol after 1813 shows the influence of French degrees on Bristol Masonry. The common likeness to the Rite of Seven Degrees stresses the similar origin.

Rite up to c 1813.	*As Revised after the Union.*
1, 2, 3 Symbolic Degrees	1. Craft Degrees.
4. Royal Arch.	2. Royal Arch (now including passing the Veils.)
5. Knights Templar of St John of Jerusalem, Palestine, Rhodes and Malta.	3. Elect of Nine.
	4. Scots Knight Grand Architect and Scots Knight of Kilwinning.
6. Knight Rose-Croix of Heredom.	5. Knight of the East, Sword and Eagle.
	6. Knight of St John of Jerusalem, Palestine, Rhodes and Malta i.e. Knights Templar.
7. Grand Elected Knight Kadosh.	7. Knight of the Rose-Croix.

The split between the high degrees and the Symbolic, including the Royal Arch, was necessary at the Union to ensure that the Craft Lodges of Bristol remained regular. The removal of the Kadosh degree, so that the Rose-Croix became the *ne plus ultra*, was also in accordance with the trend in the English Encampments.

A Templar Certificate, dated 1821, issued by the Provincial Grand Conclave of Baldwyn is signed by five different brethren, each authenticating the degree which he ruled i.e.

Grand Commander of Elect Masters.
Grand Commander of Sco. Masters.
Grand Commander of Knights of the East.
Grand Commander of Knights Templar.
Grand Commander of Kts. of Rosea Crucis.

This was to remain the order of precedence until 1845 when the list of degrees given in the 1786 Constitutions of the A & A Rite was accepted by the new Supreme Council for England and Wales.

Bristol Masons base their antiquity on a Charter of Compact which bears the date 1780 and which claims 'time immemorial' status and a sovereignty over all Knights Templar and other high degrees throughout England and Wales. It is uncertain who was responsible for this document which, it has been suggested, is actually an agreement between the Bristol Encampment and another early Encampment, that of Antiquity at Bath. There are grounds for accepting the views, given at length by Ward, that the Charter is rather later than 1780. Its seal, the only place where the name 'Baldwyn' appears, may be an even later addition, as there is no evidence that the Bristol high degree masons called themselves members of the 'Baldwyn Rite' until about 1810.

As regards the claim to primacy, this is difficult to sustain. It will be remembered that de Lintot's Rite, which included both Knights Templar and Rose-Croix degrees, started at least as early as 1772 and later turned into the Encampment of Observance of Seven Degrees which continued to work long after 1780. It is not within the scope of this book to enter into the discussion. What is certain is that, in 1791, Dunckerley accepted the Knights Templar at Bristol as having 'time immemorial' status. He was invited at that date by the Bristol Encampment to become their Grand Master and did so when he was forming the Grand and Royal Conclave. There is no information whether representatives of Bristol ever attended a meeting of the Conclave or whether Bristol ever considered itself as belonging to it. Membership, if it existed, may have ended with Dunckerley's death, but the 'Baldwyn' Encampment appears in the official list published in 1810 when Waller Rodwell Wright was Grand Master. As the Baldwyn Rite refused to have anything to do with the Grand Conclave, when it was reactivated in 1843, or with the new Supreme Council when it was formed in 1845, it possibly withdrew formally from any central control during the Grand Mastership of the Duke of Sussex, if it had not done so on Dunckerley's death much earlier.

The eventual submission of the Baldwyn Rite to the authority of the Supreme Council for England and Wales is described in Part III.

Encampment of St John of Jerusalem No 8

An octavo notebook, filled with the writings of a Cornish mason, one John Knight, is an important addition to knowledge about the early high degrees in England. The notebook is one of a series of probably twelve. Two of them, one being commented on here, are in the Library of the United Grand Lodge and the others are in the Coombe Masonic Library at Freemasons' Hall, Hayle, Cornwall. Extracts given here and in Appendix VI are inserted by permission of the Board of General Purposes.

John Knight was born about 1741 and was initiated, or possibly joined, the Druids' Lodge, No 103 of Redruth in 1766. He was exalted in 1775 in the Royal Arch Chapter of Sincerity, Peace and Prosperity, Devonport. In 1777, he was installed into the Knights Templar, probably at his Royal Arch Chapter at Devonport and, in the same year, he was 'admitted to the last seven degrees of the 26 degrees of Masonry, signing his name with his mark as a Mark Mason' (*History of Freemasonry in West Cornwall from 1765 to 1828* by Joseph Osborne, 1901). He attained high rank in all the degrees of masonry, including that of being Provincial Grand Master of Knights Templar in Cornwall from 1793 until his death in 1828.

John Knight was also the founding first Principal of the Druids' Royal Arch Chapter, No 79, of Love and Liberality and, on 17 August, 1791, the three Principals wrote to Thomas Dunckerley about the warrant for the Chapter. In the body of their letter is the following:

> We see in your letter to Bro Harrison of the 8th July a print relative to the Royal & Exalted Religious and Military order of Knights Templars & that you are the Most Excellent and Supreme Grand Master. There are some of that Order in this place & Bro John Knight of the Druids' Chapter has formerly presided as Grand Master, [presumably in the chapter where he had been installed] we would wish to know the expence of a Warrant or Dispensation & what steps it will be necessary to take for obtaining the same.

This letter was signed by the three Principals with John Knight signing as Z. Dunckerley replied from Hampton Court Palace on 26 August, a remarkable example of the speed of the mail in the late XVIII century.

> The price of a Patent for a Conclave or Chapter of Knights Templar is £1. 6s. with 5/- for every Knight, for which certificates will be sent. If there are three or more Knights among ye, I will grant you a Patent, if you can send me the first letter of the Pass Word and the last letter of the sacred word.

He also gave the cost of the sash, gilt cross and silver star to be worn by the Knights. The Patent was ready by the end of November, and was sent to John Knight, together with an impression of the Great Seal. The following month, Dunckerley sent everything needed to start—or at least regularise—the Chapter. This cost the then quite considerable sum of over £5 but included three certificates, presumably for John Knight and the two other founders. In conclusion, Dunckerley added:

> ... the last letter of the principal word was right therefore when I hear from you in return shall forward all you desire; let me have the Title of your Conclave & the names, ages & professions of the other Knights. When the next list is published of R.A. Chapters, you will know the number. I believe you have forgot the Pass Word, but I trust you will find it among your Companions to whom I present my affectionate regards.

Thus was founded the St John of Jerusalem Knights Templar Encampment with John Knight as its first Grand Master. As we know, it received the number of No 8 in the Register of the Grand Conclave and this was presumably published in the list of Royal Arch Chapters. This may indicate the close ties, even at that period, between the Knights Templar and the Royal Arch or it may just have been a matter of convenience arising from Dunckerley's close association with the latter. In the later lists, during the Grand Mastership of Waller Rodwell Wright, the Knights Templar Encampments were only given.

John Knight's notebook was written about 1811, and the second half (pp 85–189) gives many details of a Rite which must have been worked in some lodges at least in the West of England from about 1770 onwards. The degrees worked were:

1. Entered Apprentice.
2. Fellow Craft.
3. Mark Man, or Foreman of the Fellow Craft.
4. Master Mason.
5. Mark Master.
6. Master of Arts and Sciences, Passing the Chair.
7. Architects.
8. Grand Architects.
9. Excellent or 81 Deputy Grand Masters.
10. Super Excellent or Nine Supreme Deputy Grand Masters.
11. Red Cross.
12. The Sublime degree of Royal Arch Masons, given in five points.
18. The Royal Ark Masons, Marioners or Noachides.
19. Knights Templar.
20. The Mediterranean Pass.
21.–25. Knight of Malta or Malta Orders.
26. Rosy Crucian or Ne Plus Ultra.

The joint summons, illustrated on pages 133–4, does not show which degrees were worked by the Lodge, by the Royal Arch Chapter or by the Knight Templar Encampment. It seems likely, however, that the first six degrees were conferred in the Lodge. The next group, numbers 7 to 18, are more appropriate to the Royal Arch Chapter and the last, from 19 to 26 concern the Knights Templar Encampment. Appendix VII refers to the degrees in some detail but the second and third groups, which refer to the high degrees, may be summarised as follows.

Excellent and Super-Excellent degrees were worked in England from about 1730, but died out quickly, possibly from lack of support, active antagonism or their supersession by the Royal Arch degree.

John Knight's notebook shows that there were degrees with similar names in the West Country from 1770 onwards. As we do not know the rituals of the originals, it is impossible to say whether John Knight's degrees were revivals of the early English ones or new degrees from France. All the degrees in this group, including the Architect degrees, the Red Cross and the Royal Arch, as well as those with Excellent names, have to do with the completion of the Temple or its rebuilding after the Babylonian captivity. The references, though often anachronistic, are all concerned with the Old Testament. The wording of some of these degrees shows that they were translations from the French but there is no information whether they came directly from that country or through de Lintot's Rite of Seven Degrees. All the degrees have similarity with degrees of the A & A Rite. It should be appreciated that John Knight's Royal Arch degree has little likeness to the modern degree and is far more closely linked to the Knight of the East and the Prince of Jerusalem. It is also for consideration whether the English word 'Excellent' is no more than a syononym for 'Elect' or '*Elu*'—the sense is the same.

The third group is the continuous sequence of Knights Templar, Mediterranean Pass, Knight of Malta and Rose-Croix. This agrees with the Irish and Bristol procedures. The Mediterranean Pass in John Knight's Rite was based on the legend that it could only be given to a knight who had performed a year's valiant service in the Holy Land, and wished to return to Europe. There is no reference in it to St Paul, though a separate degree of St Paul is named later in the notebook, though not described. The story of St Paul and his connection with Malta must be a much later addition to these degrees.

The Knight of Malta degree was not a separate degree as it is now in the modern English ceremonial, and in John Knight's time it was one of the steps towards the Rose-Croix or Ne Plus Ultra. He gives the Malta legend in detail and it is very like the traditional history of the degree in use today. The close relationship between the two Orders at this period is made clear by the fact that the opening and closing of the Grand Conclave i.e. the Templar degree, is virtually identical with the modern opening and closing of the Malta degree, and has no reference to the Knights Templar or the Rose-Croix. As far as Redruth was concerned, all three degrees were part of a series through which the candidate passed in his progress towards the Ne Plus Ultra. This provides an explanation for phrases in the modern Rose-Croix ritual such as 'a courageous and valiant knight' or 'the illustrious heroes of former ages' which might seem inappropriate.

It is possible that the degrees in this series had their origin, in many cases, in the Rite of Seven Degrees brought to England about 1766 and passed to the West Country through Ireland or Bristol. This does not, however, give a satisfactory answer to all the questions John Knight's notebook raises. At the end, he adds to the puzzle by writing 'There is a very beautiful order (of which I have the honour of being one) called Grand Scotch Masters'. He quotes a meeting of this degree which was held in Falmouth in 1773. This could hardly be part of de Lintot's Rite. Was it an *Ecossais* degree direct from France or a reawakening of one of the Scots Masters degrees worked in England in the 1740s? We do not know.

The Royal Kent Chapter, Newcastle

The story of the Royal Kent Chapter of Newcastle is another important link in the chain of information about the spread of high degrees in England, particularly in the 1820s to 1840s. (*The Royal Kent Chapter of Knights of the Pelican and Eagle and Sovereign Princes of Rose-Croix of HRDM No 8* by W. Waples and W. G. Bird is the basic reference). The story is complicated because, in the north-east of England, the much older Order of Harodim was being worked, certainly up to the Union. From about 1805, when the Grand Conclave started to reassume control of the Knights Templar Encampments, the majority of which also conferred the Rose-Croix degree, the Harodim Order, where it existed, had to be assimilated or suppressed. As an example, in the St Bede's Lodge at Morpeth, the Harodim ceremony was inserted after the Royal Ark Mariner in a list of high degrees which was similar to that used by St John of Jerusalem at Redruth. As the Harodim ritual included a bridge crossing ceremony, this was quite unnecessary duplication in a series which already had this legend. The confusion may have been almost at its worst in the early days of the Royal Kent Chapter where Waples in *AQC* 60 suggests that there were probably a Rose-Croix Chapter and a Harodim Order working side by side.

The Royal Kent Chapter of Newcastle was a breakaway by Newcastle masons from the Joppa Encampment of Sunderland, in 1812. Joppa Encampment had started at Edinburgh in 1807 and only became part of the London organisation in 1811. The Royal Kent Warrant from the Grand and Royal Conclave in London was dated April 1812 with the usual title of 'Knights Companions of the Royal Exalted Religious and Military Order of the Temple and Sepulchre of St John of Jerusalem, HRDM KDSH'. Some interest in the Rose-Croix had begun earlier as 17 brethren, who must have been Knights Templar, went in 1807 to Edinburgh 'to receive from Encampment No 31 of the Irish Early Grand' the degree of Rose-Croix, Kadosh

ROSY CRUSIAN SUMMONS.

Redruth.

Bro^{r} Comp & Sir K^{r}..

In consequence of our authority as Rosy Crusians or Ne Plus Ultra, we hereby require your punctual attendance on us, at our High and Exalted Encampment, London Inn. Redruth, Cornwall on the day of 18 by 10 Oclock in the forenoon* In Order that all business may be Completed before Dinner.

I am
Sir K^{t} Commandant
With Respect
Yours fraternally

*(or Oclock in the evening.)

A.B. M.W. 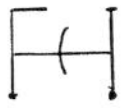

A.B. M.E.D.G.M. 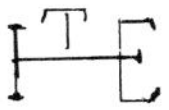

This Summons must be signed by the Most Wise of the R-Cs and also by the M.E.D.G.M. of Knights Temp^{r} as appointed

NOTE This draft summons appears in manuscript in John Knight's notebook. The fact that it has to be signed by the Sovereign of Rose-Croix Chapter and the Grand Master of the local Knights Templar shows the intimate connection between the two degrees. The Rose-Croix Signature sign may be a monogram of F, H and C while the Knight Templar sign shows the Royal Arch sign with the E on the right standing for Eques (Knight) and the tears possibly in mourning for the death of Jacques de Molay.

𝔍.𝔗.𝔑.𝔒.𝔗.𝔥.𝔄.𝔘.𝔇.𝔗.

In the East, a Place full of Light,
WHERE REIGN
VIRTUE, SILENCE, AND PEACE.

We, the Most Eminent Grand Master, and Officers of the Royal and Exalted Religious and Military Orders of H.R.D.M. Grand Elected Masonic Knights Templars, K.D.O.S.H. of Saint John of Jerusalem, Palestine, Rhodes, &c., under the Patronage of

His Royal Highness Prince Edward, Duke of Kent,
Or his Successors,

Do hereby Certify, and declare unto all men enlightened and spread upon the face of the Earth, that by the Virtue, Fidelity, Courage, Firmness, Wonderful Works, and Painful Trials in maintaining our Light in Masonry, which we have found in our Worshipful Brother and Companion John Knight, Junr., of Redruth, in Cornwall, aged Fifty years, **We** have conferred on him the Dignity and Honour of Knights Templar Hospitaller and of Malta in our Field Encampment, St. John of Jerusalem, No. 3, held at Foss's Hotel, Redruth, Cornwall.

Given under our Hands and Seal of our Order at our Field of Encampment aforesaid, the Tenth day of March, A.D. 1824, A.L. 5828, A.O. 706, A.C. 510.

The better to Identify our said Brother and Companion he hath by our direction hereunto subscribed his proper name.

JOHN KNIGHT, *M.E.G.M.*
P. PENDER, *1st Captain.*
PEARCE ROGERS, *2nd Captain.*
THOS. HICHENS, ⎱ *Standard*
GEO. ARNALL, ⎰ *Bearers.*
R. KNIGHT, *Registrar.*

John Knight.

Druid's Lodge of "Love and Liberality," No. 103.

Druid's Chapter of "Love and Liberality," No. 79.

Masonic Knights Templars, "St. John of Jerusalem,"
No. 8.

Their Conclave or Field of Encampment, having assembled this day, June 17th, 1806, to go thro' the several Degrees, as undermentioned, when the following Brothers Compans. W. Sir Knights were Initiated into the several Degrees, as undermentioned, viz. :—

	Mark Man.
Knights of Malta.	Mark Mason.
Knights Templars.	Architect.
	Grand Architect.
	Excellent.
	Super Excellent.
	Red Cross.
	Royal Arch 4 Extra Points.
	Royal Ark Mariners or Ark Masons.
	E.W.N. and Southern Knights.
	Mediterranean Pass.
	Rosy Crucian or Ne Plus Ultra of the Grand Universal Science.

and Ne Plus Ultra. There was then a gap of more than ten years in the records, but it was a tradition, according to Waples, that the Rose-Croix degree was conferred on every Good Friday on those Knights Templar who had been installed during the year. The period was a disturbed one for high degree masons with the Union of the two Grand Lodges and the arguments about the high degrees with the final decision that they were not part of 'pure Masonry'. As explained earlier, owing to the difficult position in which the Duke of Sussex found himself, there was virtually no central control.

The Chapter, however, continued to meet and, in March 1817, a Knight Companion signed the Minutes as a Sovereign Prince Rose-Croix. In the following year 'a meeting of the Ne Plus Ultra was held'—presumably a meeting of those who already held the Rose-Croix degree—but no ceremonies were worked. Not until 1822 was there another Grand Conclave of Rose-Croix and Ne Plus Ultra, on the Good Friday, recorded in the minutes when 17 out of the 22

Previous Pages

Page 132 **Knight Templar Certificate (1824) of John Knight, Jr, issued by St John of Jerusalem Encampment, Redruth.**

The seal on the *certificate* is of interest and can be explained as follows. The letter M at the foot of the ladder implies Masonry, and the N at the top, the Ne Plus Ultra of the Order. At the foot is the date of the start of the Order, 1118, which being deducted from the current year, gives the A.O. The 11M 1314 on the left is the date of the martyrdom of Jacques de Molay, the Grand Master (11 March, 1313) which deducted from the current year gives the A.C. on the summons.

The letters P and K denote Palestine and Kadosh. The initials I.D.M. on the left, signify Jacques de Molay. The figures 3, 5, 7, 9, 27 and 81 are masonic numbers ending with the square of the highest arithmetic digit and denote the periods in the ages of a mason, from three years as an EA to the 81 of the Ne Plus Ultra, the seven steps in masonry.

The ladder has two sides and seven steps. The two sides refer to Philip the Fair, King of France and Bertram Got, Archbishop of Bordeaux. The seven steps symbolise the seven conditions which the former imposed on the latter when he had him elected Pope under the title of Clement V. The seventh condition by which the Archbishop was bound, but which he did not know until after his election, was the destruction of the Knights Templar.

Page 133 **Note of a meeting in 1806 of St John of Jerusalem Encampment, Redruth, listing the degrees controlled and worked. Both reproduced from *The History of Freemasonry in West Cornwall 1765–1828* by J. G. Osborn, 1901.**

present received the Rose-Croix degree, and presumably became Ne
Plus Ultra in addition. A year later, there was another Grand
Conclave and six more 'Knights Companions' were:

> admitted and passed through the three parts of the Rose-Croix, were
> admitted Knights of the M. and R. [?] Pelican and Eagle, created
> Sovereign Princes Rose-Croix and declared 'Free of Heredom'. They then
> were received into the Ne Plus Ultra and took their stalls in the Chapter.

The very elaborate sounding ceremony may have been more developed than that practised in the West Country where John Knight's
ritual hardly mentions the Pelican, and the Eagle not at all. It is
possible that the Knights of the M. and R. are no more than bad
minuting for the Knights of the Military (or Masonic) and Religious
Orders of the Pelican and Eagle. Carlile in his exposure *The Manual of
Freemasonry* of c. 1825 gives two separate degrees, Knight of the
White Eagle or Pelican which he states 'in Scotland has been called
that of the Knights of the Rosy Cross of St Andrew, and has been
taken as the *ne plus ultra of Masonry*'. His second degree, The
Rosicrucian or *Ne Plus Ultra* Degree, is so similar to the former in
ceremonial and ritual as to suggest that both are, in fact, the same
degree as worked in Templar Encampments in different parts of the
country. There is, however, no clue to the expression 'declared free of
Heredom'. It might have been a relic of the days when North-East
Country masons were declared 'Free of Heredom' after taking that
degree. Both Free of Heredom and Ne Plus Ultra seem to imply a
status which, by this period, was imaginery.

There was another gap in the Rose-Croix activities at Newcastle,
according to the Knights Templar minutes, until 1830, though it is
possible that the usual Good Friday meetings of the Rose-Croix were
held but not recorded. According to Lindsay, the ritual used in the 18°
at the Royal Kent Chapter was written for them by a Scotsman,
Alexander Dalziel, who had settled at Newcastle. This may have been
the reason for the recrudescence of activity as, from 1830 to 1846, nine
further ceremonies were held. In 1858, the Rose-Croix element of the
Royal Kent Chapter submitted to the Supreme Council for England
and Wales, and was given a warrant as No 8. The Knights Templar
part of the Chapter is now No 20 under the Great Priory.

The various meetings given above seem to have been typical of the
procedure in England in the years just before the foundation of the
Supreme Council. At the start of its life, the Royal Kent Chapter
presumably adhered to the rules laid down by the central organisation. When however this ceased to function, it was inevitable that
differences between the various Encampments should have crept in.

The trend towards uniformity did not start until 1846. Until then, the procedures seem to have been as follows:

> (a) All Knights Templars, who had to have been Royal Arch Masons, were entitled to receive all the degrees up to and including the Rose-Croix.
> (b) The Rose-Croix was given to all who wanted it on Good Friday each year. This implies only one meeting a year, and here the Royal Kent Chapter may have been abnormal. John Knight's ritual stresses that the 3rd Point was only to be worked four times a year, and this implies more frequent meetings.
> (c) Meetings always opened as a Grand Conclave of Knights Templar. After the opening, the Mediterranean Pass was conferred, followed by the Malta degree. Presumably the meeting then closed. When the Rose-Croix was conferred, it had a special opening. This was followed by the 1st and 2nd Points and all candidates were declared 'Free of Heredom'. As Rose-Croix Masons, they automatically acquired the right to claim the title of 'Ne Plus Ultra'. On some occasions, the 3rd Point was also worked.

The expression 'Ne Plus Ultra' seems to have been associated in British masonry with the Rose-Croix degree as this was the highest degree that any mason could obtain until 1845, except in Ireland (which was c. 1826). Elsewhere, the 'Ne Plus Ultra' was associated with the highest degree of the rite concerned i.e. in Morin's Rite, the Sublime Prince of the Royal Secret 25°, and the Rose-Croix was only important as the first Christian degree.

The Royal Kent Chapter must have acquired a reputation for orthodoxy and ritual skill as, in 1846, it was asked to provide information on the Rose-Croix degree for the newly formed Supreme Council for Scotland. This it did, and the Dalziel ritual still forms the basis of that used in Scotland.

By the time that the Supreme Council for England started in 1845, there were a number of Chapters, similar to the Royal Kent and the St John of Jerusalem, mostly calling themselves 'Encampments', spread over the country. Twenty-five of these are still shown on the books of the Great Priory of England and Wales. As some of the early ones have died out, the number working about 1845 must have been considerably higher. The Rose-Croix elements of all these bodies were to form the nucleus of the new Ancient and Accepted Rite of England and Wales.

Some of the degrees now embodied in the A & A Rite continued to be practised for a number of years. How, in his *Manual*, 1862, suggests that they 'were conferred on brethren now living at the Crown Tavern on Clarkenwell Green. Bro. Goldsworthy [see page 159] being one of the active directors of the proceedings. We have been told that this Association was a Council of Nine Excellent Masters ... but we are unable to learn what degrees were conferred for, excepting as to the Ark Mariner or Noachite and the Rose-Croix, the survivors have no knowledge'. This is the last information about degrees of the A. & A. Rite, other than the 18° and 30°–33° being worked in England and Wales (except Bristol as already explained) but other Supreme Council work some, if not all, of the 33°.

14

THE ABORTIVE FIRST PATENT FOR A SUPREME COUNCIL

In his *Histoire, Rituels et Tuileur des Hauts Grades Maçonniques*, Naudon says 'On 13 October, 1819, the Supreme Council of France gave a patent to the Duke of Sussex to constitute a Supreme Council for England. It was never put into effect.' In his *Origin and Progress of the Supreme Council for England and Wales*, A. W. Oxford writes 'England . . . had a Supreme Council not only for England but for Great Britain, Ireland and the English possessions in America and the Indies. It was formed in 1819. . . .' The story is nothing like so simple as these two writers imply. It is evident that Naudon was unaware of the difficulties which faced the Duke of Sussex, as far as the high degrees were concerned, from 1813 onwards; while Oxford seems equally unaware of the anomalies of the French situation.

The story of the various Supreme Councils in France early in the XIX century is complicated. It starts when Comte de Grasse-Tilly returned from Charleston in 1804. He immediately conferred the 33° on a number of brethren and, by the end of the year, had established a Supreme Council for France in accordance with the Constitutions of 1786. At this time, France swarmed with independent high degree bodies, but the majority rallied at once to de Grasse-Tilly. The *Ecossais* Symbolic lodges then formed themselves into the *Grande Loge Générale Ecossaise*. De Grasse-Tilly naturally had great influence with this new body, even if his Supreme Council did not control it.

The Grand Orient had been recovering gradually from the disorders of the Revolution, but its leaders immediately started negotiations to prevent this split in French masonry. Within a few months, a Concordat was forced on the two rival masonic bodies by the government. It was arranged that there would be a sort of union, that the *Grande Loge Générale Ecossais* would disappear but that the Supreme Council would remain as a overseer with some members of the Grand Orient given 33° rank. The union was never a happy one and there seems to have been quarrelling. As a final cause of rupture, the Grand Orient created its own College of Rites to confer the 33° on its members. A few weeks later the Supreme Council denounced the Concordat and revived the *Grande Loge Générale Ecossaise*. The Government stepped in once more.

It was then arranged that the Grand Orient would control the 1° to 18° while the Supreme Council became responsible for the 19° to the 33°. At the same time, Prince Jean Jacques Régis Cambacérès, Grand Chancellor of the Empire, who was already Assistant Grand Master of the Grand Orient, was made Grand Master of the *Grande Loge Générale Ecossaise*.

These quarrels had annoyed the Emperor Napoleon and he seems to have arranged for pressure to be brought on de Grasse-Tilly, who was about to go on active service, to resign his position as Sovereign Grand Commander of the Supreme Council. Cambacérès was appointed in his place. With but one head of all the French masonic bodies, there seemed a chance of peace between them. It lasted as long as Napoleon remained in power.

The Supreme Council began to organize itself slowly in the *Galérie de Pompéi*, but moved in 1812 into the *rue Saint-Honoré*. By this time, six members of the Supreme Council for the French West Indies which de Grasse-Tilly had formed in 1802 or 1803 (see Chapter 7) were in France. Amongst them were J. B. de la Hogue, de Grasse-Tilly's father-in-law, the Lieutenant Grand Commander; and Tessier de Marguerittes, who was signing himself as Secretary General of the Holy Empire. This body wrote to the Supreme Council of France complaining that their names had not been included, as previously, as honorary members of the Supreme Council in the list following the minutes of September 14, 1812. The letter claimed that, according to the Grand Constitutions, a Grand Inspector General was always an honorary member of all Supreme Councils.

The Supreme Council replied in January 1813 that they would consider the request, but denying that it was mentioned in the Grand Constitutions; provided the signatories of the complaint would bring proof that they had been regularly appointed by an authorized person in their own territory. A similar application to the Grand Orient did not even get a reply. However curiously, the Supreme Council did include the names of de la Hogue and his colleagues in their next list two months later.

De la Hogue and his Council then moved into the building previously occupied by the Supreme Council for France in the *Galérie de Pompéi* under their original name of Supreme Council for the

French Islands in America, but were inevitably nicknamed as the 'Supreme Council of the Pompéi'.

The fall of Napoleon completely changed the situation. The Supreme Council for France was primarily affected as many of its members, including of course Cambacérès, were supporters of Napoleon and were forced to leave the country or go into retirement. The Grand Orient, with a less distinguished membership, was not so affected and immediately seized the opportunity to suggest a revival of the 1804 agreement. Some of the remaining members of the Supreme Council for France agreed. They were mostly also members of the Grand Orient and a new body was formed as 'Grand Orient, Supreme Council for France and the French possessions'. This body still exists, under the name of the 'Grand College of Rites'. Other members of the Supreme Council for France, who refused to join this new body, declared their Council to be in abeyance. The Grand Orient's action was questionable and relied for legality on the 1786 Constitutions' regulation which allowed Supreme Councils to act in accordance with a majority vote of its members. The question is still of importance as affecting the present status of the rival Supreme Councils working in France and has not been authoritatively decided.

De Grasse-Tilly returned from being a prisoner-of-war in 1814 and declared that his resignation in favour of Cambacérès in 1806 had been contrary to the Constitutions which appointed a Sovereign Grand Commander for life. It was therefore null and void. He then collected the remnants of the *Ecossais* Lodges who would follow him and set up a new body which took up residence in the *Restaurant du Prado* near the *Palais de Justice*. This became known as the 'Supreme Council of the Prado'. It started well with many members of responsible character and social position. Among them, Comte de Fernig, as Lieutenant Grand Commander, whom we shall meet again in connection with the formation of the Supreme Council for England and Wales in 1845, Vice-Admiral Comte Allemand and the Comte Decazes. Unfortunately de Grasse-Tilly had to leave France for Belgium, either on military duty or, as his detractors said, to avoid imprisonment for debt. Trouble broke out at once and he was deposed. Even if his self-appointment was legal, his dismissal was quite contrary to the Constitutions but, by this time, he seems to have been a liability to any masonic body.

When de Grasse-Tilly got back to France, he and several dissidents from the Prado Council, joined the Supreme Council of Pompéi of which he had always been Sovereign Grand Commander since he formed it in the West Indies. He started to drop the West Indian connection and began to form another French Council. However, in

Comte (later Duc) Elie Decazes, Sovereign Grand Commander, Supreme Council for France, 1818–1821 and 1838–1860.

1818, he had enough sense to resign and the position was offered to Decazes who accepted it. The Comte Decazes was an important figure in France, quite different from the usual quarrelling members of the various Supreme Councils. He was a friend of the King, Louis XVIII, was Minister of the Interior in 1818, and Prime Minister the following year.

Both the Supreme Councils of the Prado and Pompéi agreed to accept Decazes as mediator in their quarrels, while the Grand Orient at once made overtures to combine all masonry in France. After discussions, conducted by the Comte de Fernig, the Grand Orient's terms were found to be unacceptable, so Decazes decided to revive the original Supreme Council for France which had put itself into abeyance about 1815. Its members were to come from the Councils of the Prado and Pompéi. Consultations took almost two years but in 1821, Decazes announced that 'The work of the Supreme Council for long suspended for unavoidable reasons, is at last restored to strength and vigour'. Decazes then resigned, and the revived Supreme Council issued its first decree in April of that year.

This is the background to the offer, made in 1819, of a patent to the Duke of Sussex of the 33° so that he could form a Supreme Council in Britain. At the date in question there were, as has been shown, four Supreme Councils in France.

(a) The Supreme Council attached to the Grand Orient, self-founded in 1815, using some members of the 1804 Supreme Council of France to give it legality. This is the present 'Grand College of Rites of the Grand Orient'.
(b) The Supreme Council for France founded quite legally in 1804 by de ⌐ Grasse-Tilly. In voluntary abeyance since 1815 but being revived by Decazes, though not officially functioning until early 1821.
(c) The Supreme Council of the French West Indies, known as that of Pompéi. Presided over by de Grasse-Tilly until he resigned in September 1818 in favour of Decazes. It appears to have been active though it cannot have had any legal right.
(d) The Supreme Council of the Prado, a breakaway from the remnants of the legal 1804 Supreme Council. It was possibly legal when de Grasse-Tilly revived it in 1815, but forfeited most of its legality when it dismissed him in 1818. It appears to have considered itself of importance as it took the all-embracing title of the 'Supreme Council of the 33rd and Last Degree, Grand East Ecossais of the Ancient and Accepted Rite for France and the French possessions in America and the Indies'.

The offer to the Duke of Sussex was of complicated legality as there was no genuine Supreme Council for France until 1821 when the three Councils, (b), (c) and (d) united to revive (b). It came from (d), the Supreme Council of the Prado. The ostensible motive for the offer

Seals sent to the Duke of Sussex from Paris in 1819 for use by the newly formed Supreme Council.

30°—Councils of the 30° were, and in some cases, still are, called 'areopagi'. The meaning of the 'ESQ' is not known.

31°—Presumably 'G.O.SC.' is an abbreviated French translation of 'Grand Orient Ecossais'. The mistake of 31rd for 31st seems proof of French origin.

33°—It is of interest that the eagle is not crowned. Compare with the similar stamp reproduced at the end of this Chapter.

may have been to add authority to Decazes' efforts to revive and unite Ecossais Masonry. In reality, it was an attempt by the Prado body to increase its importance and prove its legality. The man behind the offer was a Frenchman who called himself Joseph de Glock-D'Obernay. Except for the few years when he was involved with masonry, little is known of his life. He is known to have been born in the small town of Obernay, at the foot of the Vosges Mountains, south-west of Strasburg in 1791. He was the younger son of a peasant farmer. It is possible that he served as a conscript in the Napoleonic armies and it is suggested that some of his time was in the French West Indies who he probably got into high degree masonry. (See *AQC* 94 where the present writer expands the story.) However, Glock appeared in Paris before 1819, calling himself de Glock-D'Obernay, claiming the 33° and high masonic rank in New Spain and Mexico. He must have had adequate diplomas to have satisfied the masons in Paris.

Glock became a member of the Garde de Corps of the new King Louis XVIII. Some time early in 1819, Glock decided to return to the New World, presumably to improve his fortunes, using masonry as a means of paying his way. Everything was in his favour; the high degrees were generally in a state of confusion, in France particularly so, and there was no one to check his activities.

D'Obernay started with a visit to Ireland where he had a letter of introduction to John Fowler, who was Deputy Grand Master to the young Duke of Leinster, Grand Master of Ireland, and also Grand Commander of the Irish College of Rites. D'Obernay tried to see the Duke of Leinster in Ireland, but he had just left. D'Obernay followed him to London. After seeing him, the Duke of Leinster wrote to Fowler:

> *19 August 1819.* I had a long communication with a Mr D'Obernay yesterday and from what I could make out of his wishes, I think it would not be right for me to receive any communications from him unless some more of our brethren were present who are better experienced than I am.

In reply, Fowler, who knew all about D'Obernay wrote:

> With respect to Mr D'Obernay . . . we have received from a Brother of our own R [ose] C [roix] Ch [apter] now in Paris satisfactory recommendations in so much that had your Grace remained in Ireland, and Mr D'O and we could have come upon terms, we would certainly have taken advantage of his full powers to have received thro' him such orders as are not yet practised in Ireland, but the terms he reqd, namely 100 guineas for the Charitable fund in France and 100 more for the Charity in Ireland were such as to the majority of the Brethren already possessed of the highest orders here appeared to be far beyond what they were inclined to accede to, the negotiations therefore fell to the ground. As Mr D'O has written to inform me he had made some arrangements for putting your Grace in possession of these orders (with power I presume to communicate the same when in Ireland to Brethren properly qualified) without putting the Order to expense, I have the honour to state that we will all feel highly gratified to receive at your Grace's hands any Masonic dignities we are not in possession of and for that purpose we will have the honour of transmitting to your Grace such full powers properly authenticated under the seal of our College as being transmitted by Br D'O to the Grand Consistoire de Paris may be there deposited in the Archives of the Order. . . .

The Duke of Leinster seemed at first to like the idea of high degrees and, even before receiving this letter from Fowler, he had written to the Duke of Sussex who was at Norwich where he was installing his friend, Coke of Holkham, afterwards Earl of Leicester, as Provincial Grand Master for Norfolk.

> . . . I had a communication yesterday with a Monr D'O who is on his way to South America. He came to Ireland, the day before I sailed, from Paris, and had powers to communicate all the higher orders, but my departure prevented the Brethren receiving them at that moment. He has been some time in London and is very anxious to show his documents to your Royal Highness when you return to town. I believe he has some idea of going to Norwich to be present at the Installation of Mr Coke & I have taken the liberty of giving him a letter to your Royal Highness that you might know who he was. I therefore trouble your Royal Highness with this letter to acquaint you of my having done so & at the same time to enclose his address.
>
> I have the
Honor to be Your Royal
Highness's Most Obedient &
Devoted Humble Svt.
>
> Harrington House,
August 19th 1819. Leinster.

The Duke of Sussex cannot have been pleased with this letter. It must have infuriated him. Since the Union of 1813, he had been trying to play down the high degrees to avoid dissension in the United Grand Lodge. Then suddenly the young Duke of Leinster introduces him to a man who could upset all that he had planned. No one will ever know what happened but it is clear that the Duke of Sussex told the young and enthusiastic Duke of Leinster of the many objections to what he had proposed. Being one of the sons of Georgee III and twice the age of the Irish Duke, he probably was outspoken. Whatever was said, the Duke of Leinster was no longer interested in high degrees and replied to John Fowler's letter welcoming the idea that he should receive such honours:

> Dear Mr Fowler, 28th August, 1819.
> I have this moment received your letter and think for many reasons which I will explain when I have the pleasure of seeing you in London that some other opportunity will be more proper for receiving the high degrees than at present. I have written to Mons. D'Obernay to that effect. [I have had a communication with the Duke of Sussex on the subject that you wrote to me some time ago but have not yet had his Royal Highness's answer.]
>
> Yours very sincerely
Leinster.

Assuming that the words in brackets refer to some quite different subject, we may deduce that the Duke of Leinster had been warned by the Duke of Sussex to avoid getting entangled with D'Obernay.

The Duke of Sussex had been placed in a very awkward position. He could refuse to have anything to do with the D'Obernay, in which case D'Obernay might have approached someone else. At the best, D'Obernay might have talked about the Duke's refusal which would have upset all the members of the high degrees in England, whose interests he was secretly guarding. The other alternative, the skilful one, was to accept all the honours and so become the only person in England who could form a Supreme Council—and then do nothing. This is what the Duke decided to do. Only a few of the Duke's closest masonic circle can have known about the plan. Leinster knew all about it but it is likely that he took no further part. The third member of the projected 'Supreme Council' was the Duke's own masonic secretary, Hippolyte da Costa. Da Costa was a Portuguese who had lived most of his life in the USA. When he returned to Portugal from a visit to London, he was arrested as a mason but his English friends arranged for his escape. He became a member of the Lodges of Antiquity and of the Nine Muses, and a protegé of the Duke who appointed him to the sinecure of Provincial Grand Master of Rutland. Whether Burckhardt and Gill, the Duke's confidants about the high degrees, knew about the scheme is uncertain. They may have done but had no ostensible part in it, all the correspondence being handled personally by da Costa.

D'Obernay's first important interview with the Duke of Sussex was on 6 September, 1819, as he wrote a letter immediately afterwards, a sort of *aide-mémoire* in what he calls '*A l'antichambre*'.

Monsieur le Duc,

After the interview with which your Royal Highness has favoured me, and after seeing Wor. Bro. Da Costa, I think I can overcome the reasons which prevented, if only temporarily, your royal agreement to the rough draft in question; an embarrassment which I flatter myself I can overcome without difficulty; by adding what I consider of the highest importance but which, in error, I forgot to insert: as long as they do not hinder the free

Opposite

Augustus, Duke of Sussex, by Domenico Pelligrini.

Grand Master, KT and HRDM, 1812–1843, Sovereign Grand Commander of Supreme Council for Great Britain, Ireland and the Possessions in America and the Indies 1819.

working of the Statutes and Regulations of the Order in England, or any other corrections which your Royal Highness considers awkward (*suscept-ibles*).

Rest assured, Monsieur le Duc, that I will consent to all that my powers allow and which I can reasonably assume to be for the full advantage of our Order. . . .

In the file in the Grand Lodge Library, dealing with the subject, there is a rough draft of the final agreed patent. It has numerous corrections in it. It is likely that D'Obernay took this back to France, as he writes the first of his begging letters:

Monsieur le Duc,   15 Sept., 1819.

I have the honour to send your Royal Highness a letter with the documents in question for Admiral Allemand [of the Sup. Con[l] of the Prado] hoping you will write to him without delay as the vessel will not sail from here before next Monday and we will not leave Gravesend before the following Wednesday evening.

It would be, Monsieur le Duc, another example of your Royal kindness if, instead of fifty guineas, you could send me a hundred because the Captain of the vessel, with whom I contracted not to pay in advance, needs it to buy provisions.

In demanding a thousand pardons for this liberty, I beg your Royal Highness to repay himself with the two hundred Louis which Admiral Allemand will surely send him next week without fail and, at the same time, would your Royal Highness send me, through our friend Da Costa, the complete regalia of 3rd Principal [*Grand Prêtre?*] of the Royal Arch with what remains of the two hundred Louis. . . .

Within a month, D'Obernay was back in London with the necessary papers and patent, presumably prepared in Paris at the Prado from the draft worked out by Da Costa and D'Obernay. We know that some masonic authorities in France had copies of the documents as they were published by the Grand Lodge of France in 1931 and are one of the sources for this Chapter. The Patent may be translated as follows:

J. de Glock-D'Obernay, of the Royal Bodyguard, Sov-Gd Insp Gen Grand Master *ad vitam* and representative of New Spain, Member and Plenipotentiary of the Sup Council for France and its possessions in America and the Indies, etc.

Having received from the Sup Council 33rd and last degree Scottish Grand East of Paris, the powers and special recommendations to make known and to spread the principles and institutions of this Ill Order, with previous and anticipated agreement of all our future actions; and having considered that it would be in the interests of the Order to establish another Supreme Council 33° for the Kingdom of Great Britain, Ireland and its possessions in America and the Indies; we have proposed to the Most Puissant and Very Mighty Prince Augustus Frederick, Duke of Sussex . . . Grand Master of English Masonry etc etc to communicate the degree to him, as well as to the below specified Ill Brn and to invest them with the high degrees of Scottish Masonry; to this end and object to create and institute in His Grace the Duke of Leinster, Grand Master of Ireland, etc etc and Mr Hippolyte Joseph da Costa, Provincial Grand Master of Rutland, the aforesaid Sup Council, which Sup Council will be independent and will enjoy the same powers and privileges as that of France and those which have been and will be established in the future, conforming always with the Statutes and Regulations of the Ancient and Accepted Scottish Rite, except for those modifications necessarily decided and agreed upon for its local government. And the Very Puissant and Most High aforesaid Prince Augustus Frederick etc etc having agreed to these suggestions, We the undersigned SGIGs and by virtue of our powers, we have solemnly conferred the 33rd and last degree and have acknowledged him Sov Gd Insp Gen and Grand Commander of the Order for Great Britain, Ireland and the possessions in America and the Indies and have also conferred the said 33° and have acknowledged the essential cofounders of the new Sup Council in very Ill Bro Duke of Sussex and Duke of Leinster etc etc etc.

The Supreme Council and Grand East of France will refrain from exercising any power of jurisdiction over England, Ireland and its Dependencies as the Sup Council of England will refrain from exercising its authority on the French dominions.

There are certain points of interest in this document. First, from the preamble, it would seem that it was issued in the name of the Supreme Council of the Prado—of very doubtful legality, as has already been explained. Secondly, its authorship is doubtful as there are a number of spelling mistakes in the original which seem to indicate that it was not written by D'Obernay who wrote very good French, as is shown by his subsequent letters. Finally, and perhaps the most important point, is the muddle about the geographical limits of the new Supreme Council, sometimes including Scotland, sometimes excluding it by calling the area England instead of Great Britain. A Supreme Council, as that envisaged in the Patent, would have united three quite separate masonic organisations into one Supreme Council and would never have worked, as its three founding members would have been perfectly aware.

The second document, also published in 1931, was a declaration by the three members of the newly constituted Supreme Council of England, Ireland, etc [Scotland now wisely being omitted]:

To all Colleges, Chapters, Councils and Lodges of Free and Accepted Masons, and to all others whom it may in anywise concern Greeting U.P.C.

We the Grand Commander and Members of the Illustrious College of Philosophical Masons of Ireland Knights of KH in sacred Conclave assembled do hereby fully empower and do moreover request of our Most Noble and Illustrious Grand Commander Augustus Frederick **Duke of Leinster** Grand Master of **Masons** in Ireland &c &c to hold communication with the Grand Consistoire de Paris or with the Illustrious Brother Joseph Glock D'O Bernay as holding full powers from the said Grand Consistoire respecting the introduction into Ireland of such degrees of Freemasonry as may not heretofore have been cultivated in this Country and for himself and for us to weave such information relating to the same as may be consistent with the established usages of the Order Done at the East of Ireland in a most holy place where Union Peace and Concord reign the 30 day of the month called Ab A.L. 505 . Anno. L.V. 5819

Ill: G: Com:

John Dumoulin Ill: S: G: W:

John Norman Ill: J G W:

Reg:

Authority to the Duke of Leinster, Grand Master of Ireland, to receive high degrees from Joseph Glock D'Obernay, dated 1819.

Wishing on this happy and memorable occasion to cement and consolidate more than ever the pleasant and fraternal association between ourselves, and the Supreme Council and Grand East of France, We, the undersigned Members, have unanimously decided, have and will nominate and recognize as honorary members of our Supreme Council of England, Ireland and its possessions in America and the Indies, Very, Very, Ill Bro J. de Glock-D'Obernay, below mentioned and the Duc d'Aumont, the Comte Decazes, the Duc de Tarante, the Baron de Marguerrettes, the Marquis de Massiac.

Given in triplicate at the Grand East in London on 13 October AD 1819 AL 5819

Signed.   Augustus Frederick, Duke of Sussex.
In the absence of and having power to do so. For the
Duke of Leinster Lieut Gd Comm
Augustus Frederick, Duke of Sussex.

Hippolyte da Costa.

In certifying this document as authentic and original, We certify and declare that, after having received the necessary obligations from the above mentioned Very Ill Brethren, we solemnly installed them yesterday evening and at the Grand East of London, the Supreme Council above mentioned.

London, this 14th day of the eigth M [presumably 14.10.1819].

Signed.   De Glock D'Obernay.

The position of the Duke of Leinster is curious. By the end of August, he knew the Duke of Sussex's plan and presumably agreed with it. Some time during September, he had received the official authority promised by John Fowler in his letter of the 19th August, permitting him to receive whatever high degrees were being offered. On the back of this certificate, the Duke of Leinster wrote:

Oct 1819
I hereby empower our Illustrious Brother His Royal Highness the Duke of Sussex to receive for me such communications in the higher degrees of Masonry as he thinks proper from Brother J. G. D'Obernay.
                              Leinster   (Seal)

This authority is among the official papers so may be assumed to have been given to da Costa for the Duke of Sussex. It is very doubtful whether, in fact, the Duke of Leinster attended his own installation into the 33°. Whether he was told to stay away by the Duke of Sussex or whether he was not prepared to co-operate any further with the farce, we shall never know. There is some clarification of this part of the story in the following letter which can be guaranteed as genuine.

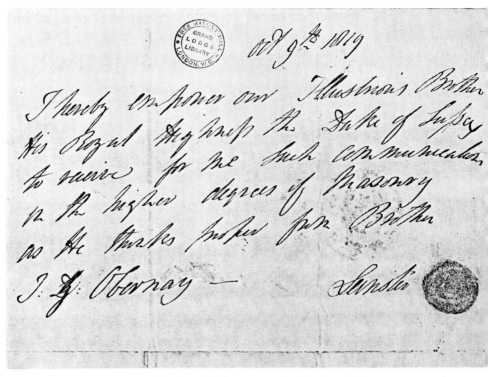

**Authorisation by the Duke of Leinster to the Duke of Sussex to receive
high degrees on his behalf, dated 9 October, 1819.**

On 27 December, 1826, John Fowler, by this time the Lieutenant
Grand Commander of the newly formed Supreme Council for Ireland, wrote to the Supreme Council of the Southern Jurisdiction
USA, their sponsoring body, saying that, on the 25 September of that
year, the Duke of Leinster had been installed as Sovereign Grand
Commander and that the Council of the 33° had been organised in
due form under letters patent from Charleston.

> ... but that it did not appear from information that he had received from
> the Illustrious Brother, His Royal Highness the Duke of Sussex, Grand
> Master of England, in a personal interview, that any Council of the 33° for
> England had not [a grammatical error for 'had'] been organized although
> His Royal Highness and two or three other elevated Brothers had received
> the degrees from France.

If Fowler had known that his own Sovereign Grand Commander had been one of the 'elevated Brothers' referred to, he would surely have said so. However, by this time, da Costa was dead and the two others concerned were not talking.

This curious story would have been incomplete without the finding of the file of correspondence which da Costa must have kept, in the Library of the United Grand Lodge. Two of the documents in it, the Certificates from Fowler authorising the Duke of Leinster to receive high degrees and the Duke's authority to the Duke of Sussex to receive them on his behalf, have been referred to. Further letters show that D'Obernay sailed for the West Indies about 23 October leaving behind him debts at his inn which he had the impertinence to ask the Duke of Sussex to pay. Like all 'bilkers', he had been let down by a debtor and, when the money did arrive, he would pay double or triple interest for the very temporary loan. Presumably the Duke paid up and there is no record of any repayment by D'Obernay.

Next month, there was correspondence with the Supreme Council in France who were anxious to know how the new body was progressing. One letter from London is of special interest as it is probably the only occasion on which the Duke of Sussex used his title as Sovereign Grand Commander. It also shows that the Duke had no intention of making any progress at all. The letter is in French and is marked as 'Copy of letters to Sup. Con France—Baron Marguerittes'. Marguerittes had been one of the leading opponents of de Grasse-Tilly in the Prado and, after Admiral Allemand's death in 1819, its leading member. The French of the letter is so much better than that usually written by da Costa that it is possible the Duke wrote it himself. The interesting preamble is given in its original French, and is followed by a translation of the remainder of the letter.

Ord; de Londres, sous la voûte céleste du Zénith, sur le point correspon-dant au 51 deg; 32 minutes Lat; Nord (Méridien de Londres) l'an de la V.L. 5819 le 29 nov 1819.

Auguste Frederick Duc de Sussex Xc. Xc. Grand Maître de la Maçonnerie d'Angleterre, Grand Commander du Sup. Con 33ᵉ Deg G.O. Ecossais pour la Gr.Bret. l'Irelande et ses possessions en Amérique et aux Indes.

Au Grands Conservateurs de l'Ordre du 33ᵉ Deg; Gr; Or; Ecossais pour le Royaume de France.

Very Ill. Brethren.

Having received the draft which you sent me, dated 14 Nov 1819 announcing the receipt of mine to the Sup: Council, I hasten to reply and to assure you of the receipt of the other documents which were with it.

The Sup: Con: for the Kingdom of Great Britain, Ireland and its possessions in America and the Indies, having just been formed, is not ready to send to members of the Sup: Con: for France, who were appointed Honorary Members, their diplomas, because the stamps, warrants and seals are not yet engraved; but they will be sent as soon as these objects are available.

It is not intended to fill the numbers of the Sup: Con: for ~~England~~ Great Britain, Ireland and its possessions in America and the Indies, until after everything has been arranged and after having chosen a suitable place, which has not yet been done; in addition, there are other difficulties which must be smoothed out carefully before it starts its work, and of which the Sup: Con: for France will be notified.

It is also essential that we receive the rituals [*cahiers?*] which we have kindly asked you to arrange and which I hope will be sent by the same hand as your letter, which is a very safe way.

I am in agreement on the caution not to receive here, and to be on guard against, all Masons and documents which do not have the authority of your Sup: Con:—precautions very necessary for the unity of the Order.

Accept Very Ill: Brn: the Masonic greetings from your affect Bro.

It is known that seals were sent from France. In 1889, a box containing 16 seals was found in Grand Lodge and was handed over to the Supreme Council. These seals may have been those referred to above and also in an unofficial letter which da Costa wrote to Baron Marguerittes about this time (see page 143).

Letters of a rather later date show that the Duke of Sussex was still to be plagued by D'Obernay. As soon as he arrived in the West Indies, he started to assert his authority, as a holder of the 33°, among high degree masons, particularly in Jamaica. Long letters that he wrote, often trying to explain why he could not remit fees that he received, are available. Mail was very slow and it was not until the middle of 1820 that the Provincial Grand Master of Jamaica wrote to the United Grand Lodge for information about what was happening. The Duke was extremely angry, and a draft of the Duke's displeasure, translated from da Costa's bad French, cannot have been pleasant reading for D'Obernay, if he ever got the original.

(*Letter to Mr D'Obernay 2 August, 1820*)
Monsieur et T.I.F. [Très Illustre Frère]
   ... From your despatches, as well as letters from Dr. Clare [Surgeon-General Sir Michael Benignus Clare, Provincial Grand Master, Jamaica 1816–31] H.R.H. has been informed of the erection of the Sovereign Gr. Consist. of Kingston, which has surprised H.R.H. very much as, according to the articles, signed by yourself on behalf of the Sup: Con: for France, the authority that you have received from France cannot be exercised in the English colonies, as is Jamaica, and you have not received, from H.R.H. as Grand. Comm. of England, powers to make similar establishments in these colonies. H.R.H. even explained to you that this

form of establishment could not be started before the Sup: Con: has been properly organized.

The consequences of your forming a Consistory at Kingston in Jamaica have been extremely disagreeable as Dr. Clare, the Pro. G.M. has written officially to the Gd. Sec. of the G.L. who has never had any information from the Gd. Master on this subject and was most surprised to get such news; all this could cause real confusion in the Grand L.

The powers which you have received from H.R.H. are limited entirely to the Royal Arch and even these cannot be exercised in the English colonies where there are Pr. Gd. Masters who inspect all their lodges and report regularly to the G.L. in London everything of Masonic interest in their respective provinces.

H.R.H. then, to prevent misunderstanding and confusion resulting from organizations set up without his authority and which could produce' a completely understandable upset in the G.L. in England, orders me to instruct you that your power is limited only to the Royal Arch; all your establishments in any other degree are nul and irregular; to tell you that the erection of the Grand Consistory of Kingston was made without H.R.H.'s authority and, as a result, all its work is to stop until fresh orders are received from H.R.H.

D'Obernay had written that he did not consider it safe to send fees that he had collected to England and, in a previous letter, he complained that he was temporarily short of money as his pocket-book had been stolen. Da Costa informed him that he must produce an account which no doubt Dr Clare would want.

But D'Obernay was irrepressible. In the same year, he was in New York where he at once got involved in local high degree affairs, writing of himself in a pamphlet and claiming, amongst other titles:

Creator and Honorary Member of the Supreme Council, Member and Senior Warden of the Grand Chapter R.A. [His name appears in no list but the Duke did give him some Honorary rank] and Representative of the Most Serene G.M. H.R.H. the Duke of Sussex, and of the Grand Lodge (of the York Rite) of Great Britain. [Which he most certainly was not.]

Seal of the Supreme Council of Paris, used in Jamaica by Glock D'Obernay. The eagle in this case is crowned.

PART THREE
The Supreme Council for England and Wales

15

THE ISSUE OF THE PATENT

THE DUKE OF SUSSEX died in 1843 and, on 22 December, a Supreme Grand Conclave of Knights Templar was summoned by W. H. White, in his capacity as Grand Chancellor and Registrar. Presumably White, the Grand Secretary of the United Grand Lodge, had been appointed to his rank in the high degrees by the Duke on the death of Robert Gill in 1822. The only other Great Officer was John Christian Burckhardt who had automatically become Acting Grand Master. The summons stated that the Supreme Grand Conclave consisted of all Great Officers, all Commanders of Encampments and two Captains from each Encampment. In spite of there being at least twenty Encampments, only eight Knights attended, besides Burckhardt and White. The *Freemasons'Quarterly Review* records their names as Spencer, Kincaid, Goldsworthy, Bauman, Fawcett, Francis, Prescott and Dr Crucefix, the last being the editor of the *Review*.

It was normal at this date for Knights Templar to have taken the Rose-Croix and Ne Plus Ultra degrees in their Encampment, so one can assume that all those named above had done so. Nevertheless, the only two to come to notice again in the formation of the Supreme Council are Crucefix and Goldsworthy, the latter never becoming a member of the Council but being involved in its beginnings.

Dr Robert Thomas Crucefix, who was a Junior Grand Deacon, had become well known in masonic circles owing to a quarrel with the Duke of Sussex in 1839, as a result of which he was suspended for six months. Though he was also concerned in the revival of the Grand Conclave, and complained in the *Freemason's Quarterly Review* that 'nothing is being done about the Grand Conclave because there are only three officers, of whom one, the Duke of Sussex, is dead,' he was also working towards the formation of a Supreme Council. On this subject, he gave his views in the *Review* '. . . there is no Red Cross Council, each Templar Encampment controlling and regulating the material of the higher degrees amongst its own members, and the regalia is not uniform.'

On 26 October, 1845, Crucefix wrote to the Secretary General of the Supreme Council of the Northern Masonic Jurisdiction United States

of America, of the Ancient and Accepted Rite requesting a patent and
explaining his position. There is no evidence as to why he wrote to the
Northern rather than to the Southern or older Jurisdiction, but it is
probable that he was aware that the Northern Masonic Jurisdiction
only admitted Christians to the Rose-Croix 18° and above, while the
Southern Jurisdiction had been theist from its start. All members of
the Rose-Croix in England were Christian, so a Supreme Council with
a theist doctrine would have been quite unacceptable. Crucefix wrote:

> To seek aid from Paris, I have certain objections in common with many
> others. Hence my attention is directed to you in the United States. As there
> are some who talk of seeking aid from Edinburgh, Dublin or Paris, I am
> most anxious that we should receive it (the thirty-third degree) from any
> other source if possible. It may strengthen my solicitation if I observe that
> I have some reason to fear that, sub rosa, there is some party who privately
> confers the thirty-third degree, and that ere long we may have the
> mortification to see a Council acting upon some illegitimate claims to
> distinction. If your Grand Council can authorize me to act, &c., it will ere
> long have the satisfaction to learn that they have been the means of giving
> existence in London to a Grand Council that will reflect honour and credit
> on themselves.

According to Jeremiah How's *Freemasons' Manual*, 1862, the man of
whom Crucefix was suspicious was another Freemason doctor, Henry
Beaumont Leeson. The *Manual* stated:

> [Leeson] ... commenced the necessary steps for the formation of the
> Council of the Ancient and Accepted Rite; while they were progressing,
> Brother Crucefix obtained a legal authority from the Supreme Council of
> New York (now at Boston) giving him the first rank. Brother Leeson ...
> was at the time in correspondence with another body for a like authority.

The 'body' could only have been the Council of Rites of the Grand
Orient or the Supreme Council for France. Either would have been
glad of the prestige of sponsoring a Supreme Council for England.
The Supreme Council of the Prado (now merged into the Supreme
Council for France) had tried, as we have seen in Chapter 14, with the
Duke of Sussex, and failed. Fortunately for Crucefix, whichever body
was interested did not act quickly enough, though he was nervous that
he would be anticipated and wrote again to America on 10 November.

> Since writing you some few days since, I am the more strongly impressed
> with the *necessity* of obtaining, if possible, the delegation of power to hold
> office as *Grand Inspector General for England*, and without delay. I pray
> you write me without delay, as my movements will mainly depend on the
> prospective, how to act with decision.

The Americans had been having trouble with the French high degree authorities and they may also have known of the project to erect a Supreme Council for Scotland. However, the Supreme Council, NMJ met on the 23 and 24 December and considered Dr Crucefix's letters. It was decided to authorise the Grand Secretary General to write officially to him in accordance with certain directions of the Sovereign Grand Commander as to how his request could be granted. After an understandable pause for Christmas, the following letter was sent:

Boston, December 29, 1845.

Dear Sir and Brother,

In answer to your notes, twenty-sixth October and tenth November last, I am directed by the Supreme Council of the Thirty-third degree for the Northern District and Jurisdiction of the United States to represent to you, that, after giving the subject matter of your communications the serious and careful consideration which its importance demands, and reposing entire confidence in your personal integrity and masonic prudence, they did on the twenty-fourth December, *Resolve*, That the interests and stability of Sublime Freemasonry, would in their judgement, be advanced by a compliance with your request. Our venerable and well beloved M:. P:. Sov:. Grand Commander *ad vitam*, J. J. J. Gourgas, Esq., merchant of New York City, directs me to express to you the great anxiety he feels that there should be a full and free understanding and a perfect harmony in the work and proceedings between the Supreme Councils of the United States, of Scotland and Ireland; and that he hopes and believes will be promoted, and the sooner secured by the cooperation of our distinguished Sublime Brethren in England, operating through a regularly and lawfully constituted Supreme Council.

The letter continued, quoting some of the troubles that the Northern Masonic Jurisdiction had been having in its international relations. These are dealt with in the next Chapter. The Grand Secretary General went on:

... I proceed with equal brevity to state the conditions and sanctions under which the Patent you desire will be forwarded to you.

You must be sensible, my Brother, that your request is to some extent peculiar and embarrassing. It asks for high and important powers which you will concede ought never to be delegated but with great caution and weighty considerations; and our M:. P:. Sov:. Grand Commander, in common with all the members of his Council, cannot but feel that the course we are pursuing in this matter is a precipitate one, and only justified by the emergency of the case. We have watched with care, and believe we understand the policy of the high masonic powers at Paris, in sending out their emissaries, and availing themselves of every opportunity to extend their jurisdiction, and to spread their innovations wherever they can obtain for them anything like a favourable reception. We are aware that they have long had their eye upon England, but have hitherto been restrained from action by the well known opposition of your late Grand Master to the *hauts grades*. That restriction no longer existing, they will soon, if they have not already directed their efforts to the attainment of this cherished object. To thwart them in this should be the desire of every friend to our pure and unadulterated Rite; and it is the consideration taken in connection with the high quarter from which the request emanates, that influences the present action of our Supreme Council.

The Council understand, that you are a member of the 'Royal Order of Palestine'; at least, a 'Grand Cross Commander Kadosh', in the Grand Conclave of England; on this belief, I am directed to transmit to you the Obligations of the 30°, 31°, 32°, 33°, all of which you will herewith receive in a separate envelope; you will, if possible, appoint Dr Oliver, your Lieut:. Grand Commander, and also appoint your Grand Treasurer of H:.E:. You will then break the envelope, each of you make separate copies of the Obligation, sign them, each signing as witnesses for the other, and return the copies so made to my care. . . . If, however, it will occasion you too much delay, or there are special reasons why you cannot appoint your officers as above named *at once*, then return copies of the Obligation signed by *yourself*, and authority will be issued to you to act individually in qualifying your own officers. The course first named is the most desirable. On the return of the Obligation, our M:. P:. Sov:. Grand Commander will forward you the necessary powers, and the whole of the thirty-third degree, together with a copy of the Grand Secret Constitutions, &c. Should anything have occurred to change your views in relation to this matter, or should circumstances have compelled you to seek authority anywhere else, you will not break the seal of the envelope, but return it to me *precisely as you received it*.

Your friend and Brother,

Chas. W. Moore,
Sec:. Gen:; H:. E:. &c.

It would seem that Dr Crucefix had already informed the Americans of his intention to appoint Dr George Oliver, DD, as his Lieutenant Grand Commander. Dr Oliver was well known throughout the masonic world for his writings and his name would have been an added assurance of the status of the new project. Dr Crucefix acted very promptly on the letter above, writing on the 6 February, 1846, and returning all the signed Obligations, including one from Henry Udall appointed as Grand Treasurer of H.E. His letter, received in Boston early in March, was as follows:

Most Puissant Brother and other Grand Inspectors General. You have not misinterpreted my zeal on the great necessity that exists in England for the exercise of a *pure practical ritual of the thirty-third degree.* I am deeply impressed with the importance of the unlimited confidence reposed in me, and shall make it my study to prove that I shall not disgrace this confidence or give you cause to regret having so far entrusted me.

I enclose the accompanying obligation, sacredly taken, in its fullest sense, and as sacredly signed by myself.

I shall critically study, with the severity of self-examination, the important papers forwarded to me, and await with anxious interest further directions and instructions.

Permit me, Most Puissant Brethren, to assure you of the highest consideration for your exalted office, of the personal respect I entertain for you, and of the very grateful sense on which I view your confidence in my *honour and fidelity as a mason.* With these *sentiments,* I subscribe myself
Your faithful servant and Brother,
Robt. Thos. Crucefix.

At the next meetings of the Supreme Council for the Northern Masonic Jurisdiction which were held on 20 and 27 March, it was reported that a most satisfactory communication had been received. Dr Crucefix was elected an Honorary Member of the Supreme Council with power to establish, in accordance with the Grand Constitutions, 'The Grand and Supreme Council of the M∴P∴Sov∴ Grand Inspectors General of the 33 degree for England, to hold their Grand East in the City of London'.

Dr Crucefix was then acknowledged as the founder and first M∴P∴Sov∴ Grand Commander and it was ordered that a Patent to that effect be sent to him, dated 26 October, 1845. The selection of this date, being that of the original application, is not unreasonable and there is no suggestion that it was antedated to ensure that the newly formed Supreme Council would have precedence over Scotland where another Supreme Council was also forming. This date has therefore become the official date of the start of the Supreme Council for England and Wales.

According to Baynard, some documents were sent with the Patent and others followed, up to August of that year. These included the full rituals of the 18° and of the 30° to 33°. Also sent were copies of the Patent issued to Stephen Morin on 27 August, 1761. This would, of course, have been an 'amended copy' produced by de Grasse-Tilly and his father-in-law, as no original has ever been found. A copy of the Grand Constitutions was also sent but it is not known whether this was the 'French' or 'Latin' version; probably the latter. A copy of an Oath of Allegiance was also forwarded which Crucefix had to sign and return.

On 23 July, 1846, the Supreme Council NMJ was advised by Crucefix that the Supreme Council for England and Wales was established. It would have been at this meeting that the new body was proclaimed 'under the C.C. of the Zenith, near the B.B.' with the comment:

> We feel as scions of a parent stock no small pride in thus having the power in some measure to repay a debt of gratitude to the memory of past worthies, by the opportunity afforded us of regenerating the scintillations that have so long been dormant in England.

In return, Crucefix dedicated the 1846 bound volume of his *Freemasons' Quarterly Review* to the Sovereign Grand Commander of the Northern Masonic Jurisdiction of the USA Most Puissant Brother J. J. J. Gourgas.

Having made his position secure as Sovereign Grand Commander, Crucefix was no longer in a hurry. He succeeded in placating Leeson who agreed to become a member of the new Supreme Council. There may have been some opposition when the names of the new Council were announced, as the *Freemasons' Review* of 30 June, 1846, hints that there were others with pretentions to the rank.

> We had hoped to give you a full account of the active operations of this highly important body, the sphere of whose utility is likely to become manifest. The *Hauts Grades* in this country have hitherto had no rallying point—no governmental discipline; but this is not the worst part of the subject. To seek for diplomas without the attainment of knowledge was not considered unbecoming—to grant them without sufficient discrimination was not held to be *infra dig.* consequently in these piping days of railroad speed and economy; it is not to be wondered at that the mania has extended to Masonry and that many a Mason, scarcely fledged from the nest, has taken wing and returned home a full grown 33°. Not but that there are very honourable exceptions but we fear they only prove the rule. It has long been a desirable point that English companions should be trained to find in their own country the means of attaining the highest possible qualifications and the names of the following brethren having transpired we give them, without hesitation, as a guarantee that they may fairly be said to possess a competent knowledge, and that they are not likely to confer any of the degrees without due discrimination.
>
> Dr R. T. Crucefix, Sovereign Grand Commander.
> Rev George Oliver, DD, Lieutenant Grand Commander.
> Henry Udall, Grand Treasurer-General.
> Dr Henry B. Leeson.
> Davyd W. Nash.
> Richard Lea Wilson.
> Thomas Pryer.
> William Tucker.

(*Short Biographies of the above are given at the end of the Chapter*)

The actual dates of appointment to the Supreme Council of the last five members are somewhat doubtful. Crucefix, Oliver and Udall had their Patents antedated to the date of the Patent of the Supreme Council, 26 October 1845. The dates of the Patents of the others are shown in the *Rules, Regulations and List of Members of the A & A Rite for England and Wales* as follows: Leeson and Wilson—April 1846; Nash and Pryer—7 July, 1846; and Tucker—1 December 1846. However, the warrants for the Grand Metropolitan Chapter No 1 is dated 24 June 1846. It has 7 signatures and one rubber stamp. The Grand Treasurer-General (Udall) and the Grand Master of the Ceremonies (Leeson) put H.E. after their names. Nash, as Grand Secretary-General used a rubber stamp. Pryer signed as Captain of the Life Guards, a title continued until 1872 when the word 'Life' was omitted. Tucker, who signs himself as Grand Almoner was not a 33° until the general meeting of the Supreme Council on 1 December 1846.

After having given the names of the new Supreme Council, the *Review* continued tactfully:

> It is hardly necessary to remark that, in the exercise of these important functions, the Supreme Council do not intrench on the privileges of the Grand Conclave, which is constitutionally limited to the degree of Masonic Knights Templar. The jurisdiction of the Grand Inspectors General commences with the Sublime Grand Lodge, and ends with their own, including all the intermediate degrees.

The Supreme Grand Conclave met twice in 1846 and, at the second meeting, a Grand Master was elected and installed. Crucefix was a member of the Conclave and acted as Director of Ceremonies at the installation. He was being careful not to trespass on the prerogatives of the older body, though there does not seem to have been any consultation with them. Actually, there could have been little enmity or jealousy between the revived Grand Conclave and the new Supreme Council as so many of those concerned belonged to both bodies. How, writing some years after the event, disagrees with this and states that the setting up of the Supreme Council was a 'severance which caused at the time much dissatisfaction and heart burning arising from which can hardly yet be said to have subsided'.

The first meeting of the Supreme Council was held on 1 December, 1846, six months after Crucefix's patent had arrived. It was an all-embracing meeting. The 33° met first and conferred the degree on Tucker and three others. This was followed by meetings of the 32° and 31° at which presumably a number of degrees were conferred. It is only possible to make assumptions as no minutes of the Council until

8 July, 1854, are available, and facts mostly come from Crucefix's *Review*. Two days later, a Grand College of Elected Knights Kadosh 30° was held. To this, all Knights of St Andrew 29° and Knights of the Sun 28° were invited to attend when they must have been raised to the 30°. There is no information how such brethren had become members of the 28° and 29° as no bodies in England are known to have conferred these degrees. The assumption is that those concerned had received them overseas and came into the category about which Crucefix had complained in his *Review* on 30 June. This was followed by a meeting of the Rose-Croix 18° and the *Review* records that a number of degrees were conferred. The proceedings ended with a banquet at Freemasons' Tavern. In this speech, Crucefix referred rather unnecessarily to Leeson's recent visit to the 'Supreme Council of the Grand Orient' and that the 'happiest results ensued'. Later, he reported to America that the banquet had been a *Chef D'Oeuvre*.

It was an auspicious start. All that now lay in front of the new Supreme Council was the difficult task of persuading the existing Knights Templar Encampments to surrender their authority to confer those degrees which had become part of the Ancient and Accepted Rite; and to take control of the Rose-Croix bodies which thus became independent. Many of the latter submitted to the authority of the Supreme Council for England and Wales soon after it started: others waited many years. The Baldwyn Encampment had resumed its freedom from the Grand Conclave and did not come under the revived body again until 1862. The Rose-Croix element waited another 19 years. In the Treaty of Union on May 1881 with the Supreme Council, it was agreed that it should become a Chapter under its authority but 'is placed at the top of the Chapters Rose-Croix'. 'The members are at liberty to continue their ancient ceremonial and it is constituted a District under an Inspector-General on whom shall be conferred the 32°.' An interesting custom retained is that the candidate in Bristol must take the degree of Knight Templar before that of Rose-Croix and has to appear at the ceremony in the Templar tunic. This custom, which had been the normal procedure in most English Encampments, appears to have ceased, except in Bristol, when the Supreme Council for England and Wales was formed. By the terms of the Treaty of Union, it is, however, not necessary for a visiting Rose-Croix Mason to have received the K.T. degree. It was also stipulated that the Templar and Rose-Croix degrees should be kept separate and not normally worked on the same night.

Finally, complete unity of the bodies working the Ancient and Accepted Rite in England and Wales was achieved when the last of the independent bodies, Antiquity of Bath, submitted to the Supreme Council in 1883, although they had in 1866 been granted a warrant.

Biographies of the First Supreme Council

Robert Thomas Crucefix MD, LLD 1797–1850. Educated at the Merchant Taylors' College and trained at St Bartholomew's Hospital. On qualifying, he went to India for a few years, but returned to London where he lived for the remainder of his working life.

Initiated 16 April, 1819, in the Burlington Lodge (now No 96), WM in 1833 and was a prominent member all his life. He was also a member of several other lodges and chapters. In 1832, was appointed Grand Steward representing Peace and Harmony Lodge (now No 60), Member of the Board of General Purposes 1832–37 and Junior Grand Deacon 1836, Grand Standard Bearer RA 1836.

He started in the high degrees while temporarily practising in Edinburgh, being installed KT in the Grand Conclave of Scotland, 1831. Joined the Cross of Christ Encampment (now Preceptory of St George No 6) 1831 and, a few months later, received the Rose-Croix and Ne Plus Ultra. In 1846, Grand Director of Ceremonies in the Grand Conclave, and 1847 was Grand Commander of Kent.

He is best known for his part in the foundation of what is now the Royal Masonic Benevolent Institution. He even launched his *Freemasons' Quarterly Review* as a propaganda vehicle for it. Infortunately the idea was not popular with the Duke of Sussex, who preferred an annuity fund. Dr Oliver, his friend, paid tribute to him:

> Dr Crucefix did not pretend to infallibility and, like other public men, he might sometimes be wrong; but his errors were not from the heart, and always leaned on the side of virtue and beneficence. He toiled unceasingly for the benefit of his brethren. . . . In sickness or in health, he was ever found at his post, and his sympathy was the most active on behalf of the destitute brother, the widow and the orphan.

George Oliver 1782–1867. Doctor of Divinity. A schoolmaster and took Holy Orders in 1813, spending most of his life in parishes in East Anglia.

Initiated probably about 1802 while a Lewis in St Peter's Lodge, Peterborough (no longer exists). (See *AQC* 97.) He was exalted in the Rodney Chapter, Kingston-upon-Hull (no longer exists), and received the high degrees in the associated bodies of this Chapter. Deputy Provincial Grand Master of Lincolnshire, 1832 to 1842, when he was not reappointed because of his involvement in the quarrel between Dr Crucefix and Grand Lodge. As a result, he withdrew almost entirely from active Craft masonry, devoting his life to writing the many books which are still found in all masonic libraries. His books, though of interest, principally for their ideas on masonic symbolism, are now

Dr George Oliver 33°, first Lieutenant Grand Commander.

regarded as insufficiently based on fact. *Kenning's Cyclopaedia* gives him a warm notice:

> As a man and a Mason, he was all that eulogy can confirm or desire. Genial and friendly, honest-hearted and sincere, just and considerate, respectable and respected in every position of duty and every aspect of life, he seems indeed a comely monument of the order to which it was his pride and privilege to belong.

Henry Udall 1808–1874. Little is known about his private life except that he was a barrister by profession.

Initiated in the Westminster and Keystone Lodge No 10 in 1835, Secretary 1841–1855 and WM 1838 and 1855. In 1855, the ceremony was carried out by the Gd Secretary W. H. White. From 1850, No 10 decayed almost to extinction, having, in 1855, only three members. It is believed that, at the suggestion of the Grand Secretary, the Lodge membership was increased by a large and continuing group of Oxford graduates who were seeking a Lodge in London. Udall's re-installation as WM by the Grand Secretary was presumably to encourage the resurgence of the Lodge. Udall continued as a member until the 1870s. It is not known when he became a member of the high degrees, but he was at one time High Pontiff (i.e. Prelate?) in the Chapter of Faith and Fidelity (ceased 1846). In July 1842, he supported Crucefix and Oliver by attacking the Prov Gd Master for Lincolnshire in an open letter to Dr Oliver in the *Freemasons' Quarterly Review*.

> I much regret there is no effectual method of teaching that brother that his elevated Provincial Rank is conferr'd on him for other purposes than that of attempting a stigma on one who is held in the highest esteem by all those whose good opinion in Masonry is worth obtaining. Be assured, dear Sir, that your character stands far too high & your Masonic virtues are too fully appreciated to be the slightest degree affected by the petty tyranny of one whose Masonic rank has been attain'd merely from his accidental circumstances of birth and fortune.

Henry Beaumont Leeson MD, FRCP, FRS 1803–1872. Educated at Repton and Cambridge, BA 1825. He was a lecturer in forensic medicine at St Thomas's Hospital for many years. Died at his home in the Isle of Wight.

Initiated in St Mary's Lodge (now No 63) but four years later joined the influential Prince of Wales's Lodge (now No 259). Represented this Lodge as Grand Steward in 1842; WM 1854. On 16 December, 1836, was installed as KT in the Cross of Christ Encampment (now Preceptory of St George No 6) and next year received Rose-Croix and Ne Plus Ultra. Also a member of Faith and Fidelity

Preceptory No 26. In 1847, appointed Past Gr Captain of Lines, Gd Conclave.

He succeeded Dr Crucefix as Sovereign Grand Commander in 1851, after a short interregnum when Dr Oliver automatically took this position and before he resigned it.

Davyd Nash 1810–1876. A surgeon and barrister whose home was at Bristol.

Initiated 1832 in the Royal Sussex Lodge of Hospitality No 187 of Bristol, but did not join the Lodge until 1838. Resigned in 1840, rejoined 1850 to 1853 but he again resigned for two months when he rejoined until finally retiring in 1858. Also a PM of Lodge of Honor and Generosity (now No 165) and Sovereign of Faith and Harmony in 1846. More of his biography appears in the text. Was made an honorary member of No 187 for 'his great kindness and usefulness while D Provincial Gd Master [of Bristol] 1854–57'.

Robert Lea Wilson c 1807–1861. His obituary states 'He was a member of a powerful county family and followed the silk trade, but for many years had no occupation.' Was a Deputy Lieutenant for Middlesex.

Initiated 1830 at Norwich in a lodge which has now disappeared. Moved soon to London where he joined several lodges and chapters, including the Burlington (now No 96) where Crucefix was also a member. WM 1836 and 1841. In 1843, was a Grand Steward representing Peace and Harmony No 60. Provincial Gd Senior Warden, Surrey 1841. Was installed KT in the Cross of Christ Encampment where he took Rose-Croix and Ne Plus Ultra on 13 April, 1835. Is stated to have withdrawn from all masonic activities in 1854 when some of his actions were criticised.

Thomas Pryer 1815–1855. By profession a solicitor, admitted 1833. His obituary states that 'He had a good practice, but was prodigal and left his family badly off'.

Initiated 20 October 1841 in Oak Lodge (now No 190) WM 1847–48. Installed KT in Mt Calvary Encampment (now Preceptory No 3) in 1843. On Trinity Sunday 1845 the Encampment was opened 'in the Superior Degrees of K.H.S.H., K. of M. and M.P., Sovn Chapter of R.C. & N.P.U. &c.' He was one of several candidates who were 'Dubbed Knts. of the above named Exalted Chevalric and Supreme Degrees in Freemasonry'. Pryer became Eminent Commander of the Encampment in 1847. He was responsible for obtaining the Warrant for the Rose-Croix Degrees of the Chapter in the following year, though it remained part of the Encampment until 1863.

William Tucker, Grand Secretary General HE of the Supreme Council, 1854–55.

William Tucker 1815–1855. Was a large landowner in the West Country.

Initiated 1842 in Lodge of Unanimity and Sincerity, Taunton, (now No 261). In 1843, was appointed Prov Grand Registrar for Somerset and next year was WM of his lodge. Founding Master of Lodge Virtue and Honor, Axminster (now No 494) and he also joined at least eight lodges in Devon and Somerset. Appointed Prov Gd Master for Dorset 1846. Deposed 1853, as explained in the text.

In 1846, was Commander of the Coryton Encampment of KT as well as being Prov Gd Master for the KT in Dorset. Presumably acquired the Rose-Croix through this Chapter, as he was conferring the degree within a fortnight of his installation. He succeeded Davyd Nash as Grand Secretary General in 1854.

16
EARLY ADMINISTRATION

DR CRUCEFIX HAD presumably invited his medical colleague, Dr Leeson, to be a member of the Supreme Council to avoid friction. He knew that Leeson had been in touch with the French and that had been the reason for his urgency in applying to the Northern Masonic Jurisdiction USA for his patent. When this arrived, Crucefix was specifically warned against the French and had been sent documents to prove their alleged misdemeanours. The American Grand Secretary-General's letter is definite:

> He [the American Sovereign Grand Commander] is the more anxious on this point in view of the irregular and unmasonic conduct which has been adopted and pursued by the Grand Orient of France: against any alliance with which so far as Sublime Masonry is concerned, he particularly desires me to caution you. He has also witnessed with grief the irregular and injudicious proceedings of the Grand Councils of Scotland and Ireland, in following the lead of the Grand Orient, in adopting and incorporating upon their own system the degrees and rites not recognized as legitimate and regular; and he desires it to be distinctly understood that such proceedings can never receive the Sanction of the Supreme Councils of the United States.
>
> As for the Supreme Council of France, it derived its origin from the US and is so far a regular body. But it has degenerated, become corrupted by French innovations, and it is not now in correspondence with the Supreme Councils in this Country.

When this letter arrived, some attention was paid to its contents as the *Freemasons' Review* reported:

> . . . The Council are proceeding with the strictest caution, and are most zealously determined not to associate with, nor admit to their alliance any other Supreme Council but such as derive their powers from the clearest possible source.

In spite of this statement, Leeson visited Paris during 1846, after the patent had been received, and seems to have been welcomed. Oxford states that an alliance had been completed between the Grand Orient of France and the new Supreme Council. It is unlikely that anything so definite as an alliance had taken place. The English Council had not actually been formed, and all that probably happened was the establishment of friendly relations. In fact both the new Supreme Council and the Grand Orient were equally unpopular with the Americans. Among the papers sent to Dr Crucefix was a copy of a letter to the Comte de Fernig, Lieutenant Grand Commander of the Supreme Council. De Fernig was a life-long enemy of the Grand Orient and he wrote to his opposite number in the Northern Jurisdiction asking why they were so angry with the Supreme Council for France. The reasons for the quarrel are not clear, but the reply sent to de Fernig certainly ended all chances of a reconciliation—as perhaps it was intended to do.

It is also difficult to understand the anger of the US Supreme Councils against the Irish and Scottish high degree bodies. Presumably the 'degrees of Rites not recognised' refer to rites, such as Mizraim and Memphis, which both took under their jurisdictions with the deliberate intention of suppressing them. Ireland had got its patent for its Supreme Council from the Southern Jurisdiction USA and Dr Morison, the first Sovereign Grand Commander in Scotland, had a patent of the 33° from Spain and then had it endorsed by both the Supreme Council for France and the Grand Orient. All this was perfectly regular according to the 1786 Constitutions.

Dr Crucefix had acknowledged all this correspondence: 'I have perused it with intense interest; indeed as a point of reference, I have taken a copy for my future reference.' His magazine, however, was reporting:

> ... A correspondence has been opened with several legitimate Councils and it is probable that our next number will develop the activities of the Supreme Council who are united as much by their Masonic reputations as by their social position. *Quis Separabit?*

Such development did take place and, at a meeting of the Council on 24 February, 1847, Bro Raymond of the USA was acknowledged as representing the Supreme Council with the Northern Masonic Jurisdiction and Henry Udall as the representative of the Northern Masonic Jurisdiction with the Council in London. There was no harm in this, but at the same time the Supreme Council was also exchanging representatives with the Grand Orient: Leeson representing it in London and a Brother Bugnot acted for the Supreme Council in Paris.

When the American authorities heard what had happened, they

were most indignant. The Sovereign Grand Commander of the Northern Masonic Jurisdiction spoke of

> the defection, contemplated and so systematically carried through and accomplished . . . we have been completely circumvented by him in a most shameless manner, it appears clearly to have been a deep-laid systematic plot, acted upon by him with great duplicity from the very moment he had received in his hands the full powers vested in him by us and solely used by him as his introduction and alliance with the Grand Orient of France.

The Americans had every reason to be angry and there is no doubt that Crucefix behaved badly. However, to accuse him of a premeditated plot is to attribute to him far more foresight than he ever possessed. He was in the hard position of a general without an army, and did not dare risk opposition by offending anyone. We shall never know if Leeson's consent to join Crucefix's Supreme Council was conditional on his continuing his visits to France, but he had to be placated, and Crucefix was in no position to stop them. Crucefix defended himself by complaining about the behaviour of the Scottish Supreme Council, which was also forming. But this had nothing to do with the matter. The new Scottish Sovereign Grand Commander, Dr Charles Morison, was fully entitled to form a Supreme Council for Scotland. The American Supreme Council were not pacified; on 23 September, 1847, they

> . . . Resolved and decreed unanimously that all intercourse or communication with the aforesaid Dr. Robt. Thos Crucefix, or his Supreme Council has ceased, and it is forbidden until he and they publicly abjure all further connexion and alliance with the aforesaid Grand Orient of France.

Subsequent proceedings of the Supreme Council for the Northern Masonic Jurisdiction do not record any cancellation of this resolution, but Dr Crucefix died in 1850, and this may have ended the quarrel. By 1853, relations were sufficiently cordial for their Supreme Council to have stated:

> Our Daughter Council of England . . . is progressing far beyond any reasonable expectations which could have been entertained in the period of its establishment . . . The present indications are that it is destined at no very remote period to take its stand at the head of all the Supreme Councils in Europe, for character, ability and efficiency. This Council can never feel other than the highest regard for its welfare, nor witness its prosperity with other than feelings of gratification.

This praise was certainly not ironical, but it is odd that, when it was written, Dr Leeson had succeeded Dr Crucefix, and it was his close association with France which caused all the trouble in the first place.

The Use of the words 'Holy Empire' with signatures

Since the start of Supreme Councils about 1800, Grand Treasurers General and Grand Secretaries General, when signing their names officially have placed the words '*Saint Empire*' or 'Holy Empire' (usually abbreviated as HE) after their titles. The words conform to the legend of the Rite and its association with the Empire of Frederick II of Prussia. Those who wrote this legend into the Constitutions of the Rite must have confused the new Prussian Empire with the centuries older Holy Roman Empire. The term 'Holy Empire' which referred to the Habsburg Empire, appeared about the XIV century and this was still in being, centered on Austria, when Frederick the Great was King of Prussia. It had become known as the 'Holy Roman Empire' many centuries before the era of Frederick, because it had the patronage of the Pope: again nothing to do with the Protestant Frederick. Frederick never assumed any title but that of King of Prussia.

The first time that 'HE' is found is in documents signed by the Secretary-General of the Supreme Council of America which was formed at Charleston at the start of the XIX century. This must have been at the suggestion of de Grasse-Tilly and his compatriots who had probably used the French version of the term, towards the end of the previous century, in documents of the Supreme Council for the French West Indies; and had probably invented it. They may have been guided in their choice of the title by their recollection of the early association of the Rite with the defunct Emperors of the East and West and possibly by the idea that the words would suggest the exercise of an extreme and extensive masonic dominion. The term may be found in the abridged edition of the Constitutions of 1786, certified as correct in March 1813 by de la Hogue. There is also an earlier entry of the Treasurer being '*du Saint-Empire*'. The final paragraph can be translated:

> The present ritual of the reception [of the 33°] and the Constitutions that follow it, have been drawn up in eighteen articles by US, Frederick II, William II, King of Prussia etc. . . . Sovereign Grand Commander of the Council, Supreme Council of the 33° degree, made at Our Royal Residence at Berlin on the first day of May, *Anno Lucis* 5786, year of grace 1786 and fortieth of Our reign.
>   Signed.   Frederick.
>   On behalf of the King.
>   Count Finckenstein von Hertzborg.
>   Secretary of the Holy Empire.

Frederick the Great, King of Prussia. Born 1712, died 17 August, 1786.

Count Finckenstein von Hertsberg was a name, well known among masons, as the signatory of the decree of 16 July, 1744, in which Frederick proclaimed himself protector of the masons in his kingdom. Von Hertsberg was an influential member of the Rite of Strict Observance, but had no connection with the A & A Rite. His name was probably used by the compilers of the 1786 Constitutions as he was known to have a position at Frederick's court, but the title after it confirms its use in the earliest days of the Rite.

The term also appears in the Latin version of these Constitutions, printed in 1834, in Article IV, in dealing with payment for a patent, which is to be made '. . . to the Very Illustrious Treasurer of the Holy Empire'. This is repeated in Article XVI, while in Article XVIII, there is the phrase 'The Illustrious Secretary and Illustrious Treasurer of the Holy Empire.' That this tradition was continued is confirmed by the fact that Baron Tessier de Marguerittes, who was an early member of the Supreme Council of the French West Indies, continued to sign himself as 'Secretary-General of the Holy Empire' for many years, as did the early Secretaries of the Supreme Council of Charleston. Thus we see that these interesting titles, though incorrect historically, are fully justified by usage and by the Constitutions of the Rite.

In the very early days of the Supreme Council for England and Wales, most of the members seem to have put HE after their signatures on Chapter warrants. This practice on the Warrant of the Grand Metropolitan Chapter No 1 has already been referred to on page 165. On the Warrant of Mount Calvary (now No 3) five of the signatures have HE after their names. It is not known when this ceased. The present custom is for only the Grand Treasurer-General and the Grand Secretary-General to use this title. The reasons for the title are explained in the address on the presentation of a candidate's certificate. Much useful information about the degree is lost if this optional address is omitted.

Secretarial Difficulties

Dr Crucefix's selection of the first Grand Inspector General to help with the office work of the Supreme Council was unfortunate. Davyd Nash was an odd choice as he had been initiated in Bristol in 1836 and had joined the fiercely independent Baldwyn Chapter four years later. It is possible that Crucefix had expected that the non-Templar elements of the Baldwyn Encampment would submit to his jurisdiction and he may have hoped that Nash would persuade them. If this was so, he was to be disappointed, as they did not do so, and therefore, in the view of the Supreme Council for England and Wales, became irregular.

When Dr Crucefix died in 1850, Dr Oliver took his place in accordance with Article III of the Constitutions of 1786 but, in a few months, he gave way to Dr Leeson and reverted to Lieutenant Grand Commander. Dr Oliver had resigned somewhat unwillingly, but there is no doubt that it was the sensible decision. He was a charming old gentleman, wrapped up in his extensive writing and not at all the type of man who could push the fortunes of the newly formed Supreme Council. Regrettably, little is known about the events of this period. It is possible that Nash kept minutes but, if so, he must have taken them away to Bristol when he retired, and the first available are dated 5 July, 1854, presumably written by his successor.

When Nash retired in that year for reasons now unknown, his place was taken by William Tucker of Coryton Park, Dorsetshire, who was then aged 38. In 1846, Tucker had been appointed to Grand Lodge and Grand Chapter rank and, in the same year, he was installed as Provincial Grand Master of his county. He seems to have been a popular choice and to have carried out his duties efficiently but in 1853, he attended a Provincial Grand Lodge meeting dressed, according to the *Freemasons' Quarterly Magazine*, 'in the full robes of a Sovereign Grand Inspector General of the 33°'. One can only conjecture what these robes were. According to some early rituals, the Sovereign Grand Commander of a Supreme Council could wear crimson robes on certain occasions, such as the installation of a member of the 33°, but there is no evidence that this has ever been the custom of the Supreme Council for England and Wales. Tucker made no denial of the charge when later he was asked to explain his conduct by the Grand Master:

> The Robe also I did wear, but with and in addition to my full clothing as a Prov. G.M. .... it appears that the union of Craft jewels with the dress and decorations of Christian Masonic Degrees, not recognized by the Book of Constitutions, and decided by your Lordship as opposed to them, is one ground for offence. If your Lordship can take the trouble to make the inquiry, it will be found that the late George IV, and also the Duke of Sussex wore non-Masonic jewels with the full Masonic costume of G.M. This combination of non-Masonic with Masonic decorations is by no means uncommon in many Provinces, and not always discountenanced by P.G. Masters. I am aware that it is irregular ...

Tucker was apparently a member of at least two Encampments of Knights Templar, including one which worked at Coryton Park and he was also Provincial Grand Master of the Knights Templar for Dorset. In September 1846, a few days after his Installation as Provincial Grand Master of the Craft for Dorsetshire, he exalted four brethren into the Royal Arch at Axminster. The following morning, at his home, Coryton Park, he installed three of these brethren into the Knights Templar and Knights of Malta degrees and in the afternoon installed them into the Rose-Croix and Ne Plus Ultra degrees. At this stage there was less differentiation in the high degrees than at present so it is a reasonable suggestion that the 'robe' he wore was, in fact, the mantle of a Knight Templar and not that of a Sovereign Grand Inspector General. No doubt, he also wore some of the regalia of the 33° with his uniform as a Provincial Grand Master. His picture shows him as a fine looking man and he stood six foot three in height, he must have been a most imposing figure, whatever he wore.

In wearing the wrong regalia, he was defying the Craft Regulations of 1847, which he would certainly have known about, but he offended much more seriously in the speech he made to the Provincial Grand Lodge. He had been advocating Christian Masonry in his Province for several years and, as we have seen, had taken an active interest in promoting it. Whether the brethren of his Province agreed with him on this issue is not known but, in his address, he made his views very clear:

> To all young Masons, to all who take an interest in the history of our Order, I do most strongly recommend an advancing course. I recommend them to take the higher degrees, for on the Continent, and in Scotland and Ireland, they will find a greater respect paid to these degrees than to any other: I have succeeded in establishing a *Rosea crux* in Weymouth. Many of my Masonic friends belong to it and I hope to see it increase every year.

Later, in his long address, he went even further:

> We, the Supreme Grand Council of the Sovereign Grand Inspectors General of the 33rd degree, work silently and slowly but surely, we uphold in every way the Grand Master and the Grand Lodge of England, we uphold every institution of the Order; we solemnly renounce the slightest interference in any of the Degrees under the Grand Lodge, Chapter or K.T. Conclave; we merely take up Masonry where it has been let drop in England; and endeavour, as far as in us lies, to grant those degrees without which no Mason can be called perfect, nor can he be received with those honours he would wish to have given to him on the Continent.

The story of the result of this meeting is told by F. J. Cooper in *AQC* 83. The Grand Master acted with remarkable promptness in deposing

Tucker from his office as Provincial Grand Master. The punishment was a drastic one, and only the second occasion in English masonry where a Provincial Grand Master was removed from his office. The reasons for the punishment were obvious. First, there was the wearing of regalia of a degree not recognised by Grand Lodge; second, the crime of expressing views contrary to the accepted universality of the Craft; and lastly, advocacy of high degrees when acting as a Provincial Grand Master of the Order.

Cooper suggests that the severe punishment was really dictated by a fear, in the minds of the authorities in Grand Lodge, of the growing importance of the Supreme Council and the Supreme Grand Conclave. They wished to avoid a situation, similar to that in France, where members of high degrees had established a right to wear their regalia in Craft lodges and to exercise certain powers of supervision and discipline. This is ostensibly an adequate reason, but there was a background which made it unlikely that Tucker could expect his case to be considered with justice tempered by mercy.

The Earl of Zetland, the Grand Master, seems to have been the first to have learnt about what had happened when he read an account of the meeting in the *Freemasons' Quarterly Magazine*. He instructed the Grand Secretary to write to Tucker for an explanation. At the same time, the Grand Registrar, Alexander Dobie (who was also Provincial Grand Master for Surrey) and the President of the Board of General Purposes, R. G. Alston, were consulted. The Grand Secretary, W. H. White, had been in office since 1809, and had also acted as Grand Secretary of the Supreme Grand Conclave from 1822 to about 1846. He had summoned the original meetings after the death of the Duke of Sussex, and thus become the target for the complaints about dilatoriness in Crucefix's *Review*. He had been in office as Grand Secretary during Crucefix's original trouble in Grand Lodge. Even though he was the most important figure in English Masonry, Crucefix does not appear to have consulted him about the formation of the Supreme Council, so it is unlikely that he had great sympathy for Crucefix's project, the A & A Rite. Dobie and Alston had been doing 'Box and Cox' with their appointments for the previous ten years and, with White, had established an unpopular and dictatorial regime which Gould (Vol III, p 23) describes as 'the entire English Craft being in a state of great insubordination and discontent'. Tucker's conduct must have seemed almost a personal affront.

Relations between the United Grand Lodge and the Supreme Council cannot have been improved when, soon afterwards, Leeson, then Sovereign Grand Commander, indicated his views about what had been done to Tucker by appointing him Grand Secretary

General. Tucker only held the appointment for a year as he died unexpectedly, aged 39, and was succeeded by Charles John Vigne, who also only held the appointment for a short while before becoming Grand Treasurer General.

When Davyd Nash retired from being Grand Secretary General in 1854, he was appointed Deputy Provincial Grand Master of the Province of Bristol. He was also appointed Grand Superintendent of the high degrees of Bristol. As a result, he was committing the offence, in the eyes of the Supreme Council, of holding communication with bodies not recognised i.e. the Baldwyn Chapter of Bristol and the Antiquity Chapter of Bath. No action was taken quickly but, in July 1857, members of the Supreme Council were summoned to hear charges against him. Before the meeting could be held, some letters were written in the *Freemasons' Magazine*, culminating in one from Nash. This is given in full as it shows the attitude, generally then held by members of the Badlwyn Rite, which caused them to remain independent of the Supreme Council and Grand Conclave for several more decades:

> ... as Deputy Provincial Grand Master for Bristol and Grand Superintendent of the degrees of the Ancient and Accepted Rite established in that city, and held and practised there since the year 1800, I am also in possession of the evidence relating to the condition of the A & A Rite in this country before the erection of the Supreme Council, of which Dr Crucefix was the head, by the Supreme Council of the Northern Jurisdiction USA.
>
> In the year 1800 those degrees of the A & A Rite which included the 18th degree of Rose-Croix were acknowledged by the Grand Orient of France, and introduced into Bristol by some French refugees, members of the latter body, and the Chapters of Encampments so formed registered with the Grand Orient in Paris. The Templar K——h which, if it is not the 30th degree of the A & A Rite, it is difficult to distinguish from it, appears from the Bristol documents to have been conferred in the Baldwyn Encampment of Knights Templar, an Encampment which has existed in Bristol from a very remote period.
>
> It is not true that the members of the Degrees of the A & A Rite held in Bristol designate themselves Knights Templar. They have no other connection with the Knights Templar than arises from their holding their meetings in the same hall, subscribing to a common fund for the maintenance of that hall, under the terms of a trust deed, for the benefit of all Masonic bodies in the province of Bristol and being placed under the authority of an officer who unites in his person the Grand Mastership of the KT Rite and Superintendent of the degrees of the A & A Rite.
>
> It would have been more correct that the Baldwyn Knights Templar of Bristol do not acknowledge the Grand Conclave than that the Grand

Conclave do not acknowledge them. There are officers in the Grand Conclave who were installed Knights Templar in the Encampment of Baldwyn at Bristol and no one knows better than your correspondent that every effort has been made by myself to bring about the union of the Baldwyn Knights Templar with the Grand Conclave and that such union would have been effected to the satisfaction of the Grand Conclave but for the triumph of local and personal feeling over the true issues of the Order.
20 June 1857   D. W. Nash.

There is no evidence to support the suggestions made by Nash that the origin of the A & A Rite in Bristol stems from the Grand Orient. The known story, which is very different, is given in Chapter 13. His case was considered by the Supreme Council early in the next month when a letter from him to the Sovereign Grand Commander and the letter given above were read and discussed. Even though he was, in his capacity as Superintendent of the Baldwyn Rite, issuing warrants, his case was once more adjourned to give him an opportunity to explain his conduct as a Soveriegn Grand Inspector General of the Supreme Council for England and Wales. The adjourned meeting was held in the following January and, though Nash had written asking to be reconciled, it was found that he had meanwhile issued a pamphlet which apparently precluded any further negotiations and he was expelled. The writer has been unable to find a copy of the pamphlet mentioned and one can only assume that he justified his own conduct by the right of the Baldwyn organisation to be independent.

The notification of the expulsion of a member of the Supreme Council is by what is known as a 'Red letter'. This dates back to the earliest days of the A & A Rite when a candidate for Sovereign Grand Inspector General had to swear obedience to the Order with one of the penalties being that 'of having my name exposed in red letters in the councils and lodges throughout the world'. The notice, printed on a paper about two foot long and nine inches wide, was sent to all Chapters in England and Wales and to Supreme Councils in amity. A copy of the one used in the case of Davyd Nash is in the archives of the Supreme Council in London.

The last change in appointments was caused by the failure of the Grand Treasurer General to carry out his duties. Henry Udall was one of the three original members of the Supreme Council. He presumably was Treasurer from the start. Unfortunately little is known about him, except that he was a distinguished mason whose career, given in Chapter 15, shows that he was Master of his Lodge for the second time in 1855 when he was honoured by having the ceremony carried out by the Grand Secretary. Yet, a year later at a meeting of the

Council on 8 August, 1856, it was decided 'for repeated neglect in regard to the presentation of his accounts, the imperfect manner in which these accounts have been kept, his frequent absences without forwarding such accounts although requested to do so, that there was no alternative but to dismiss him from the Council'. His duties as WM of Westminster and Keystone Lodge may have caused him to neglect his work as Treasurer. It is also possible that he lost interest in the Rite, particularly after the death of Dr. Crucefix, a personal friend. There does not seem to have been any question of a red letter in this unfortunate case. There were, however, complications as Henry Udall had been the representative of the Supreme Council of the Northern Masonic Jurisdiction USA from 1846. A letter was accordingly sent to America 'hoping that they will continue their friendly relations with the Supreme Council'.

This was not the last of the teething troubles in administration. As late as 1868 when Dr Leeson retired, and was succeeded by Lieutenant-Colonel Henry Atkins Bowyer, (appointed to the Council ten years before), he went to his home in the Isle of Wight with official papers which were only extracted from him with much difficulty.

17

INTERNATIONAL RELATIONS

THE FIRST INTERNATIONAL convention of Supreme Councils was held in Paris in 1834. Three of the existing Councils took part though Ireland, the only Council then in Britain, was absent. The Supreme Councils for England and Wales or for Scotland are not, therefore, affected by the Treaty of Alliance which emerged from discussions; but there is nothing in the Treaty to which exception could be taken. Its provisions were mainly aimed at binding each Supreme Council to respect the others' individual sovereignty and the existing Constitutions, Rules and Regulations. Probably the most important result was the publication by Saint-Laurent of the 'Latin' version of the Constitutions of 1786. (See Chapter 8 and Appendix V.) As this was circulated without comment with the Treaty, it must have been approved in place of the 'French' version which had appeared in the 1804 rituals of the Supreme Council for France, and which had been adopted by some Supreme Councils, principally those sponsored by France.

The international relations of the Supreme Councils in the United Kingdom were complicated, all through the XIX century, by the terms of these 1786 Constitutions which laid down that 'In each great Nation, Kingdom or European Empire, there will only be one Supreme Council.' Such a generalisation, probably produced in America at the start of the century by men with little knowledge of international relations, did not fit high degree Masonry in a state in which there were already three independent Grand Lodges. The French attempt, described in Chapter 14, to erect one Supreme Council for Great Britain and Ireland did not have a chance of starting for a number of reasons, but one of the most important was that masons in Ireland and Scotland would never have agreed to be under a Supreme Council ruled from London. This, however, would have been quite in order under the Constitutions of 1786.

The Supreme Council for Ireland was set up in 1826 under a patent from the Supreme Council of the Southern Jurisdiction USA. This latter, previously the Supreme Council of Charleston, constituted in 1813 at New York the Supreme Council for the Northern Masonic

Jurisdiction USA splitting the United States into two high degree spheres of influence, and itself became the Supreme Council for the Southern Jurisdiction USA. As we have seen in Chapter 15, it was the Supreme Council for the Northern Masonic Jurisdiction USA that granted the patent to Dr Crucefix for England and Wales in 1845. The Scottish Supreme Council was formed by a Dr Morison who, at one time, had been personal physician to the Duke of Sussex. Dr Morison received his 33° from the Supreme Council of Spain, founded in 1813 by a brother of Comte de Grasse-Tilly. Dr Morison, who had had his patent ratified both by the Supreme Council of France and the Grand Orient, acted in accordance with Article II of the Constitutions. This permits any Sovereign Grand Inspector General to create a Supreme Council in any state or kingdom where none exists. The regularity of the Supreme Council for Scotland was ratified formally in 1846 by the Supreme Council for France.

The complications of the formation of the three Supreme Councils in the United Kingdom have been smoothed out by time, and there can now be no doubt as to their accepted legal status as fully sovereign Supreme Councils for the purpose of the Grand Constitutions of 1786. One might quote Albert Pike, admittedly in regard to Scotland in particular, in 1877 as saying 'The peace and well being of Freemasonry requires that long and undisturbed possession shall be accepted as equivalent to original title in due form, or as conclusive right to such title.' This view was supported in 1964 by the distinguished jurist, Judge Luther Smith of the USA. On the other hand, it can be said with equal certainty that international recognition would not be given to any newly created body which purported to exercise Supreme Council jurisdiction over an internal division of a sovereign state.

The anomalies of the formation of the three Supreme Councils in the United Kingdom did, nevertheless, cause a quarrel between England and Scotland which was to last for 20 years. The trouble arose when the Council for Scotland started to consider the formation of a Chapter in India which had been asked for by the local Scottish District Grand Master of the Craft. The English Council wrote at once to Scotland expressing the hope that there would be no 'authorising of any Brother to confer degrees in any country under the Jurisdiction of the Supreme Council for England'. This claim by the English Council to have exclusive rights in India and, as it turned out, in practically all the British possessions overseas, did not commend itself to Scotland.

Discussions on the subject started amicably but gradually got more acrimonious. Any possibility of a reasonable tripartite agreement was impossible as the Supreme Council for Ireland had no authority over the 18°, which had its own ruling body and, in any case, Ireland had no interest in expansion overseas. Thus the problem became a direct confrontation between the Supreme Councils for England and Wales and for Scotland. It is not proposed even to summarise the voluminous correspondence which lasted until final agreement was reached in 1889. Unfortunately, for most of the period, there was a clash of personalities between the two Grand Secretaries General, both men of strong character. The views of the Scots were:

> The British Colonies are as much Scottish or Irish territory as they are English, and either Council is quite entitled to establish Chapters in them for their own countrymen. This is the view in St John's, Royal Arch and Templar Masonry, and it does not work badly. It is difficult to conceive any proper motive for seeking to introduce a different rule into the Ancient and Accepted Scottish Rite. Scottish and Irish Masons are as much entitled to the higher degrees as are English Masons; and they are entitled, if they prefer it, to seek these degrees from bodies holding under the Supreme Councils of their native lands.

It is difficult to accept this view as unreasonable, particularly as the already much larger Supreme Council for England and Wales, with a number of Chapters established overseas, would have gained exclusive rights in practically all the British possessions, if it had been accepted. However, the English argument is in analogy with Article V of the Constitutions of 1786 in that it is unwise to have more than one Supreme Council operating in one country. The pity is that the two Supreme Councils appear to have been unable to divide up their claims into reasonable spheres of influence. We can now see that, had the English view prevailed, many of the complications which affect masonry in parts of the world which were formerly the British Empire, would not now be arising. It is true that, in most cases where there are three Constitutions working together (in South Africa four), complete harmony is normal, but there are wide divergences in the ceremonies, regalia, conditions for promotion, etc. These are not to the advantage of any branch of masonry, the Ancient and Accepted Rite, governed by the Constitutions of 1786, possibly being more affected than any other.

The complexity of the legal position is shown by the formation, about this time, of a Supreme Council for Canada. As early as 1867, Albert Pike had written to the Supreme Council in London on this subject. In reply, he was told quite rightly that Canada was a dependency of the British Crown. He was also told, though with less justification, that Canada must obtain its high degrees from England.

In the following April, a Colonel McLeod Moore, who already held the honorary rank of 33° in the Northern Jurisdiction USA, with some other Canadian brethren, petitioned the Supreme Council for England and Wales for a charter to work the A & A Rite up to a Consistory 32°. The petition was immediately granted and Moore, and later four more brethren, having the 33° conferred upon them. In the December, Moore resigned and one of the four, Thomas Douglas Harington, succeeded him. During the next few years, the Rite spread in Canada and included a Council 30° under a charter from the Supreme Council for Scotland. Here was the same position of rivalry which was to bedevil relations between the Supreme Councils in Britain for the next 20 years. In this case, on receiving a request from Canada to form an independent Supreme Council, the Council for England and Wales ordered a referendum to be held. This naturally resulted in a majority for independence. A Patent was therefore issued to Harington and a Supreme Council for Canada was formed under Articles III and V of the Grand Constitutions. The Scottish members of the Rite in Canada joined in. As Canada was still part of the British Empire, though self-governing, this may have been technically irregular, but all other Supreme Councils accepted the position. It is a pity that such a satisfactory result did not extend to the quarrel, between the English and Scottish Councils, about overseas jurisdictions in other parts of the world.

It was during the period that the Supreme Council for Canada was under consideration that the Supreme Council for England and Wales issued a patent to Chile. The patent was issued on 8 February, 1870, and the new Supreme Council was constituted on 11 May the same year. Unfortunately, it only had a short life and was reconstituted in 1899 by the Supreme Council for the Argentine. All this was quite uncontroversial.

In 1875, the quarrel between the Supreme Councils for England and Wales, and for Scotland broke out again on a somewhat different subject and was to have most unhappy results. In January, a letter from the Supreme Council for Switzerland was received by all regular Supreme Councils announcing that there would be an international congress in the September. Oxford dismisses the Congress summarily; 'This Congress, instead of making union, did little except cause dissention'. It is true that it did no good and caused much ill feeling. In fact, it was probably the direct cause of the temporary break in the relations between the Supreme Councils for England and Wales, and Scotland. On the other hand, it had important consequences, not only for the whole Rite, but also in determining the place in the international organisation that the three British Supreme Councils were to choose for themselves in the future.

Eleven out of the existing 22 Supreme Councils attended. England and Wales sent three representatives while Scotland sent their redoubtable, but hot tempered Grand Secretary General, who also represented Greece. Ireland was not represented. The work carried out was very extensive and included a revision of the 1786 Constitutions, a manifesto which included a declaration of the principles of the Rite, a new set of rituals for the various degrees, the revision of regalia and, finally, a treaty of Alliance and Confederation.

The real difficulty of the Lausanne Conference, that which wrecked any chance of there being a comprehensive organisation of Supreme Councils, was the definition of the Deity. It must be appreciated that the period was one of extreme liberalism, even agnosticism, in Europe, particularly in France. The Conference was held only two years before the removal, by the majority of the French Symbolic lodges, of the Bible from their ceremonies and the name of the GAOTU from their obligations, thus causing a rupture within Craft Masonry which has not yet been healed. Trouble started before the end of the Conference. On the 8th September, the Scottish representative announced that he had to leave before the final day, and on the 13th, he told the Conference that he could not accept the suggested definitions of the GAOTU as none affirmed a belief in a personal God. It is not clear whether his early departure was genuinely due to more pressing business, or whether it was a gesture of dissent. However, at some stage, the Conference also decided to allocate to England the sovereignty over all British colonies and dependencies. This decision is recorded in the proceedings of the Conference, issued by Switzerland after the meetings had dispersed. It is felt that it could not have been made while the representative of Scotland was still attending as he would certainly have protested.

In October 1875, the Scottish delegate reported his unfavourable reactions to his Supreme Council. By this date, he would have received the proceedings of the Conference, including the adverse decision about Scottish sovereignty in the British Empire. His views, particularly about the religious question, appear also to have been received sympathetically by some other Supreme Councils, notably the important Southern Jurisdiction of the USA presided over by Albert Pike who was irritated that the Conference had decided that Hawai was under French masonic jurisdiction while the US maintained that it was already occupied by them. It was decided to hold a meeting in Edinburgh of the five Supreme Councils who agreed i.e. Southern Jurisdiction US, Ireland, Scotland, Central America and Greece. The other Supreme Councils either refused to attend or did not reply. The US produced Articles of Federation where were published in their official Bulletin (Vol III—Jan 1876–May 1878) and reported them as decided at a meeting held in Edinburgh in September 1877. The Articles, circulated in advance, had a new definition of the Deity.

> Freemasonry proclaims as its necessary and fundamental principle, a belief in the existence of a true and living God. It requires from its members an acknowledgement of such belief, leaving to each to worship God in the manner and form in which in his own conscience he believes to be most acceptable to him.

As the A & A Rites in Scotland and Ireland were at that time, and presumably intended to remain, Christian while the Southern Jurisdiction was not, it appears that the object was to leave practical decisions to individual Supreme Councils. It was also laid down that disagreements between Supreme Councils were to be settled by a Tribunal of Adjudication composed of one member from each Council belonging to the projected League. These formula, rather than those decided at Lausanne, appeared to have satisfied the metaphysical mind of the Scottish Grand Secretary General. As a result, the projected meeting was never held, nor was one held subsequently. However the relations between the Supreme Councils for Scotland and for England and Wales were not improved.

It is not known how much the English delegates to the Lausanne Conference knew about the proposed new Federation but, in May 1876, less than two months later, they circulated all English Chapters a note in which they reiterated their views that the definition of the Deity given at Lausanne was adequate. However, in a further attempt to clear up the matter, the Supreme Council for England and Wales sent a suggestion to the Swiss Supreme Council, who were the *rapporteurs* for the Conference, that the definition might be changed in the proceedings to:

> Freemasonry proclaims, as it has done since its start, the existence of God, the Great Architect of the Universe, and the immortality of the soul.

This change was agreed to grudgingly by the other Councils in order to attain some semblance of unity within the Rite, but this can only have been lip service in the case of some of the European Councils.

Relations between the Supreme Councils for England and Wales and for Scotland had been becoming increasingly strained and, on 9th October, 1877, the former broke off relations. This was an individual gesture and it had not been able to persuade any other Supreme Councils to follow its lead.

Three delegates from the Supreme Council for England and Wales visited France in October 1878 to a festival organised by the *Ecossais* Lodges of France in honour of foreign masons attending the Paris Exhibition of that year. Seventeen countries sent delegates, and the highlight of the festival was a meeting held at the Trocadero. The Sovereign Grand Commander of the Supreme Council for France at this time was Isaac Adolphe Crémieux, an important figure both in French liberal history and in French masonry, who had been Minister of Justice and also imprisoned by the Emperor Louis Napoleon until 1870. He had led the French delegation at the Laussane Conference. Naudon reports that he made 'a remarkable speech in which he spoke of the universality of the Scottish Rite and gave an eloquent definition of the symbolism of the Great Architect of the Universe according to the Conference of Lausanne'. According to Oxford, the London delegates were not impressed, reporting that 'he hardly touched on the question of a Supreme Being, but was very decided upon the immortality of the soul from his point of view'. One wonders if the delegation appreciated the difficult time that this was for the Supreme Council for France and its Jewish Sovereign Grand Commander. The previous year, the lodges of the Grand Orient had suppressed the obligation in the name of the Great Architect and had removed the Bible from their ceremonies. These views were spreading to the Symbolic lodges of the Supreme Council and strong reference by their Sovereign Grand Commander on the question of a Supreme Being would have precipitated a crisis. In fact, within two years, 12 lodges broke away and founded an independent Grand Lodge of France. This body, which still exists, has never been recognised by the United Lodge of England and is in fraternal relations with the irregular Grand Orient.

As a sequel to this event, and to the difficulties caused by the Lausanne Conference, the Supreme Council for England and Wales, on 10 May, 1881, decided to withdraw from the Confederation of Supreme Councils. It did not wish to be subjected to pressures to change its Christian traditions in the A & A Rite. It also wanted to avoid the risk of finding itself in amicable relations with a Supreme Council which might draw its membership from Symbolic lodges which are not considered regular according to the Landmarks of English masonry and the decisions of the United Grand Lodge of England. In its new situation, the Supreme Council for France clearly came into this category.

There have been several conferences of the A & A Rite since 1875, but no representatives of the British Supreme Councils have attended; Scotland and Ireland also having withdrawn from the Confederation about that date. A well-attended one was held in 1907, presided over by Comte Goblet d'Alviella, a distinguished Continental Mason, well known to British masons as a scholar of repute who contributed interesting papers to the Transactions of the Quatuor Coronati Lodge. This Conference did not achieve anything spectacular, but it laid the foundations for further meetings which have been held since that date. It passed one important resolution which decided that the Constitutions of 1786 were to remain as the rules and regulations for the government of the Rite. Thus it abrogated the Lausanne text. This is in entire agreement with the views held by the Supreme Council for England and Wales and most other Councils of importance who have dissociated themselves completely from its decisions.

In 1889, after much negotiation, relations were restored between the Councils for England and Wales and for Scotland. The resulting treaty provided:

> (a) No Chapter was to perfect a brother for less than three guineas, or perfect a brother from a sister jurisdiction without its permission. (This seems to have been the first time that the expression 'to perfect' was used officially.)
> (b) The 30° (or higher degrees) was not to be conferred on any brother unless he was elected to it by the Supreme Council of his allegiance. No Consistory was to be held abroad, except for the purpose of conferring degrees on brethren so elected, and then only under special authority from the Supreme Council.
> (c) No brother was to receive, from any other masonic body, any degree, except with the permission of his own Supreme Council.

It will be seen that the Treaty makes no mention of the claims of either Supreme Council about their rights to form Chapters overseas. This omission was only accepted with difficulty by some of the Supreme Council for England and Wales. One member resigned and the previous Grand Secretary General, who was then Captain General, opposed the omission, but accepted the majority vote. In spite of this, harmony was soon restored and, since that date, has been maintained.

Ireland was not able to adhere to the Treaty when it was signed. The Supreme Council for Ireland did not then control the high degrees up to that of Prince Mason (18°) which had its own Grand Chapter. About 1903, the dual control became inconvenient. It was found that the Irish brethren going overseas were not being recognized as regular Prince Masons as they were not under the jurisdiction of the Supreme Council as in all other jurisdictions. Accordingly, by mutual consent, the government of the Rose-Croix degree was vested in the Supreme Council for Ireland. In 1905, the treaty became tripartite and these three British Supreme Councils have held regular meetings since that date.

After the second World War, an International Conference was held at Havana in 1956. The British Supreme Councils did not attend but, before this conference, there was held a preliminary meeting of the English-speaking Supreme Councils in August 1954 at Montebello, Canada. There were present the representatives of the Supreme Councils of Canada, the two US jurisdictions and the three British ones. It was intended to discuss matters of common interest but, as a preliminary, each jurisdiction gave an account of its organization and its activities.

It was during these preliminaries that the English Grand Chancellor (representing the Supreme Council for England and Wales) made it clear that the Ancient and Accepted Rite in his country was a Christian order. The Irish and Scottish representatives confirmed that this was also the case in their jurisdictions. The delegations from Canada and the Northern Masonic Jurisdiction, USA explained that they had such a small percentage of non-Christians in their areas that the matter was not of constitutional importance and could, if necessary, be controlled by admission to the degrees concerned.

The Sov. Grand Commander of the Southern Jurisdiction USA took an opposing view, referring to the Grand Constitutions of 1786 and the fact that members of the original Supreme Council had included non-Christians. The representatives of the British Supreme Councils stressed that this was not a question for discussion and the matter was taken no further. It is clear, as a result, that the question of recognition does not depend on such factors which are the concern of the Supreme Council concerned.

The next step in international relations was when, in 1958, meetings of the English-speaking Supreme Councils (actually the same composition as at Montebello) were held. These now take place at intervals of about four years in Britain and America alternately. (Quebec, 1958; London, 1964; Washington, 1971; Edinburgh, 1974; Boston, 1978, and Dublin, 1983.) On the last two occasions, the scope of the meeting has been widened to include representatives, attending by invitation, as observers, from the Supreme Councils of the Netherlands and Finland, and the 'Scandinavian Group' comprising the Grand Lodges of Sweden, Denmark, Norway and Iceland. These meetings are quite informal and no decisions are taken which might infringe the sovereignty of each Supreme Council, but useful exchanges of information take place.

Craft masonry in Finland was reopened when that country gained its independence from Russia after World War I, but no further degrees or Rites were developed until after World War II. In 1957, the Supreme Council for England and Wales was flattered by an approach from senior brethren in Finland to assist them in starting the A & A Rite. A number of brethren were perfected in London and, in 1960, the first Chapter was consecrated in Helsinki. Progress was continuous, new Chapters being formed, and in 1962, these were constituted into a District with an Inspector General. Expansion continued steadily until there were 20 Chapters in four districts. In 1970, a Finnish Regional Council was constituted as a prelude to complete independence which took place with the formation of the Supreme Council for Finland in 1973. Previously, a referendum had been held asking each Chapter to decide whether it wished to place itself under the jurisdiction of the Supreme Council for Finland or remain under the Supreme Council for England and Wales. The not unexpected result was 100 per cent in favour of the jurisdiction of the Supreme Council for Finland.

At the formal ceremony which was held, each Most Wise Sovereign of a Finnish Chapter surrendered his English Warrant to the Sovereign Grand Commander of the Supreme Council for England and Wales. On the authority of his patent, the new Sovereign Grand Commander for Finland, Most Puissant Brother Toivo Tarjanne (formerly Most Worshipful Grand Master of Finland), was installed and appointed his Supreme Council. He was then given the Warrants of the 20 Finnish Chapters and announced that they constituted the authority for them to work under the new Supreme Council and would be endorsed accordingly. Possession of an original English Warrant is now highly prized in Finland and the names of each of the Finnish Chapters are still retained in the English list. The Supreme Council for Finland has since been recognised by all Supreme Councils with which the Supreme Council for England and Wales is in amity.

It is obvious that none of the existing Supreme Councils can comply with all the minor details of the Grand Constitutions of the Rite, and probably have never been able to do so. There are far too many local complications to make this possible. The Constitutions must be considered as laying down principles, particularly in international relations and, as such they are essential. An example of this arose recently in connection with the request for a Supreme Council to cover the territory of the Republic of South Africa. In that country, as a relic of the events in the colonial era, there are districts and chapters from the Supreme Councils of England and Wales, Ireland, Scotland and the Netherlands, all of which work together in amity. The chapters of the last Supreme Council wished to form their own independent Supreme Council, as the Netherlands Craft lodges had done quite legitimately, a few years earlier, to form the Grand Lodge of Southern Africa. The matter was referred to the Supreme Council for the Netherlands by the Netherlands Chapters. This resulted in a conference being held in London on 27 September, 1971, between the Supreme Councils for Ireland, England and Wales, Scotland and the Netherlands. It was then agreed that, under the Grand Constitutions of 1786, there could only be one Supreme Council for the whole of Republic of South Africa, and that a 'composite' one could be established provided that

(a) The Christian basis of the A & A Rite was maintained.
(b) An agreed plan acceptable to the Supreme Councils could be formulated.
(c) Any Chapter that desired to remain under its present jurisdiction should be permitted to do so.

Such a plan was formulated and put to all Chapters in all four jurisdictions in the Republic of South Africa in the autumn of 1976. It provided that the first Supreme Council should consist of nine members, four of whom would be appointed by the Supreme Council for England and Wales, three by that of Scotland and two by that of the Netherlands. This proportion was approximately in proportion to the strengths of the various bodies concerned. The plan pointed out that such a new organisation would have to be self-financing and the cost was estimated at that time, at an annual levy of about eight Rand (£5) per member.

A referendum was then conducted by secret ballot. Each member of the A & A Rite in the Republic was asked whether he wished his Chapter to be placed under the suggested new Supreme Council or to remain as at present. The member then placed his vote in a sealed envelope. As far as the English Chapters were concerned, these envelopes were sent to London where the votes were examined and counted by two Sovereign Grand Inspectors General, 33° (one a Judge) and the result was 33 Chapters wishing to remain as at present and 5 to go under a Supreme Council for the Republic. Similar arrangements were made for the Scottish and Netherlandic Chapters with the results that all Scottish Chapters voted to remain under the Supreme Council for Scotland and all Netherlandic Chapters, not unexpectedly, voting for independence.

The overall result was therefore a considerable majority in favour of the *status quo* and the four Supreme Councils concerned decided that they would not permit the question to be reopened for a considerable time ahead.

Note. The referendum held by the Australian Chapters is referred to on page 201.

18

THE RITE AT THE PRESENT TIME

The Title

IN THE MANIFESTO which announced the formation of the Ancient and Accepted Rite Supreme Council at Charleston in December 1802, the founding Americans called themselves 'The Supreme Council of the United States of America'. This title was short lived and was changed when it constituted, in 1813, a Supreme Council for the Northern Masonic Jurisdiction of the USA, the original Council restricting itself in accordance with the Grand Constitutions of 1786 which allowed the division of North America into two parts. The word 'Scottish' only appeared in the names of some of the degrees and never in either title. It only became popular after the publication in France in 1834 of the Latin version of the text of the 1786 Constitutions. Some of the Councils which were then forming took the word 'Scottish' into their titles. The French had, as far as can be seen, always used it with the word *Ecossais* being normal for high degree lodges and rites. It is still used by a number of Supreme Councils, including that of Scotland.

The word 'Scottish' was not in the patent issued to Dr Crucefix in 1845 by the Supreme Council of the Northern Masonic Jurisdiction USA. In spite of this, the Supreme Council for England and Wales used the word occasionally in correspondence, without any apparent justification, and it appears on some certificates issued by the Council in the mid-XIX century. As mentioned in the Introduction, the Supreme Council decided in 1909 to remove the word officially from its title, and it has not been used since.

In 1977, a further change was made from 'The Supreme Council 33° of the Ancient and Accepted Rite for England and Wales, the Dominions and Dependencies of the British Crown' to 'The Supreme Council for England and Wales and its Districts and Chapters overseas'. The new title is felt to be a better description of its present responsibilities. Its jurisdiction now extends over its own Chapters everywhere in the British Commonwealth, except in Ireland, Scotland, Canada and Australia, which have Supreme Councils of their own. It also controls its own Chapters in a number of countries which are no longer part of the Commonwealth, but which do not have their own Supreme Council. The most noteworthy of these is the Republic of South Africa.

The Grand East

The administrative headquarters of a Supreme Council is known as its 'Grand East'. It is referred to as such in warrants, patents, certificates, etc. and is the place where the Supreme Council normally meets. In the early years of the Supreme Council for England and Wales, the Grand East usually coincided with the office of the Grand Secretary General. It is a custom in the A & A Rite to give the latitude and longitude in official documents. When the patent was issued to Dr Crucefix in 1845, the Northern Masonic Jurisdiction gave the position of the new Grand East in London as West 0° 05' 37" and North 51° 31' 00" and this was used in early documents. It is actually a point in the City of London, probably in St Paul's Churchyard, and it is suggested that, in the absence of any definite location, this reference was arbitrarily chosen. There was, however, a footnote: 'If these figures are not right you will correct them.' The actual figures used were rounded off to West 6' and North 51° 30'.

Accommodation was first acquired in John Street (now divided into Upper and Lower John Street) and little is known about it. This street is off Golden Square in which there was a house, with the appropriate number of 33, which was to become the headquarters of the Rite for many years. The minutes of the period are unhelpful as to dates, but the first book of Rules and Regulations to be issued from this address is dated 1869. An interesting photograph now in the present Supreme Council room shows the Council of about 1890 seated in a group in the garden of Golden Square, opposite the front door of No 33. Neither the house nor the number now exist, being absorbed into the offices of new commercial development.

Early in this century, the question of rebuilding arose. It was not practicable at Golden Square and, after various sites had been considered (including the vestry site of St James's Church, Piccadilly) 10 Duke Street was selected. The old XVIII-century house, with its gardens and stables, was demolished and a new purpose designed building constructed. The foundation stone was laid with masonic ceremony by the Sovereign Grand Commander, the Earl of Dartrey, on 1 December, 1910, and the building was opened in October 1911.

The Grand East

The Supreme Council for England and Wales and its Districts and Chapters Overseas, has its administrative headquarters in St James', London, and is known as the Grand East. The present building has been in use by the Supreme Council since 1911.

Nearly every 'London' Rose-Croix Chapter meets now at Duke Street which has two suites of rooms in which the 18° can be held under ideal conditions, and a further room in which an Enthronement ceremony can be worked. All rooms are available for other masonic bodies, provided they are not needed by Chapters of the Supreme Council. The Grand Hall has a fine organ made by Bevington which was brought from Golden Square but its previous history is not known. In addition, the building houses the offices of the Grand Secretary General and the Supreme Council room, round the walls of which is a library of valuable books and documents, supervised by an Honorary Librarian.

Later warrants and documents still have the map reference as West 6' and North 51° 31'. Actually, this was not correct either for John Street or No 33 Golden Square. These two houses are so close together as to have the same reference which should have been West 0° 07' 33" and North 51° 31' 00". Duke Street has the identical westing but is North 51° 30' 37"'. Documents were not altered when the move there took place.

Masons Yard, on to which the stables of the original property gives, is sometimes thought to be so named because of its masonic connections. This is not so, but it was the yard of the Mr Mason, whose association with Mr Fortnum led to the well known establishment in Piccadilly.

The Supreme Council and its Organisation

The Supreme Council started with eight Sovereign Grand Inspectors General 33° but the membership was increased in 1851 to the number of nine specified in the Grand Constitutions of 1786. It has remained at this number, though the titles of the members have changed from time to time. At present, they are:

Most Puissant Sovereign Grand Commander
Very Puissant Lieutenant Grand Commander
Most Illustrious Grand Treasurer General of the H:E: (Holy Empire)
Most Illustrious Grand Prior (who is normally in Holy Orders)
Most Illustrious Grand Chamberlain
Most Illustrious Grand Chancellor
Most Illustrious Grand Captain-General
Most Illustrious Grand Marshal
Most Illustrious Grand Secretary General of the H:E: (Holy Empire)

Other Sovereign Grand Inspectors General 33° are entitled 'Very Illustrious'. Members of the 32°, 31° and 30° are 'Illustrious' and of the 18° 'Excellent and Perfect Prince'.

The ceremonial duties of the Council are supervised by a Grand Director of Ceremonies who is normally a Sovereign Grand Inspector General 33°, assisted by a Deputy and two assistants. There is also a Grand Organist, with an Assistant, and a Grand Outer Guard. The Grand Secretary General has a small staff of clerks to assist with the secretarial duties.

When a vacancy occurs in the Supreme Council, the new member is elected by the remaining eight whose vote must be unanimous. It is now a necessary qualification that the candidate must be a Grand Officer or a Past Grand Officer of the United Grand Lodge. The

Sovereign Grand Commander and the Lieutenant Grand Commander are appointed for life, the latter having the right to succeed if the former dies or resigns. Other members of the Council serve for a five year term, but they are eligible for re-election. The seniority of the members of the Supreme Council is determined by simple rules. The Sovereign Grand Commander, followed by the Lieutenant Grand Commander, are automatically the senior. The other members rank according to their date of appointment, not of office. The Grand Secretary General, if he is a paid official, as is now normal, remains the junior member of the Council, irrespective of how long he has been in office.

It will be noted that the Supreme Council seems to be a self perpetuating body with irremoveable leaders. In theory, this is undemocratic and unlike most masonic bodies, where the rulers have to be elected—at least theoretically—at fixed intervals. This procedure is, of course, in accordance with the Constitutions of 1786 and there is the added provision that, in the election of members, there must be unanimity. In practice, the procedure works well and it is difficult to suggest an alternative which would equally suit the Rite in England and Wales. Some foreign masonic bodies, where the rulers have to submit themselves for re-election to a wide franchise at regular intervals, have experienced, and are still experiencing troubles, which the Ancient and Accepted Rite for England and Wales have fortunately been spared.

In 1872, the Supreme Council decided to divide England and Wales into Districts under the direction of Inspectors General, though this rank had actually been conferred two years earlier on an Inspector General for India. Since that date, the system has been extended, both at home and overseas, and there are now about forty Districts. Each is ruled by an Inspector General who is automatically made a member of the 32°, but is almost invariably promoted to the 33°. Inspectors General are appointed for five years, but are eligible for reappointment. They have certain powers, normally exercised by the Supreme Council, delegated to them, and they can be assisted by a District Recorder, but there is no District organisation similar to that in the Craft, Royal Arch, Knights Templar, etc. Districts are usually small, 22 Chapters being a large number, with the majority much smaller. This enables Inspectors General to have a valuable and pleasant personal contact with the members of the Chapters they supervise, something that would not be possible if they were responsible for more. It is too be hoped that the rapid expansion of the Rite will not make this impossible in the future.

For the unattached Chapters in London, the position is different.

As long ago as 1874, the Supreme Council appointed an Inspector General for London but there remains no record of his duties. About 1940, Inspectors General were again appointed for London but with no specific tasks. In 1957, the matter was raised once more but inquiries from the London Chapters indicated that there was no demand for such appointments, so no action was taken.

In 1980, the Supreme Council decided that, with the number of London Chapters progressively increasing, the present situation was unsatisfactory as it was impracticable for members of the Supreme Council to visit all the London Chapters. It was also considered that the present arrangement did not ensure an equitable distribution of the 31° and 32° on the basis of merit. Further that, in the ordinary course, London brethren had no avenue of promotion to the 33°.

Accordingly, in September 1980, the Supreme Council decided to split the London Chapters into five groups and to appoint five able and experienced brethren to undertake the duty of maintaining liaison between them and the Supreme Council. The duties of these five brethren of the 33° are to maintain close personal relations with their Chapters, to visit them occasionally, to give them advice and guidance when required and to submit to the Supreme Council recommendations for promotions to the higher degrees. Unlike the procedure in Districts, the routine paper work will continue to be dealt with direct with the Grand Secretary General. The groups are each named after a saint particularly associated with the ritual of the Rite e.g. 'The St John Group of London Chapters'.

The increasing responsibilities of the Supreme Council are shown as follows:

In 1884, there were about 100 Chapters
    1918, there were about 200 Chapters
    1934, there were about 300 Chapters
    1948, there were about 400 Chapters
    1956, there were about 500 Chapters
    1964, there were about 600 Chapters
    1971, there were about 700 Chapters

In July, 1985, the Supreme Council granted a Warrant to No 952. Chapter numbers have not been closed up and, with Finland and Australia forming their own Supreme Councils, bear no relation to the number working.

The Australian Chapters

The rapid expansion of the Rite in Australia from the 1940s began to pose special problems of control and supervision. As early as the 1960s, the Supreme Council decided that its century old relationship with the Australian chapters had to be reviewed. After consultations, it was found that, while there was no desire on the part of the Australian brethren to sever all connection with the Supreme Council, it would be advantageous to delegate some authority to a body in Australia established for that purpose.

As a result, an Australian Branch Council was established by special regulation, and inaugurated in 1969. However, by the 1980s, the situation had again changed and it was clear that there was now a desire by many of the chapters under the Supreme Councils of England and Wales and of Scotland to form their own Supreme Council. Accordingly a referendum was held in November 1984 in Australia. The result was a significant majority (some 80%) of the Chapters, both English and Scottish, to place themselves under a Supreme Council for Australia.

The Supreme Councils then jointly designated M:. Ill:. Bro. J. K. Lawrence 33° to be the first Sovereign Grand Commander, and he was invested at a ceremony held in Sydney on 12 October 1985 by the Sovereign Grand Commanders for England and Wales, and Scotland. He immediately formed and constituted a Supreme Council for Australia, which will have some two hundred chapters. Only eleven chapters in that country will remain under the Supreme Council for England and Wales, and they will be unattached, working directly under the Supreme Council.

Membership of the Rite

It is a rule among Supreme Councils that Candidates for the Rite must have received the symbolic degrees and be at least of the rank of Master Mason. In some countries, the Supreme Council controls its own symbolic lodges and so gives these degrees under its own authority. In England and Wales (and also in Ireland and Scotland), the Supreme Council has no symbolic lodges, and these degrees are given in lodges of the United Grand Lodge, though affiliation by a Master Mason of another regular obedience is normally allowed.

The religious characteristics of the Supreme Council which formed itself at Charleston are curious. Four of its members were practising Jews. John Mitchell, the first Sovereign Grand Commander was an Irishman by birth, so he may have been a Roman Catholic; Frederick Dalcho, the first Lieutenant Grand Commander was a Protestant; while the other three, Americans by birth, were certainly Christians but their denominations are not known. The rituals of the degrees from the 18° onwards had, in many cases, a distinctly Christian tendency. However, by 1845, the Supreme Council of the Southern Jurisdiction, as it had then become, was theist in character i.e. the religious qualification for membership was a simple belief in an all controlling Great Architect of the Universe. On July 16, 1845, the Northern Masonic Jurisdiction had ruled that all members of the 18° must previously have been installed as Knights Templars, a Christian degree in the USA. This was the similar sequence to that in England and meant that they had to be Christians for the 18° and upwards. It is a reasonable presumption that this was the reason why Dr Crucefix applied to this Supreme Council for his patent. The original members of the Supreme Council for England and Wales would have received their Rose-Croix and Ne Plus Ultra degree through English Knights Templar Encampments, which were entirely Christian. There has never been any suggestion—as far as is known—that the Ancient and Accepted Rite in England and Wales (or in Ireland or Scotland) should deviate from Christianity; and this has always been an essential qualification for membership. Nevertheless, it will be noted that the Supreme Council is in amity with some Councils which are theist in character and Christianity not an essential qualification for membership.

The first degree to be conferred under the authority of the Supreme Council for England and Wales is the 18°, with the degrees from the 4° to the 17° being communicated by name only. This is the same in Scotland but, in many countries, some or all of the intermediate degrees are conferred in full. During the last century, it was normal to confer the 18° on a number of candidates at the same time, and early rituals always refer to 'the candidates'. This practice has now died out as Regulations (no. 29) forbid there being more than two candidates at the same ceremony without a dispensation from the Supreme Council. It is usual, however, for Chapters to perfect only one candidate, thus ensuring that he obtains the maximum from the ceremony. The higher degrees (30°–32°) are normally conferred on a number of brethren at a time, one selected brother acting as the representative candidate, the rest only taking part in essentials while watching the remainder of the ceremony.

The degree of Grand Elected Knight Kadosh, Knight of the Black and White Eagle 30°, is conferred by the Supreme Council on Past Sovereigns of the 18° on the recommendations of their Chapters. Before the 30° is conferred, the 19° to 29° are communicated by name to the candidate. The degrees of Grand Inspector Inquisitor Commander 31° and Sublime Prince of the Royal Secret 32° are strictly limited in membership. Admission to these degrees is by election by

the Supreme Council. There are time qualifications which are sometimes altered, but length of service is not a recommendation in itself,
outstanding work on behalf of the Rite being essential in all cases. The
degree of Sovereign Grand Inspector General 33° is reserved for the
Supreme Council and Inspectors General of Districts, though it is also
very occasionally given to other distinguished members of the Rite. It
will thus be seen that the higher degrees in the Rite are limited in
England and Wales (also in Ireland and Scotland). This is not the case
with some other Supreme Councils where promotion to the 32° is
automatic and promotion to the 33° is often proportionally higher
than in England and Wales.

In England and Wales, the 30° to the 33° are always conferred at a
ceremony conducted by the Supreme Council personally. By the
Constitutions of 1786, no Grand Chapter of Grand Elected Knights
Kadosh can be held, except in the presence of three Sovereign Grand
Inspectors General, and such Grand Chapters are regularly held in
London to confer the degree. There is also a meeting of the 31° and 30°
at a differing provincial centre in England each year. The 30° can also
be conferred when it is possible, as in South Africa, to get three
Sovereign Grand Inspectors General together. Tribunals of the 31°
and Consistories of the 32° are held regularly in London. Where it is
possible, outside England to get three SGIG together outside England, the 31° and 32° are also worked but, at present these degrees are
still conferred by Patent, so the ceremonies are really demonstrations.
The 33° is only conferred in London by the Supreme Council though
it, and all other degrees of the 30° and above, can be conferred by
patent in exceptional circumstances, when it is not possible for a
candidate to attend.

Visitors

Qualified visitors are always welcomed at ceremonies of the Ancient
and Accepted Rite. The differences in the degrees worked by other
Supreme Councils and the consequent differences in methods of
recognition complicate the reception in a Chapter of a visitor from
another Supreme Council. Apart from these obvious difficulties, it is
important to realise that, in some Scandinavian countries, all of
whose degree Rites are in amity with the Supreme Council for
England and Wales, the organisation of their Rites has little similarity
with the A & A Rite. While this makes visits by members of such Rites
very interesting, it may be hard to prove their standing. The author,
when called upon in such cases, has found that a reasonable solution
is to test the visitor as a mason (always remembering that certain

matter may be reversed) and then to remind him that he is bound by his obligation not to visit any masonic body to which he is not entitled.

As a guide, it may be noted that a member of the Swedish Rite, which covers most of Scandinavia, other than Finland, holding at least the following degrees, can be admitted as shown below.

Swedish Rite	*A & A Rite*
VIII—Knight of the South, or Favourite Brother of St John.	32° and below.
VII —Knight of the West or Favourite Brother of Solomon.	31° and below.
VI —Knight of the East.	18°.

Because of the religious variations between the different Supreme Councils, even when a visitor is proved, it is a kindness to warn him that the degree which he will be attending is of a Christian character; and so give him the opportunity to withdraw if he feels that this will cause him embarrassment.

Regalia

The regalia now worn by members of the order is described in detail in the *Rules and Regulations* issued by the Supreme Council for England and Wales. Actually, all the 33 degrees of the Rite have regalia but, except for those degrees which are conferred in full, this is only seen in the Chapters of Improvement under the Supreme Council for England and Wales at demonstrations. The regalia worn by other Supreme Councils differs in minor matters, though the regalia of the Swedish Rite is entirely different. Other Supreme Councils, of course, may work degrees not conferred in full by the Supreme Council for England and Wales, and then the regalia is worn.

Early manuscripts give descriptions of the regalia of their period and this has probably been changed as often as the details of the degrees themselves. At the start of the XIX century when the Supreme Council for France was set up by the Comte de Grasse-Tilly, regalia began to become stabilised. A French magazine, dated 1837 (*L'Universe Maçonnique*), describes the regalia of all the degrees and shows that they are basically similar to those used at present. The earliest description of an 18° jewel is given in a French ritual dated about 1765 i.e. about the date that the Rose-Croix degree was first developed.

The jewel of each brother is a compass with its points on a quarter of a circle. The head of the compass should be a rose with its stem merging into

Early Rose-Croix jewels.

Early 32° apron of the Netherlands Supreme Council.

one of the legs. In the centre of the rose is the letter G, and the rose is topped by a small column. In the centre of the compass is a Cross with its top touching the head of the compass and its arms the legs of the compass, and its feet the quarter circle. On each side of the Cross is a mosaic pavement of gold and silver.

On the middle of the Cross is an eagle with its wings extended on the arms of the Cross and its feet drawn back against its body.

On the reverse is a Pelican, also with its back to the Cross, its wings spread around its feet. Seven chicks are under its raised beak to receive the blood that the Father draws from his chest. . . .

The jewel worn in John Knight's Encampment about 1800 was similar though the emphasis is altered as the Pelican is now on the obverse and the eagle has disappeared. In both cases, the jewel was worn suspended from a collar, red on one side and black on the other. With regard to the wearing of jewels, How, writing in 1862, stated '. . . at the present day, so desirous is the Supreme Council to disavow the Knights Templar, that the candidate for the Rose Croix is, at the time of receiving the degree, allowed to wear the jewels of any Masonic rank he may have attained, except that of Knights Templar'. The suggestion that there was real enmity seems curious as so many brethren belonged to both bodies. However, a wish, in the early days, for a complete break between two bodies which had previously been so close, is understandable. It is of interest to note that the wearing of jewels, not of the A & A Rite, by candidates continued until about the end of the century. Even now, there is no mention of a prohibition in the present Rules and Regulations. Standardized centenary jewels and jewels for past Most Wise Sovereigns are authorized and frequently worn.

Swords formed part of the regalia of all degrees when the Rite was first formed, presumably a relic of the days when the 18° formed part of a Knights Templar Encampment. These have gradually disappeared from use during the next hundred years. In the Chapters of the Supreme Council for England and Wales, swords are no longer worn, though unsheathed swords are still used by some officers during the ceremonies. Other Supreme Councils have, in many cases, retained the use of swords in their Rite.

Little is known about the early regalia of the 30° to 32°. The first Kadosh type degree in England must have been that in de Lintot's Rite of Seven Degrees of about 1770. One must assume that the regalia was one of those worn in France. Other Kadosh degrees appeared later, in such places as Bristol, but no information is available about the regalia worn. A French ritual of 1765 of the degree gives a description of the candidate being clothed in a form of

Crusader costume. Whether this was ever used in England is not known. It had been replaced by something more like the present regalia early in the XIX century. The 31° and 32° did not come into English Chapters until the Supreme Council for England and Wales was formed in 1845, but there is evidence that some Englishmen had had these degrees conferred upon them by foreign Chapters. The regalia for these degrees would therefore have been known and may have been adopted by the Supreme Council. There is no evidence that descriptions of regalia were sent to England by the Northern Masonic Jurisdiction in 1845 with the documents about the ceremonies. It seems likely, therefore, that adaptations of the regalia worn in France was used. How, purporting to quote early Rules and Regulations, describes early regalia. That of the 18° includes each brother wearing a dalmatic i.e. tunic, of white cloth, bordered in black, with a Latin cross in red on the front and back. For the First Point, the jewel of the collar was to be covered with black crepe. Brethren of the 30° wore a white mantle, bordered in black. He also states that the dress of the Sovereign Grand Commander includes a 'royal robe of crimson satin' and a regal crown, though it is not clear if the last applied to the Supreme Council for England and Wales.

In the early days of the Rite, aprons were worn with regalia of the 18°, 31° and 32°. In the French 1837 list of regalia worn, members of the 31° had a white apron with a red cross on the flap, while the 32° apron had the badge of the degree on its flap. The 32° apron can only have been in use for a short while, as the French rituals of the early XIX century often omit it. The 31° apron also had a short life in France. It is known that members of these degrees in England wore aprons during the XIX century, but the practice was short lived. The 18° apron, which has no symbolic importance, except to show a general association with masonry, and which duplicated part of the jewel, lasted longer. In 1957, it was made optional by the Supreme Council with a view to its being phased out to avoid the invidious discrimination with the higher degrees in which the apron had been discarded so much earlier. It may be presumed that the Supreme Council gave this option to individual members so that those who, perhaps having inherited an apron, would be able to continue to wear something of personal sentimental interest. The system does not seem to have worked satisfactorily and the wearing of 18° aprons has now been stopped.

The original regalia for a member of the 33° was described in complete detail in the Appendix to the Latin version of the Grand Constitutions of 1786. As has been explained, this did not appear until 30 years after the formation of the first Supreme Councils, but there is

Early English XIX Century Rose-Croix apron reputed to have belonged to Dr Oliver.

no reason to doubt that the regalia, as described, was that actually worn by the original members of these Supreme Councils. The jewel of the degree was laid down as: 'An Eagle similar to that on the Standard: [of the Order] it wears the golden crown of Prussia.' The Eagle on the Standard is described as a 'Black double-headed eagle, (*un aigle noir à deux têtes*) with wings outstretched, the beaks and legs are of gold; it holds in one claw the golden hilt and, in the other, the steel blade of an old-fashioned sword, placed horizontally from right to left.'

The history of the double-headed eagle is given in *AQC* 24 by W. T. Chetwode-Crawley.

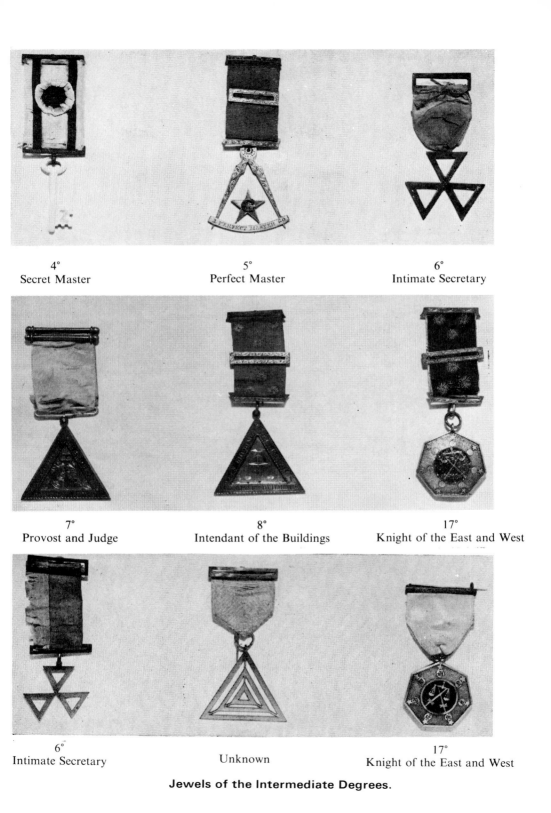

| 4° | 5° | 6° |
| Secret Master | Perfect Master | Intimate Secretary |

| 7° | 8° | 17° |
| Provost and Judge | Intendant of the Buildings | Knight of the East and West |

| 6° | | 17° |
| Intimate Secretary | Unknown | Knight of the East and West |

Jewels of the Intermediate Degrees.

'No heraldic bearing, no emblematic device in wear to-day, can boast such antiquity. It was in use a thousand years before the Exodus from Egypt, and more than two thousand years before the Building of King Solomon's Temple.'

The story begins on two terra-cotta cylinders found near the ancient city of Lagash, chief city of the Sumerian kingdom which spread over the area now known as the Middle East. It is related by the King of Lagash:

'The waters of the Tigris fell low and the store of provender ran short in my City.'

The King dreamed a dream in which the will of the Gods was revealed to him. There came to the King a Divine Man whose stature reached from earth to heaven and whose head was crowned with the crown of a God surmounted by the Storm Bird that extended its wings over Lagash, and the land thereof. This Storm Bird was the Double-headed Eagle, the visible emblem of power and dominion. It is thus the oldest royal crest in the World.

Some time after 2800 B.C. the Sumarians were driven out of their country by the men of Akhed, a Semetic tribe. They, in their turn, had to give way to the eventual founders of Turkey, the Seljukian Sultans whose conquest of Palestine led to the Crusades. It was the Crusaders who brought the emblems to the Emperors of the West and East, the Habsburgs and the Romanoffs.

The double-headed eagle is first mentioned in masonry—as far as is known—in a letter from brethren in Metz to other brethren in Lyons in June 1761. The reference is to a 'golden eagle with wings out-stretched wearing princes' crowns on both its heads and holding a dagger'. It is not known how the badge became adapted to the higher degrees. When there was the schism in France about 1763 and the body calling itself 'Emperors of the East' broke away from the Council of the Knights of the East, it may have taken the double-eagle as its badge. It seems more likely that this happened a year or so later when the same body had assumed the title of 'Emperors of the East and West' as this badge would be symbolic of how much wider was its dominion than that of the Council of the Knights of the East.

There is no evidence that Morin was in any way concerned except that his suggestion of the involvement of the Sovereign of Sovereigns in Prussia in the 1762 Constitutions probably led those responsible for the Constitutions of 1786 to adopt the badge and link it quite erroneously with Frederick. What, however, is quite certain is that Frederick would never have allowed any document in his name to have, as its badge, his own crown in association with anything other than the single eagle of Prussia. He had spent most of his life fighting for survival against the double eagles of the Empire and of Russia. The Prussian Eagle has its head turned to the left, its claws tucked up, or spread and often holding a sceptre and an orb.

Nevertheless, though this is clear proof that Frederick had no personal connection with the Ancient and Accepted Rite, it does not detract in any way from the present badge of the Supreme Councils of the Rite. Many heraldic emblems are the result of oddities and, in spite of its curious origin, the double eagle, holding a sword in its claws, is a fine badge and worthy to be used by Supreme Councils. The Supreme Council for England and Wales describes its badge officially as 'a double spread-eagle, surmounted by a crown, and holding a sword in its claws'. This badge is also the neck decoration worn by members of the 30° and above, its colouring and that of its supporting collarette varying with the rank of the wearer.

The Rituals of the Degrees

In English Craft masonry, the rituals are not standardised, and great latitude is allowed, provided they conform to the Landmarks of the Order and impart the necessary information. This attitude is emphasised by the word 'ritual' appearing nowhere in the Book of Constitutions of the United Grand Lodge. Other ruling masonic bodies think differently, laying down ceremonies which must be adhered to. This is the course adopted by the Supreme Council for England and Wales. The Baldwyn Chapter has permission to use its own long established ceremonies, but all others are compelled to conform to the printed version issued by the Supreme Council and to embody amendments as they are issued. However, the rubrics of the printed ritual are not as detailed as in many other rites and allow a certain variation in gesture and movement though not, of course, of wording. The latest ritual gives more guidance than previous ones.

The King Edward VII Chapter of Improvement, which meets regularly in London, on dates given in the *Rules and Regulations*, to give instruction in the ceremonies, works strictly in accordance with the wishes of the Supreme Council. Its primary object is to instruct individuals but it will give guidance to any Chapter. New Chapters, or old established ones, if not certain of procedures, are well advised to send representatives to learn what is correct. In the case of Chapters which work outside London, and require information, the Chapter will give written advice. It also gives annual demonstrations of the Intermediate Degrees in London and in the Districts. There are other recognised Chapters of Improvement in the Districts, and details of most of them are also given in the *Rules and Regulations*.

When the Supreme Council was constituted, the Grand Secretary General of the Northern Masonic Jurisdiction, USA, sent the obligations of the 30°–33° with his letter of 29 December 1846. He promised to send 'the whole of the thirty-third degree' when these obligations had been returned to him signed. As has been stated in Chapter 15, full rituals of the 18° and of the 30° to 33° were sent in the following August. The minutes of the Supreme Council for England and Wales are missing until 1854 and, as the rituals are not mentioned after this date, we do not know what was decided.

The 18° ritual that was sent from America must have been derived from early French rituals translated and revised by Morin or Francken. All the rituals of the Rite were eventually de-Christianized by the Supreme Council of the Southern Jurisdiction, USA, but before this was done, high degree chapters had been erected in the north of America, and the Northern Masonic Jurisdiction continued to use Christian rituals, at least for the 18°–33°. Thus the 18° ritual sent over to England in 1845 was Christian in character and perfectly acceptable. The newly formed Supreme Council would certainly not have wanted to anger any English Rose-Croix Chapter, who might wish to join it by imposing a new ritual. It seems probable that, to start with, English Chapters would have been allowed to continue with the ritual they were using. Eventually—we do not know when—a change had to be made. We can only speculate what English ritual was used. Some of those in use in England can be ruled out. The Baldwyn Rite is known and, in any event, this Chapter was not in amity with the Supreme Council for England and Wales, even though the latter's Secretary General was a member of it. The ritual used by the Royal Kent Chapter at Newcastle was adopted as the basis for the Scottish ritual for their Rite and can equally well be discounted. At the time, there were many Knights Templar Encampments working the Rose-Croix degree and the members of the new Supreme Council would have received their Rose-Croix degree in one of these. All the rituals probably varied slightly as there had been no central control since 1813.

About 1870, or possibly earlier, the Supreme Council issued each Chapter with a hand-written ritual. A number of these, beautifully written in copperplate and bound in red leather, exist. Some copies have later printed amendments inserted. Whether these books were the first official ritual on paper is not known, but nothing earlier has been found or is in the archives of the Supreme Council.

Printed exposures of the 18° dated 1845 are referred to on page 135.

These are the collected works of the rather disreputable printer, Richard Carlile, published after his death. They were therefore in use before the start of the English Supreme Council, possibly by KT Encampments, and not its choice. A later, well-known exposure, *The Text-Book of Advanced Masonry*, 1873, may have been plagiarized from the official manuscripts referred to above.

The rituals now used by the Supreme Council for the 30° to the 33° are slightly modified forms of those used in the Northern Masonic Jurisdiction USA. Some English Chapters may have been working elementary forms of the Kadosh 30° (originally 24°) or Prince of the Royal Secret 32° (originally 25°) so parts of these might have been taken into the final versions adopted. Whatever rituals were used from 1845, they have been revised from time to time, and will continue to be adjusted as necessary.

The Intermediate Degrees, worked as Demonstrations by the King Edward VII Chapter of Improvement are the 4°–17°. These rituals and their ceremonies are based on the Francken Ms of 1783. *Resumés* of the degrees have been printed in the pamphlet *The Intermediate Degrees, 1°–17°* which all Chapters are requested to give to candidates after they have been perfected to the 18°. The 19°–29° are communicated to candidates for the 30° by name only before the ceremony. *Resumés* are available to members of the 30° in the pamphlet, *The Intermediate Degrees 19°–29° and a Resumé of the 30°*. Only the 28° of this series has so far been demonstrated.

Full rituals of all the Intermediate Degrees are held in the archives of the Supreme Council.

Conclusion

It is difficult to write a conclusion to a history of the A & A Rite as so much of the story has yet to be resolved. The author has been fortunate enough to be able to throw new lights on some events. This edition contains also the results of additional research, particularly about the early days of French high degree Masonry.

The 1771 copy in English of the Constitutions of 1762 recently discovered in the Library of the Supreme Council for England and Wales is important as being the earliest known. Though it proves almost definitely that these Constitutions were antedated, it also makes it clear unfortunately that some of those who developed the Rite were not prepared to accept documents as they were originally written. The later 'copies', until now considered as genuine, do no service to the Rite and are a menace to historians.

The rediscovery of the pamphlet, written by Brest de la Chausée, only a few years after the events described, assists in unravelling a complicated story about the high degrees in France between approximately 1755 and 1765. Amongst other matters explained, his writings confirm that the Emperors of the East and West had no part in the issue of the Patent to Morin, the production of the Constitutions of 1762 or the formation of the Rite; though some of their high degrees may eventually have found their way into it.

A study of a file in the library of the United Grand Lodge, holding papers about the formation of the abortive Supreme Council for Great Britain in 1819, also clarifies a curious episode. It shows that the part played by the Duke of Sussex, after the Union, had not been to neglect the high degrees, but to keep them running in a quiet way until they became more acceptable to the newly organised United Grand Lodge. Complaints made about him at the time have often been doubted, and are now proved to be unjustified. The file also shows how anxious, at this time, were those reorganising the high degrees in France to increase their prestige by drawing Britain into their circle. It also reveals that their emissary was a bad choice as he was primarily a peddler of degrees and financially dishonest.

There is still much to discover. In spite of work on documents dealing with the early history of the high degrees in Bordeaux, the reasons for the birth of the high degrees and whether they started in England or in France remains a matter of conjecture. In the same way, in spite of much research, the real history of what happened in Charleston between 1795 and the birth of the American Supreme Council in 1801 has yet to be discovered. Finally, more information as to how the high degrees returned to England about 1770 is also needed to complete this part of the story. Work on these subjects is being done, and there is no doubt that the next decade will see the publication of books far more informative than the present one. In the meanwhile, the author hopes that what he has written will help members of the Ancient and Accepted Rite (and masonic students generally) to understand a little more clearly how the degrees, of which they are so fond, were developed.

In England and Wales, and in some other Supreme Councils, the Rite has always been Christian in membership. In its early form, it was Christian, and may actually have been started as a sort of protest against the universality of the English Grand Lodge of 1717. Since 1801, a number of the Supreme Councils of the world have come into line with Craft masonry and have made the Rite universal in membership. This book explains how this has never happened in England and Wales. But any idea that the Ancient and Accepted Rite is in opposition to those rites, where universality is the rule, is nonsense.

All members of the Rite in England and Wales are practising members of the Craft; many of them holding high office in the United Grand Lodge. For them, however, Christian masonry is an extension that they choose to join in the knowledge that it will take them further towards what they are seeking in their masonic lives.

Early French 18° Rose-Croix apron depicting Faith, Hope and Charity.

CHRONOLOGY OF THE EVENTS IN THE TEXT
PART I

Note—References are given only if they do not appear in the text.

Date	Event and References
1717	Foundation of the Grand Lodge of England.
1723 or 1724	Foundation of the Grand Lodge of Ireland.
1732	Foundation of *Loge L'Anglaise* (No 204 later) at Bordeaux..
1733	A Scots Masters Lodge held at the Devil's Tavern, Temple Bar, London on the 2nd and 4th Mondays. Lodge was erased in 1736. Cited in the *Rawlinson Ms* in the Bodleian Museum, Oxford and also in Pine's *Engraved List* and Smith's *Companion*.
1735	At the Bear Inn, Bath, Lodge No 113, on a special occasion, the WM both Wardens and 9 Brn were made Scots Masters. References as above. A similar meeting was held in 1747, and then only rarely until 1758.
1736	Foundation of the Grand Lodge of Scotland.
c 1736	Chevalier Ramsay's Oration written, mentioning the relationship between Crusaders and Masonry..
1737	The *Journal de l'Avocat Barbier* cites French courtiers making up a Masonry different from the English and using such expressions as *'chevalier'*, *'chevalerie'* and *'chapitre'* *AQC* 32, etc..
1737	A Baron Scheffer received in Paris at the Comte de Clermont's Lodge the three Symbolic degrees and two *Ecossais* degrees *AQC* 32 (somewhat doubtful).
1738	Duc d'Antin appointed as the first French GM of France.
1740	Lodge of Antiquity (then No 1) made 9 Brn into Scots Masters. Recorded in Lodge history.
1740	5 MMs were 'Rais'd Scots Masters' in No 137, Bristol *AQC* 40.
1740	5 Brn made Scots Masters at Salisbury.
1740	An *Ecossais* Lodge formed at Bordeaux by *Loge la Française*, an offshoot of *Loge l'Anglaise*.
1741	Scots Lodge opened in Berlin *AQC* 9 & 33.
1743	Death of Duc d'Antin, succeeded as GM of France by Prince Louis of Bourbon-Condé, Comte de Clermont.
1743	Issue of regulation condemning *Ecossais* Masonry by the GM's personal Lodge, *Loge Saint-Jean de Jérusalem*.

1743	Baron von Hund claimed to have been given high degrees in Paris.
1744	French exposures start references to high degrees.
1744	Scots lodge opened at Hamburg *AQC* 9.
1745	Fictitious date of opening of Chapter of Arras.
1745	Failure of '45 Rebellion in Britain ends Jacobite influence in Freemasonry.
1745	Regulations reissued by *Loge Saint-John de Jérusalem* giving *Ecossais* masons supervisory powers.
1746	Estienne Morin claims to have founded a high degree lodge, *La Parfaite Harmonie*, at Bordeaux.
1747	Scots Lodge opened at Leipsig *AQC* 9.
1747	*Loge Elu Parfaite* founded in Paris by Lamolère de Feuillard.
1748	Appearance of Knight of the East as highest *Ecossais* degree.
1752	Lamolère de Feuillard appointed its Deputy by the Bordeaux Mother Lodge.
1757	Dr Manningham, DGM England, denies presence of high degrees in England or Scotland, but admits knowledge of their existence overseas.
1758	Jacques Lacorne claims to be appointed by Comte de Clermont as *Substitut Particulier*.
1760	Schism among Paris Masons from Lacorne, by Martin Pény and his supporters.
1761	Chaillon de Jonville appointed by Comte de Clermont as *Substitut General*.
1761	Patent to Estienne Morin as Insp Gen by GL of F to propagate masonry overseas.
1761	First mention of Sov Prince Rose-Croix applied to holders of the degree of Kt of the Eagle.
1761/2	Probable start of Emperors of the East (to become later Emperors of the East and West).
1762	Date given to first Constitutions of A A Rite.
1762	Morin's ship captured and he is taken to England.
1763	Morin arrives in W. Indies. He receives documents from France, probably Statutes and Regulations of the GL of F of 1763.
1763	Morin appoints H. A. Francken as his Deputy in Jamaica.
1763	Scots Lodge formed at New Orleans.
1765	Possible completion of Rose-Croix ritual by Willermoz at Lyons.
1766	Circular by GL of F and Council of Kts of the East limiting powers of Mother Lodges over high degree lodges. Also condemns Kadosh degree.
1766	Possible date when Morin began 1762 Constitutions and supporting documents.
1766	Morin replaced by Bro Martin by GL of F and goes to live in Jamaica. About this date forms Grand Council in Jamaica.
1766	Baron Tschoudy publishes *L'Etoile Flamboyante*.
1766	Publication of *Les Plus Secrets Mystères*.

1767	Francken forms Lodge of Perfection and Council of Princes of Jerusalem at Albany, New York.
1767	A letter written by Comte de Clermont refers to Rose-Croix degrees, wishing to restrict them to a few masons of high rank.
1767	GL of F closed by Government following constant disturbances.
1770	Morin forms Grand Chapter of Princes of Royal Secret in Jamaica.
1771	Death of Comte de Clermont.
1771	Death of Morin.
1771	Francken writes manuscript book which includes 1762 Constitutions (in English) and rituals of 15°–24°. Now in Sup C Library, London.
1772	Union between GL of F and Emperors of E & W to form a Grand Lodge.
1773	Some members of Paris Lodges form Gd Orient.
1773	Duc de Chartres appointed GM of GL of F.
1781	Publication of *GIGE Chevalier Kadosh*, probably written c. 1769.
1783	Francken writes a second Ms book, somewhat similar to his 1771 Ms. Now with Sup C NMJ USA..
1783	Lodge of Perfection opened at Charleston, USA.
1785	Publication of Vol II of *Recueil Precieux* which included high degrees.
1786	Reputed date of Grand Constitutions of 1786 of A & A Rite.
1786	Death of Frederick II, King of Prussia.
1788	Council of Princes of Jerusalem opened at Charleston.
1789	Comte de Grasse-Tilly reaches San Domingo from France.
1791	Start of Negro rebellion in San Domingo.
1793	De Grasse-Tilly, his father-in-law, de la Hogue, and their families move to Charleston.
1795	Francken dies in Jamaica.
1797	De Grasse-Tilly, with French colleagues, forms Grand Consistory of 25° at Charleston.
1799	De Grasse-Tilly probably visits San Domingo.
1801	Sup C possibly opened at Charleston.
1802	Sup C issue 'letters of credence' of 33° to De Grasse-Tilly and de la Hogue.
1802	De Grasse-Tilly returns San Domingo, and sets up Sup C for French West Indies.
1803	De Grasse-Tilly captured but taken to Jamaica where he sets up Sup C for Jamaica.
1803	De Grasse-Tilly leaves Charleston for Paris.

PART II

1765	Probable date of arrival of Lambert de Lintot in England.

1766	Unattached French masons in London, led by de Lintot, buy warrant, probably of No 331.
1772	Mention of Kts Templar in Bristol paper.
1776	Probable date when Maj Charles Sherriff received 25 degrees of Morin's Rite and made DIG at Fort Augustine, Florida.
1778	KT degree conferred in Phoenix Lodge No 257 at Portsmouth.
1778	Bristol Charter of Compact claimed this date of origin.
1779	De Lintot appointed WM of St George de l'Observance and takes it as No 1 of Preston's Grand Lodge South of the River Trent.
1782	De Lintot writes to Scotland about high degrees, but is not understood. Matter is dropped.
1782	Emmanuel Zimmermann and Pierre Laurent confer Rose-Croix degrees in a KT lodge in Dublin.
1783	Major Shirreff retires from army and settles in Shropshire.
1785	Shirreff starts to interest Gd Sec Moderns and other leading masons in high degrees.
1785	Five masons, including the Gd Treasurer Moderns, attend convention of Rite of Philalethes in Paris.
1786	Revival of Grand Encampment KT in Ireland.
1788	Shirreff forms Lodge of Perfection in London.
1791	Thomas Dunckerley assumes position of GM of KT in England and invites Duke of Kent to become Patron of the Order.
1791	St John of Jerusalem Encampment KT founded by John Knight at Redruth.
1793–1813	French prisoners of war work high degrees in the camps in UK and confer degrees on many Englishmen.
1795	Death of Dunckerley, succeeded by Lord Rancliffe.
1800	Death of Rancliffe; no successor.
1804	Robert Gill reassembles Grand Conclave. Duke of Kent appointed Grand Master KT.
1807	Duke of Kent resigns and is reappointed Patron. Waller Rodwell Wright is appointed Grand Master.
1812	Wright resigns and is succeeded by Duke of Sussex.
1812	John Knight's notebook on high degrees written.
1812	Royal Kent Chapter KT formed at Newcastle.
1813	Union of Moderns and Antients.
1817	United Grand Lodge declare high degrees not to be part of true masonry. Duke of Sussex puts Grand Conclave into abeyance, but retains small central organisation.
1819	Duke of Sussex, Duke of Leinster and H. da Costa installed 33° by Glock D'Obernay on behalf of French Supreme Council. New body does not function. (The complicated chronology of events in France leading to this event is given in text.)
1820	Glock D'Obernay reprimanded by the Duke of Sussex for founding a Consistory in Kingston, Jamaica.
1820	Robert Gill's house burnt and archives of KT apparently destroyed.

1826	Supreme Council for Ireland formed with Duke of Leinster as Sov Gd Commander.
1830	Duke of Sussex reassumes active control of KT but does not summon Grand Conclave.
1843	Death of Duke of Sussex.

PART III

1813	Supreme Council, Northern Masonic Jurisdiction USA founded.
1843	English Grand Conclave summoned.
1845	Sup C NMJ USA adopts Christianity for 17° and above.
1845	(26 Oct and 10 Nov) Dr R. T. Crucefix applies to NMJ for patent.
1845	(29 Dec) Sup C NMJ grants patent to Dr Crucefix ante-dated to his letter of application 26 October.
1846	Grand Conclave KT installs a Grand Master.
1846	First meeting of Sup C for England and Wales.
1846	Sup C for Scotland formed.
1847	Sup C NMJ breaks off relations with Sup C E & W until about 1851.
1850	Death of Dr Crucefix, succeeded as Sov Gd Comd by Dr Oliver.
1851	Dr Oliver resigns and is succeeded by Dr Leeson.
1853	W. Tucker 33° is dismissed as Prov GM Dorsetshire by Gd Master.
1855	Tucker appointed Gd Sec Gen. Dies 1855.
1869	Probable date of move of Sup C to 33 Golden Square.
1870	Sup C sets up Sup C for Chile.
1871	Sup C sets up Sup C for Canada.
1872	District organisation with Inspectors General started.
1875	Lausanne Conference of Sup C.
1876	Sup C breaks off relations with Sup C for Scotland.
1881	Sup C withdraws from world confederation of Sup C (as later did Scotland and Ireland).
1881	Treaty of Union with Baldwyn Chapter.
1883	Chapter of Antiquity, Bath, last independent Chapter, submits to Sup C.
1889	Treaty re-establishes relations between Sup C of England and Wales, and of Scotland.
1905	Sup C Ireland adheres to 1889 Treaty and tripartite meetings started.
1911	Sup C moves to 10 Duke Street, London SW1.
1958	Tripartite meetings extended to include 'English speaking' Sup C on a four yearly basis.
1969	Australian Branch C set up.
1973	Sup C sets up Sup C for Finland.
1976	Referendum by Chapters in Republic of S. Africa decide against a Sup C for that country.

1980   Sup C divides London Chapters into five groups.

1985   Sup C for Australia erected jointly by S G Cs for England and
              Wales, and for Scotland.

Notes

(a) In *A Letter from the Grand Mistress, 1724* is; 'The Knights of St John of
Jerusalem, or the Knights of Malta in which two Lodges I must nevertheless
allow the Honour of having adorned the ancient Jewish and Pagan Masonry
with many religious and Christian Rites'. This is sometimes accepted as a
very early reference to high degrees.

(b) The reference to early high degree masonry in Belgium in *AQC* 32, citing
La Franc-Maçonnerie Belge du XVIII siécle, by P. Duchaine, has been found,
on checking, not to exist.

REGULATIONS FORMERLY GIVING SPECIAL POWERS TO MASONS HOLDING CERTAIN HIGH DEGREES

Notes

(a) Regulations giving special powers of inspection and discipline to brethren holding some of the high degrees were basically similar. Such degrees were Scots Master, Master *ad vitam*, Prince of Jerusalem, and several others.

(b) The following are extracts from regulations for *Ecossais* Master, one of the lowest of the high degrees, and from the Grand Master *ad vitam*, one of the more senior. The first extract is from rules issued by the Grand Lodge of France, dated 1748, taken from a copy in the *Bibliothèque Nationale* in Paris. The remainder are from the *London French Ms* and are probably of later date.

    x All *Ecossais* Masters will be Grand Wardens of masonry automatically and, as such, every *Ecossais* Master has the right to establish Lodges and to make masons of the first degree in places where there is no regular lodge established by *Ecossais* Masters or by a Grand Lodge of Great Knights of the East.

    x A *Grand Ecossais* presides in the lodge of the first three degrees, but cannot award any punishment against another *Grand Ecossais*, who is at fault. They will reserve this punishment to be carried out in an *Ecossais* Lodge; and it will not be light.

    x When there is any question of inflicting a punishment on a *Grand Ecossais* for a fault committed, one will go to. . . . [Presumably Knight or Commander of the Temple].

    x In admitting a brother to a new degree, the rules and policy laid down in that Statutes, Regulations and Constitutions of the Order will be considered. No lodge will be regular unless all the brethren who belong have been summoned. If it should happen that there are disagreements in the deliberations, the Knights of the East will be called in to adjudicate, or the matter will be referred to a superior *Ecossais* Lodge. It can be referred to the Commanders of the East who are their superior.

    x *Ecossais* lodges will visit each other by deputation, will exchange correspondence regularly and will reciprocally spread the light which they have acquired. Each *Grand Ecossais* will have a copy of these regulations and also of the Regulations of the Grand Lodge of the first three degrees, so as to be able to supervise and comment, as necessary, in accordance with his powers and rights.

Certificate of Authority of a Grand Ecossais

We, the undersigned, excellent leaders of knowledgeable men, certify that the present Regulations and Statutes conform to the original sent to us from the Grand Lodge of Grand Masters *Ecossais* of Paris. In proof of this, we have put our signature and the official seal of our Sublime Lodge.

Given to the Very Excellent and Very Powerful Brother ....
who has signed in the margin of the present Statutes and Regulations, *ne varietur*.

At Le Havre, this 19th day of November, 1761.

        (signed)   ? Jaime

        Chevalier of the Royal and Military Order of Saint-Louis.

        Grand Ecossais and Master of the Lodge.

(The Lodge at Le Havre was one of the *Mères Loges Ecossaises* which owed nominal and spasmodic obedience to the central authority in Paris).

Extracts from the Regulations for the Degree of Grand Master ad vitam

x When there are several Grand Master [*ad vitam*] in a town, they must assemble from time to time to discuss the problems and abuses which could arise in any one of their lodges. It is important that, if anything unusual happens in a lodge, the Grand Master of that lodge informs the most senior, who will call together the other Grand Masters to consider the whole matter.

x It is to be noted that there may be more than one Grand Master in any lodge.

x When the Grand Masters are all assembled, they seat themselves where they wish, except the senior who is their commander and who will occupy the first place, with the two Wardens in the West. Then the Very High, Very Powerful and Very Sublime Grand Masters, if they have anything to propose, raise the matter, and the case is decided.

x When a Grand Master visits a lodge of another Grand Master, he must place himself on the throne, which the other must vacate for him, and place himself on his left, giving the right to the visitor. The visitor's Wardens place themselves to the left and right of the throne, and all sit. If the Grand Master visitor has no Wardens with him, he should ask for two from the Master of the Lodge, who will know those who are capable of filling the office. The Wardens of the Grand Master should be, at least, Scottish Masters [*Maîtres Ecossais*].

x A Grand Master [*ad vitam*] received and accepted in a Lodge never changes and remains permanently. No one has the power to cancel [his appointment] or to remove him from the rank of Grand Master.

x The Grand Masters must hold their feasts on the day of St John the Evangelist together with all the Worshipful Masters and their Wardens in the town in which it is their duty to shed the light.

NOTES ON THE DEGREES OF THE ANCIENT AND ACCEPTED RITE

Introduction

Almost from their first appearance, high degrees were formed into various combinations by mother lodges to form rites. Most of these were short lived. As shown in Chapter 4, Morin started to collect existing degrees into a rite as soon as he got to the West Indies in 1763. By about 1770, his rite had grown to 25 degrees. His rite was then increased from 25 to 33 degrees some time before the Charleston Supreme Council was started in 1801. The authority for the increase was ostensibly the Constitutions of 1786.

Most of the degrees were of French origin but there was some German influence.

From the time of their original developments, the degrees have had many revisions:

(a) Normal changes by the various high degree bodies that used them in the early formative years.

(b) Development, revision and translation of the degrees of Morin's Rite i.e. 4° to 25° by Morin and Francken after 1765. (See Chapter 6.)

(c) Further revision and renumbering of some of the degrees from about 1795 onwards to comply with the Constitutions of 1786. Some further revision, if not invention, of the 30° to 33° by de Grasse-Tilly and his associates about 1800.

(d) A revision in mid-XIX century in America by a Frenchman, Charles Joseph Jean Laffon de Ladebat. It is not known what Supreme Councils used his revised rituals, but they were certainly used for a time in America. The rituals used by the Supreme Council for England and Wales were not affected by his revision.

(e) Complete revision and de-Christianisation a little later by Albert Pike, Grand Commander, Southern Jurisdiction USA. These are not used by the Supreme Councils in Britain and by few Continental Supreme Councils, though they got wide publicity because of the extensive writings and influence of the author.

The rituals now used by the Supreme Council for England and Wales are mentioned in Chapter 18. The following notes make no attempt to describe the rituals which are in use at present. Full written versions are available to those who require this information, with the authoritative copies being held by the Supreme Council. The object of this Appendix is to describe what is known of the history and development of each degree.

The Intermediate Degrees 4° to 17°

A full description of the degrees from the 4° to the 17° is given in the pamphlet, *The Intermediate Degrees*, which every member of the 18° of the Supreme Council for England and Wales receives when he completes this degree. The degrees in this pamphlet are based on those in the *Francken Manuscript 1783*.

4°—Secret Master. The author has not been able to find a version of this degree earlier than the one given by Francken in 1783. The jewel of the degree is an ivory key but this symbol first appeared in the Craft exposure, *Masonry Dissected* of 1730, and also appears in several other masonic degrees. *Masonry Dissected* was quickly translated into the majority of European languages and so does not help in finding the origin of the Secret Master degree. Naudon suggests that the underlying idea of the degree is the seeking of knowledge of truth. This is probably more apparent in the French than in the English version.

5°—Perfect Master. Here, we find a return to the Traditional History of the 3°. This is one of the oldest degrees in the Rite, possibly developed about 1740 when high degree masons in France were made *Parfait* (perfect) as the start of their *Ecossais* masonry. An early version of the symbolic part of the degree appears in the *London French Ms*. In the Francken version, the lesson is the respect due to the memory of a worthy brother.

6°—Intimate Secretary or Perfect English Master. The origin of this degree is not known. It is presumably based on the Old Testament quotation, 1 Kings, Chapter IX, verses 11–13. 'And Hiram came out from Tyre to see the cities which Solomon had given him; and they pleased him not. And he said, What cities are these that thou hast given me, my brother? and he called them the land of Cabul to this day.' The lessons of the degree are the anomalies of zealousness and care not to offend by prying into another's secrets. There are many versions reasonably similar.

7°—Provost and Judge, or Perfect Irish Master. This is another of the early degrees of unknown origin which probably originated with the 'true system' of the Bordeaux high degrees. It deals with work on the Temple after the death of Hiram. There seems to be no reason for the alternative title of Perfect Irish Master in any of the versions found, except to distinguish it from the degree of Scottish Master.

8°—Intendant of the Building(s), or Master in Israel or Scottish Master of JJJ. This degree appears in Paris some time before 1748. The JJJ, the early title, derives from the initials of two early sacred words, Jakini and Joo, and a profane word, Jourdain. All this has disappeared from later versions. This degree includes an examination of the candidate, after which the Scottish Master title was conferred, giving certain powers of inspection and discipline as shown in Appendix II. The *Francken* version removed many of the New Testament references in the early versions, though, possibly by oversight, some are retained.

The title of this degree should be 'Intendant of the Building' not 'Building*s*'. The 1771 *Francken Manuscript*, now in the possession of the Supreme Council in London, shows the word in the singular. The manuscript book that Francken wrote in 1783, and which gives the impression that he wrote in a hurry, shows the word in the plural, an obvious mistake as the building concerned is the Temple. The 1783 manuscript is in the archives of the Supreme Council, Northern Jurisdiction, USA—a copy having been sent to the Supreme Council in London. The list of degrees issued in the 1802 Circular does not repeat Francken's 1783 error but refers to the degree as 'Intendant of the Building.' However the wide distribution of the 1783 Ms appears to have perpetuated an obvious mistake.

9°—Elect of Nine, or Master Elect, or Perfect Master Elect, or Elect of Perignan. (The title Elect of Perignan was removed in the later Francken Ms.) The three Elect degrees in the A & A Rite are a digest of the many Elect degrees which started in France in 1740 and the following years. They belong to the type of high degree masonry which Sitwell termed 'false' implying that it did not emanate from the Bordeaux group of lodges. The 'true' and the 'false' schools did not join up until about 1765, or even later. All the degrees are extensions of the Traditional History of the 3°.

The *Elu* degree is still worked in full by at least two Chapters of the Netherlands Constitution in South Africa. In the Goede Hoop Chapter at Capetown, special caverns produce a ceremony which must be alarming for the candidate and is gruesome, even for spectators. The *Francken* version is not so dramatic. The degree, which was the first in *Les Plus Secrets Mystères*, is not now worked in most Continental Rites.

10°—Elect of Fifteen or Grand Elect. This is very similar to the previous degree and is also not normally worked in Continental masonry.

11°—Sublime Elect or Sublime Prince Elect. Early versions of the degree continue the story and include the legend that the Elect were those masons who took the Order to Scotland when masonry finally disintegrated at Jerusalem. This is expanded in the 20° and is one of the earliest links in masonic tradition with Scotland and the Crusaders.

The three 'Vengeance Degrees' have little now to recommend them, except as historical curiosities handed down from early masonry.

12°—Grand Master Architect. The degree is the sole remaining representative of a score or more of Architect degrees which were produced in the XVIII century. The 4° of *Les Plus Secrets Mystères* is 'Little Architect, first degree and Apprentice *Ecossais*'. Its 5° is 'Grand Architect' and this is divided in the *Recueil Précieux* into 'Grand Architect or Companion *Ecossais*' and 'Master *Ecossais*'. In the *London French Ms* there are three Architect degrees of Apprentice, Companion and Master.

John Knight's Notebook of c 1811 (see Chapter 13) shows that a degree of Architect was worked in England, probably as a result of the introduction of the Rite of Seven Degrees by Lambert de Lintot in 1766. These degrees faded out, except in the Baldwyn Chapter, when the high degree bodies in England submitted to the authority of the Supreme Council some time after 1845, even if they had not disappeared before.

None of the Architect degrees referred to above has more than a vague similarity with the *Francken Ms* degree which must have been a comparatively late version. This is a pity as some of the early ones are of great interest while the present version is somewhat colourless.

13°—Royal Arch of Enoch or Royal Arch. Versions of this degree have always been of special interest because of the possibility of connection with the Royal Arch degree worked in Royal Arch Chapters. It must be made clear that few have any historical backing. There is nothing in the Bible or in Josephus' *Antiquities of the Jews* associating the Patriarch Enoch with any form of vault or arch. The Genesis 5, verses

21–24, references merely tell us that 'All the days of Enoch were three hundred and sixty and five years: And Enoch walked with God: and he was not: for God took him.'

Mackey's *History*, which is often so much out of date factually, has a very good Chapter on the Legend of Enoch. His summary is:

> . . . it would appear that the *Legend of Enoch*, being wholly unknown to the Fraternity in the Middle Ages, unrecognized in the *Legend of the Craft*; and the name not even mentioned in the old records [i.e. the Old Charges] was first introduced into the rituals of some of the higher degrees which began to be fabricated towards the middle of the 18th century . . . and that in its fabrication very copious suggestions were borrowed from the Rabbinical and Oriental traditions on the same subject. It is impossible to assign to this Legend the slightest historical character.

The various arch and vault degrees in masonry had common sources as Mackey mentions. One of the most important comes in the XIV century *Ecclesiastical Histories* of Nicephorus Callistus (Vol ii, Book x, Cap xxxiii) which tells the story of the finding of St John's Gospel in a cavern beneath the Temple.

14°—Scotch Knight of Perfection, or Grand Elect Perfect and Sublime Master, or Grand Elect of the Sacred Vault, of James VI or the Sublime Mason, or True and Perfect Scotch Mason. It is not known how all the degrees named above became the single, last degree in the Lodge of Perfection. Morin's Rite ended with 25 degrees with his Lodge of Perfection only including the degrees up to the 14° or 15°. However, Morin's Rite is called the Rite of Perfection in the Constitutions of 1786 and this incorrect designation has been used by the majority of writers for the whole series up to the 25°. All the early versions are varieties of a vault story. In the True and Perfect Master's degree in the *London French Ms* which may have been one of the sources of the final degree, there is a curious story, nowhere else mentioned, of the Sacred Word being turned into Samaritan characters, which no foreigner could understand, by St Jerome when he translated the Bible. Modern French versions of the degree change all the religious allusions into Cabbalistic ones, and the version produced by Albert Pike is naturally also de-Christianised.

15°—Knight of the East, Knight of the Sword, Knight of the Eagle, or Knight of the East or of the Sword, or Knight of the Sword and of the Red Cross. The degree of Knight of the East appeared before 1750 to allow those, upon whom it was conferred, to control the Perfection and Elect degrees. It was an extension of a degree which first appeared in *Les Plus Secrets Mystères* under the title of Knight of the Rose-Croix. The latter had no connection with the 18° and never became part of the Morin's Rite or A & A Rite.

The degrees of Knight of the Sword or of the East and the 16° and 17° were all originally known as Orders of Chivalry, but this title is no longer applied to the 17°. Earlier, they were also known as Red Cross degrees and, in Scotland, two similar ones are part of the Royal Arch series. The 15° also has certain similarities with a degree known as the Red Cross of Babylon, conferred still by other masonic rites. The legends of all these degrees are really simplified stories of the Biblical history to be found in the books of Ezra and Nehemiah. A better historical account will be found in Josephus, Book XI. In French, the motto of the degree is the initials LDP which are usually expanded to 'Liberté de passage' in reference to a river crossing. According to Naudon, this was changed during the Revolution, in some lodges, to *Lillia destrues pedibus* (Crush the lilies under foot), an unpleasant reference to the massacre of the French royalty and aristocracy; and later to *Liberté de Pensée* (Liberty of Thought) in the agnostic lodges.

A similar degree, also called the Red Cross, was being worked in England as late as 1811. Its origin is not known, except that the wording shows that it was a translation from the French. It is also thought that the Rite of Harodim, practised in the north-east till the Union, had degrees which were basically the same.

The Francken Ms of c 1786 has the curious descriptive title:

'15th Degree Masonry renew'd, or the Sword Rectified, such as is practised in the Grand Lodge of Prussia and France, the Islands of Hispaniola, Jamaica and in the Province of New York, viz. Bordeaux, Marseilles, Toulon, Cape Francois, Cayes de Fonds, St. Mark, Port au Prince, Kingston in Jamaica and Albany in the Province of New York established by the Most Illu. Bro Stephen Morin Prince of the R.Secret &c &c &c grand Inspr. genl. and Revived by H.A. Francken Prce. of R. Sret. Depy Inspr. general of all Superior Lodges over the 2 Hemispheres.'

16°—Prince of Jerusalem, Chief of Regular Lodges. All the known versions of this degree are substantially the same. It is the 24° of the *London French Ms* and is explained in some detail in Mackey's *Encyclopaedia*. There is no doubt that the 15° and 16° are basically of very early origin, with references to their legends appearing as early as 1740. As history, they follow more correctly and less anachronistically the known stories than do other masonic rites.

In the French system, the Prince of Jerusalem had very considerable powers of inspection and control of inferior lodges, including the symbolic.

17°—Knight of the East and West, or Knight of the West. The origin of this degree is not known. It probably appeared about 1762 with the increase in degrees caused by the schism in the Knights of the East "either" by Pény or it may have been one of the degrees produced by Pirlet's Emperors of the East and West. From its title, the latter seems to be the most likely. It is suggested that it was of Templar origin, in which case its early roots may have been in the Rite of Strict Observance in Germany. According to Mackey, the degree started as a non-masonic Crusader Order which he attributes—almost certainly incorrectly—to the Chevalier Ramsay. Whatever the source of the degree, it is very appropriate as a fitting prelude to the principles and precepts of Christianity.

18°—Rose-Croix of Heredom, Knight of the Pelican and Eagle. This degree is fully discussed in other parts of the book, notably Chapter 3.

The Intermediate Degrees 19° to 29°

These degrees are communicated by name to candidates for the 30°. They are not used in full and have not been demonstrated, so far, by the King Edward VII Chapter of Improvement, except for the 28°. Synopses of the degrees are available to members of the 30° and above. The official versions of the rituals are held in the archives of the Supreme Council. Most of these degrees are based on the Francken Mss of 1771 and 1783, though their numbers may have been altered by the Constitutions of 1786. The rest of the degrees come from various XVIII century manuscripts. It must be appreciated that the degrees used by some foreign Councils differ considerably from those in the *Francken* series. It must also be realised that the Southern Constitution USA uses a completely different set of rituals which were de-Christianised about a century ago by Albert Pike, the then Sovereign Grand Commander of that Council. His object was to make the A & A Rite as acceptable to men of all religions as are the Craft degrees. At the same time, he took the opportunity to rewrite degrees which he considered obscure or with whose symbolism and lessons he did not agree. The reader must decide for himself whether he considers Albert Pike was justified. There is clearly much to be said for and against his work.

19°—Grand Pontiff, Sublime Scottish Mason, Grand Commander of the Temple. The Christian version of this degree uses the Book of Revelation for its symbolism. The mystical sentiments are not easy to follow, but the main intention is to bridge the gap between the Old and New Testaments—the word 'Pontiff' being derived from the Latin '*Pontifex*', a bridge-builder. This is one of the degrees completely reconstructed by Albert Pike who returns to the Old Testament and the search for a new Covenant. In Morin's Rite, this degree had the additional title of 'Master for Life' but the Preface to the 1786 Constitutions combines that degree with the 23° of the Primitive Rite and the title is dropped. The later Francken Mss had already made this change. As stated earlier, the Primitive Rite may not have been functioning at this time.

20°—Grand Master of Symbolic Lodges, Grand Master ad vitam. In the original Morin's Rite, this degree was the Gd Patriarch Noachite or Prussian Knt (now the 21°). The change seems to have taken place in the later Francken Ms. To conform with what appears already to have happened, the Grand Constitutions of 1786 ordered a new degree to be formed from the 19° and 23° of the Primitive Rite—a Rite that probably did not then exist. The new degree's legend is a theme that appears in the Francken degrees.

The catechism of the degree, which seems to have little bearing on its theme, is important as it embodies one of the early versions of the story of the Scottish origin of masonry. This was used by the Chevalier Ramsay in his Oration and is described briefly in Chapter 3. The following extract takes up the legend from the time that the Elect are finally driven from Jerusalem when that city was destroyed. The Elect fled to Rome:

> ... most of them died there and the remaining Masons divided themselves and went to several parts of Europe, but the greater part of them went to Scotland where they built a town called Kilellin where at the present time there is a lodge of that name. 27,000 of these Masons in Scotland resolved to assist the Christian princes and knights that were at that time in Jerusalem in a Crusade in order to take the Holy City and land from the Barbarians who were in possession of it. And they obtained leave from the Scottish monarch.
>
> Their bravery gained them the esteem of the Order, and all the great officers took a resolution to be admitted into the secrets of these Masons which, when they had received them, they also admitted those Scottish Masons into their Order, by the name of the Rose-Croix or Pelican.
>
> After the Crusade was over, everyone retired to their respective coun-

tries at which Masonry was spread all over Europe and was for a long time in full vigour in France and England, but after the destruction of the Temple [presumably the Order of Knights Templar c 1300] they neglected the Craft for many ages in England and France but the Scottish, to their praise be it said, were the only ones that kept up the practice of it.

A Scotch nobleman, who went to France, became for a long time resident of Bordeaux, where he established a Lodge of Perfection.

A curious alternative legend for this degree is based on Frederick the Great and General Welhaven. Frederick as Master of the Three Globes Lodge in Berlin and Welhaven one of its members. At a certain meeting, Frederick was aware that Welhaven, who was present, was a traitor. The King called upon the traitor several times to confess, but he did not do so. In due course, Welhaven was denounced and sentenced to life imprisonment. The lessons are naturally loyalty, truth, forgiveness, etc. but there is no basis historically for the story. There may, however, be some truth in the idea that anger at Welhaven's disloyalty could have been the cause of Frederick ceasing to be an active mason. This version is given fully and studied in *AQC* 40 pp 166 and 199.

21°—Noachite or Prussian Knight. This degree was the 20° of Morin's Rite but was moved to the 21° in the later Francken Ms. The original title of Morin's 21° was Grand Master of the Key of Masonry but that was added to the 23° in the later Francken Ms. This move was confirmed in the 1786 Constitutions where the degree was stated also to be the sixteenth degree of the Primitive Rite. The degree of Prussian Knight is so different from all the other degrees that its retention in the Rite at all is curious. Francken states that the degree was translated from the German in the XVII century, but this is most unlikely. Most versions have allusions to Frederick (1712–1786) and this probably is why something so apparently out of place should have been retained at all. In the *London French Ms* the story is told that Frederick formed the degree as an Order to reward knights who had served him well in the Seven Years' War (1757–63). The degree first appears in print in *Les Plus Secrets Mystères*, published in 1766 and this makes the connection with the Seven Years' War just possible, but unlikely as the degree seems to have been of earlier development. The degree appears frequently after 1766 with minor variations. The legend is the story of Peleg, who built the Tower of Babel. It is given in *Genesis XI*, but a much fuller version, from which the degree may have been taken, appears in *Josephus (Book I, Chap iv)*. An English version of the degree, found in John Knight's notebook of 1811 (see Appendix

VII) stresses the drunkenness of Noah and the wickedness of Ham, a variation appearing nowhere else. In this version, the degree is also called the 'Royal Ark Masons, Marioners, or Noachites, also sometimes called the Prusian Masons'. Ham, as the wicked son of Noah, is repeatedly connected with necromancy by early writers, down to the XVII century.

The degree, as revised by Albert Pike, used a completely new theme, presumably based on some other legend. He changes the Prussian Knights into the Westphalian Free Knights. One of them, Adolphus the Saxon, on his return from the Crusades, demands justice against a Count Reinfred de Loéngrin and the Bishop of Vienna. This seems no more appropriate in the A & A Rite than the original, and does not have the merit of antiquity.

22°—Knight of the Royal Axe or Prince of Libanus, or Grand Patriarch. This may have been one of the degrees produced by the Council of the Emperors of the East and West sometime between 1762 and 1768. There is nothing to say whether it was an early degree revived or a new development. It had, however, reached a form which was sufficiently final to be included in a narrative form by Morin or Francken in the Manuscript book of 1771. Mackey suggests the degree is particularly interesting 'in consequence of the mystical association of the Druses with the Crusaders'. It is hard to follow his reasoning about a degree which does not appear to be based on any form of early legend and is completely imaginary.

23°—Chief of the Tabernacle and 24°—Prince of the Tabernacle. Naudon suggests that these degrees, and the three following, are part of a series from the Rite of the *Ecossais Trinitaire* of 1765. This Rite was quite independent of the Grand Lodge of France or of the Council of Knights of the East. However, there was a connection with the Emperors of the East and West through their leader, Pirlet, who was also a member of the *Ecossais Trinitaire* Rite. The Rite was one of those absorbed by the Philosophical Rite, founded about 1775 in Paris, thus confirming Baynard's views about the origin of these degrees. The five degrees would have become known to de Grasse-Tilly when they came out to the French Lodges in the West Indies and so chosen by him for the A & A Rite.

Waite suggests that the two degrees above had no place in the Rite after the Christian degrees. Albert Pike's versions seem to be entirely his own idea, though possibly based in Jewish legend, and covers the testing of Aaron and his sons for priestly office. It is not known whether his degrees were used anywhere else than in the Southern Jurisdiction, USA.

25°—Knight of the Brazen Serpent. The early versions record the Biblical story given in Numbers 21, verses 4–9, with Christian references from St John 3, verse 14. Its provenance is also connected with the Rite of *Ecossais Trinitaire*. Mackey and others give the degree a legend of the time of the Crusades with an Order of the Brazen Serpent in the Holy Land. The obligation of its members was to care for travellers, heal their sick and escort them to and from Palestine, this being the allusion to the healing and saving virtues of the Brazen Serpent. The similarity of this legend with the known duties of the Hospitallers of St John makes it unconvincing.

26°—Prince of Mercy, formerly Scottish Trinitaire. This degree also comes from the same source as the previous three. In its early form, it had high mystical and Christian qualities. Inevitably the removal of all traces of Christianity from such a degree turns it into a legend of hermetism and imagination. This is what happened in those Supreme Councils which do not accept a Christian theme. However, for some unexplained reason, Pike's version hardly affected the Christianity of the degree. On the Continent of Europe, there have been a number of unusual themes, such as the *Ordre des Trinitaires*, founded in theory in AD 1118, or the *Pères de Merci* of AD 1218, who brought back captives from Algeria, while still another version deals with Buddha, Lord or Mercy and Compassion.

27°—Knight (or Commander) of the Temple, or Sovereign Commander of the Temple. This degree is the last of the *Ecossais Trinitaire* series. There have been a number of different degrees with these names. That now in the A & A Rite has nothing to do with any Knights Templar degree or with the degree of the same name in the *London French Ms.* This was another of the degrees which gave its holders certain powers. Waite says that the 'alleged privileges of the Commanders of the Tmple' included the right (a) to remain seated, and with their hats on in ordinary lodges, at the North of the Master and (b) to come and go at pleasure and (c) to have seven votes at all ballots. Whether 'ordinary lodges' always accepted their claims is another matter— some certainly did.

28°—Knight of the Sun or Prince Adept or Philosophical Lodge or Chaos Disentangled. This degree was the 23° of Morin's Rite until it was changed to its present position by the 1786 Constitutions. There are a number of versions and, in some form, it was one of the earliest of the high degrees. It was used by Morin in the West Indies when he lived there before 1760, and contemporary letters show that he conferred the degree on several occasions. Naudon quotes a version of 1765, a slightly later one is in the *London French Ms* and, of course, it appears in the *Francken Mss*. All the known rituals are long and complicated but none shows evidence of its origin. It is certainly one of the most interesting of the degrees of the Rite but it is not possible to precis its theme which relies on symbolic mysticism, with a basis of Rosicrucianism, to impart its lessons.

The lesson of the degree may be summed up: 'While God, by the use of his superior powers, maintains perfect balance in the forces of nature in the world, the equilibrium between good and evil in a man's life has to be maintained by the man himself. He, who has the ability to achieve this, has the right to be called a Prince Adept.'

Mackey writes of Albert Pike's de-Christianised version, 'There is not in the wide compass of masonic degrees, one more emphatically Rosicrucian than this.' One wonders if this is particularly important. However, he continues: '. . . Of all the high degrees, it is perhaps the most interesting to the scholar who desires to investigate the true secrets of the Order. The old catechisms, now too much neglected, are full of suggestive thoughts, and in its modern ritual, to which we are indebted to the genius of Bro Albert Pike, it is far the most learned and philosophical of the Scottish degrees.'

Naudon disagrees: 'We do not think that it has gained by it,' while Waite, with his usual forthrightness, says that Pike has ruined the degree.

The Supreme Council for France also had a non-Christian version until the middle of the last century. In this, the Knighthood of the Sun was represented by a school of natural sciences, or an academy in which the Book of Nature was interpreted and its laws studied. The universal spirit was represented by the symbol of a dove, and it was said to supply life to the three kingdoms—animal, vegetable and mineral. A less mystical and more easily understood theme was substituted in due course.

29°—Grand Scottish Knight of St Andrew or Grand Patriarch of the Crusades. Mackey says that the degree 'was composed by Tschoudy, and bequeathed with other manuscripts to the Council of Emperors of the East and West'. It is not known when this happened, if it did, but it is not improbable as the Emperors were at the height of their importance in 1769 when Tschoudy died. This was three years after he had written *L'Etoile Flamboyante*, and the degree *Ecossais de Saint*

André, contenant le développment total de l'art royal de la Franc-Maçonnerie was not published until 1780—ample time for it to be included in the A & A Rite. Nevertheless, there were early versions of this degree, all endeavouring to prove a relationship between Scotland and Masonry, particularly Templarism. An example is given in Chapter 3 where an early Rose-Croix degree is found to have 'Knight of St Andrew' as part of its title. The version eventually used, according to Baynard, was the 25° of the Primitive Rite.

It is pointless to select any one of the many early versions for description. A French one, given by Naudon, recalls the events of the building and rebuilding of the Temple, and then repeats the theme that freemasons were originally Templars who were themselves masons, descendants of Hiram. The task of these masons was to rebuild the Christian churches.

The degree is a transitional one, theoretically taking the candidate from the philosophies and Christianity of earlier ones to the realities of the Knights Templar. Albert Pike has produced his own version. It inculcates equality and represents the Knights of St Andrew as exponents of truth. Toleration is stressed as a fitting climax to all preceding degrees.

30°—Knight Kadosh (or Kadosch) or Ne Plus Ultra. The degree is worked in full by the Supreme Council for England and Wales for the promotion of Most Wise Sovereigns of the 18° Rose-Croix degree. Candidates are those who have been recommended for this promotion by the Chapters, and elected by the Supreme Council to the 30°. Before the ceremony of the 30°, the intermediate degrees of 19° to 29° are communicated and conferred by name only. This is always done by the Supreme Council or by its authorised representatives. Information about the ritual used at present is available to those entitled to it. The past history of the degree is, however, of much interest to students of the A & A Rite. The actual Kadosh degree may have been the last of a series of *Elu* (Elect) degrees. These Elect degrees are called the 'Vengeance Degrees' but there is some doubt whether the original Elect degrees dealt with earthly punishments. A 1765 version of the *Chevalier Elu* finds the Master telling the candidate 'You know well the persecutions which wiped out the Templars. . . . Our leader, in the middle of his torments, said no more than that God was too just to leave this crime unpunished.'

There is considerable evidence that the origins of this type of Kadosh degree lie in Germany and were a development of the Rite of Strict Observance. The degree was probably introduced into France through Metz, with the inspirer being the same Master of a Metz

Lodge, Meunier de Précourt, who gave the information to Willermoz about the 18° (see Chapter 3.) The degree had a bad reception in Paris and was condemned by the Council of the Knights of the East as 'false, fanatical, detestable, not only because it was contrary to the principles and duties of the State and the Church.' It was, however, accepted by the Council of Emperors of the East and West. Its actual date may be fixed by the fact that, as late as 1767, the Comte de Clermont wrote that the 'limit of the Sublime Degrees in Masonry' was 15 of which the summit was the Rose-Croix, while by 1771 it was the Kadosh degree mentioned in Francken's *Ms*.

A legend in early versions was that the Elect (either Nine, 15 or 70) had descendants who were Kadosh (probably a Hebrew word implying holy or consecrated). In due course, 70 of these Kadosh were translators of the Bible under the orders of Ptolemy, King of Egypt. Later, under the leadership of St John the Almoner, they and their descendants tended the sick and needy, but they decreased in numbers until there were only a few remaining. These joined the Crusaders. Such a story has, of course, no historical foundation. The persecution of the Templars appears in many of the versions of the Kadosh type degrees, with the remnants fleeing to Scotland. Unfortunately most versions include gruesome and unpleasant penalties and these have been used by anti-masonic bodies in the same way that the penalties in the Symbolic degrees have been used to denigrate Craft masonry.

In the *London French Ms*, the candidates has to swear never to stop hating the Knights of Malta because they became rich with the wealth of the Knights Templar. This is historically untrue and the story was probably invented as an attack on the Roman Catholic Church, which has always been in amity with the Knights of Malta, and still is.

Towards the end of the XIX century, when relations in France between Church and State were at their lowest ebb, the 'liberal-minded' members of the Grand Orient and its Council of Rites changed the ritual of this degree and used it for deliberate attacks on the Church. Fortunately, most of these contentious rituals have disappeared and the high degrees in France are now adaptations of more reasonable versions.

31°—Grand Inspector Inquisitor Commander. The degree is only conferred by the Supreme Council for England and Wales. Candidates are elected to the degree, on the recommendation of their Chapters and District Inspectors General, by the Supreme Council. The number of holders of the degree is limited.

As the title of the degree implies, certain judicial powers are conferred, but this is theoretical as far as the Supreme Council for

England and Wales is concerned, as such work is carried out by the Supreme Council itself. It is not known whether the implied judicial powers are used, or ever have been, by other Supreme Councils.

The degree was inserted in the Rite by the Constitutions of 1786 and it is reputed to have come from the French Philosophical Rite. It is certain that it was adapted by de Grasse-Tilly and his associates about the end of the XVIII century. A copy of the ritual was sent to the forming Supreme Council in London in 1845 by the Northern Masonic Jurisdiction USA.

32°—Sublime Prince of the Royal Secret. The conditions under which this degree is conferred are the same as that of the 31°, but the number of holders is even more limited.

This degree was originally the 25° and the senior of the rite formed by Morin in the West Indies. In this book, the rite is called 'Morin's Rite'. Most masonic writers call it wrongly 'The Rite of Perfection' though the perfection element went no further than its 14°. Morin never refers to it as 'of Perfection' and the error probably has arisen as this wrong title appears in the preface to the Constitutions of 1786— for the first time as far as the present writer can discover.

Until the A & A Rite was formed, all Inspectors and Deputy Inspectors were of the rank of Sublime Prince of the Royal Secret. Morin and Francken conferred the degree in the West Indies as early as 1768 and they may have developed it there, or it could have been brought by one of the many travellers from France. What is certain is that Francken knew of the degree in 1771 and had some sort of ritual for it, but the earliest ritual known is the version given by Naudon dated 1765. A more up-to-date version appears in the *Francken Ms* of 1783. This would have been that sent to London by the Northern Masonic Jurisdiction in 1845.

Early French rituals had a completely different theme from the present version. The former are interesting as showing a further attempt to associate Scotland with high degree masonry. It is a story of a Templar degree with the ancestors of masonry being the Magi— something that the author has never heard suggested before. Their descendants became Crusaders and, when Jerusalem was in danger of capture by the Infidels, King Baldwin II instituted them into the Order of Grand Knights of St Andrew or Princes of the Royal Secret. The members of the Order then became the guards of the royal treasure. When Jerusalem was taken, these Prince Masons took part of the treasure with them and hid it. Their place of refuge was Scotland, and the 'royal secret' was where the treasure lay.

The ritual of the modern degree, which has changed little from the original one, suggests that Frederick the Great was involved in the Rite as early as 1761. At that date, Frederick was heavily engaged in the Seven Years' War; and any idea of an association between himself and any the masons of various countries—some with which he was at war—is so impossible as to prove that the degree was developed later. The real date is some time after 1765.

In the early days of Morin's Rite, one finds the Templar legend that keeps up the hatred of the Knights of Malta for the part they were reputed to have played in the Templars' destruction. However, in this degree, the last in Morin's 25 and the 32 in the A & A Rite, we find a complete reversal with the Knights of Malta taking part in a reunion with other masons and the old ritual saying:

'The Knights of Malta who have been admitted to our mysteries and have shown themselves faithful guardians of the Order . . . are united with the Knights of the Black and White Eagle" (Morin's Kadosh).

Alain Bernheim in Renaissance Traditionelle of January 1985 (No 61) suggests that Morin's object seems to have been to unite all branches of Freemasonry into his Rite.

33°—Sovereign Grand Inspector General. The qualifications and appointment of members of the 33° are referred to in Chapter 18. The degree can only be conferred by the Supreme Council. A copy of the ritual was sent to the Supreme Council for England and Wales from America in 1845. The rank possibly originated, as has been explained in Chapter 7, as early as 1795 when Comte de Grasse-Tilly may have conferred the rank upon himself, though other rituals in France may have had 33 degrees earlier. It seems to have taken a more genuine guise three years later when he possibly formed the first Supreme Council, that of the French West Indies. The real start, however, can be put at 1801 when the American Supreme Council formed itself at Charleston. It is not known what ceremonies, if any, were used to confer these early 33°. There is evidence that the ritual for the ceremony was not completed until about 1805, or even later. Even then, there seem to have been two distinct forms, one being used in most of the English-speaking Councils and a different one in France and probably other Continental countries. The present ritual used by the Supreme Council for England and Wales is naturally restricted to members of the degree. However, a ritual of the early XIX century is given by Naudon. In this are two points which are worth considering by masonic historians. Neither is part of the ceremony as used by the Supreme Council for England and Wales.

The presiding officer represents Frederick and he is assisted by the Comte de Clermont (Prince Louis de Bourbon-Condé)—a surprisingly incompatible pair. The Comte de Clermont, a past Grand Master of France had died in 1771, many years before the 33° was thought of or the Grand Constitutions of 1786 written. In addition, he was the defeated French commander at the Battle of Dettingen and therefore an active enemy of Frederick's. His name can have been of little interest to the Americans of the Charleston Supreme Council, even if they had ever heard of him. His inclusion suggests the pen of de Grasse-Tilly, working with his father-in-law, though why they should have included a Bourbon, during the French Revolution, is difficult to understand.

The second curious point is the return to the blaming of the Knights of Malta for benefiting from the destruction of the Templars. The Knights of Malta, in a few countries, did obtain some Templar property, but the real wealth of the Knights Templar were seized by their destroyers, the Pope and the King of France, and by any other rulers who could lay their hands upon it. These accusations of misdeeds by the Knights of Malta started much later, as has been explained in the note on the 30°.

The actual position about the two Orders of Chivalry was quite different in Britain. At the end of the XVIII century, the degrees of Knights of Malta and Knights Templar were being worked together and were as united as they are today. The position in the USA at this time is not quite so clear. We know that there was an Order of Knighthood, which included the Malta degree, in Charleston in 1826 and possibly earlier and, according to the American exposure *A Ritual and Illustrations of Freemasonry* of about mid-century 'the degrees of Knights Templar and Knights of Malta are given together'. All this makes it difficult to understand why the American members of the Supreme Council allowed the myth of differences between the two Orders in their new degrees. It can only have the result of their using the Francken rituals as a precedent. It is a pity that propaganda, instigated by a few agnostics, should have been allowed to influence important masonic degrees—and it is pleasant to know of its subsequent removal.

Appendix IV
THE PATENT TO ETIENNE MORIN, 1761

Note   This is the copy authenticated on p. 40. Morin's patent would have been in French and the authenticated copy in English. It was retranslated into French for insertion in de Grasse-Tilly's 'Golden Book'. The translation below is that given in Gould's History.

To the glory of the GAOTU, etc., and by the goodwill of HSH the very illustrious Brother Louis de Bourbon, Count de Clermont, Prince of the Blood Royal, Grand Master and Protector of all Lodges.

At the Orient of a most enlightened place where reign Peace, Silence, and Concord, *Anno Lucis* 5761, and according to the common style 27th August 1761.

Lux ex tenebris. Unitas, concordia fratrum.

We, the undersigned, Substitutes General of the Royal Art, Grand Wardens and Officers of the Grand and Sovereign Lodge of St John of Jerusalem, established at the Orient of Paris; and we, Sovereign Grand Masters of the Grand Council of the Lodges of France, under the sacred and mysterious numbers, declare, certify and decree to all our very dear Bros., Knights, and Princes scattered throughout the two hemispheres, that being assembled by order of the Substitute General, President of the Grand Council, a request was communicated to us by the worshipful Bro Lacorne, Substitute of our very illustrious G.M., Knight and Prince Mason and was read in due form.

Whereas our dear Bro. Stephen Morin, Grand Perfect Elect (*elu parfait*) and Past Sublime Master, Prince Mason, Knight and Sublime Prince of all Orders of the Masonry of Perfection, member of the Royal Lodge of the "Trinity", etc., being about to depart for America, desires to be able to work with regularity for the advantage and aggrandisement of the Royal Art in all its perfection, may it please the Sovereign Grand Council and Grand Lodge to grant him letters of constitution. On the report which has been made to us, and knowing the eminent qualifications of Bro. S. Morin, we have, without hesitation, accorded him this slight gratification in return for the services which he has always rendered this Order, and the continuation of which is guaranteed to us by his zeal.

For this cause and for other good reasons, whilst approving and confirming the very dear Brother Morin in his designs, and wishing to confer on him some mark of our gratitude, we have, by general consent, constituted and invested him, and do by these presents constitute and invest him, and give full and entire power to the said Bro. Stephen Morin, whose signature is in the margin of these presents, to form and establish a Lodge in order to admit to and multiply the Royal Order of Masons in all the perfect and sublime degrees; to take measures that the statutes and regulations of the Grand and Sovereign Lodge, general or special, to be kept and observed, and to never admit therein any but true and legitimate brethren of sublime Masonry:

To rule and govern all the members who shall compose his said Lodge, which he may established in the four quarters of the world wherever he may arrive or shall sojourn, under the title of St John, and surnamed "Perfect Harmony"; we give him power to choose such officers as he may please to aid him in ruling his Lodge, whom we command and enjoin to obey and respect him; do ordain and command all Masters of regular Lodges of whatsoever dignity, scattered over the surface of land or sea, do pray and enjoin them in the name of the Royal Order, and in the presence of our very illustrious G.M., to acknowledge in like manner as we recognise our very dear Bro. Stephen Morin as Worshipful Master of the Lodge of Perfect Harmony, and we depute him in his quality as our Grand Inspector in all parts of the New World *to reform the observance of our laws in general*, etc.; and by these presents do constitute our very dear Bro. Stephen Morin our G.M. Inspector, authorizing and empowering him to establish perfect and sublime Masonry in all parts of the world, etc., etc.

We pray, consequently, all brothers in general to render the said Stephen Morin such assistance and succour as may be in their power, requiring them to do the same to all the brothers who shall be members of his Lodge, and whom he has admitted and constituted, shall admit or constitute in future to the sublime degrees of perfection which we grant him, with full and entire power to create Inspectors in all places where the sublime degrees shall not already be established, knowing well his great acquirements and capacity.

In witness thereof we have given him these presents, signed by the Substitute-General of the Order, Grand Commander of the Black and White Eagle, Sovereign Sublime Prince of the Royal Secret, and Chief of the Eminent Degree of the Royal Art, and by us, Grand Inspectors, Sublime Officers of the Grand Council and of the Grand Lodge established in this capital, and have sealed them with the Grand Seal of our illustrious G.M., His Serene Highness, and with that of our

Grand Lodge and Sovereign Grand Council. Given at the G.O. of Paris, in the year of Light 5761, or according to the Vulgar Era, 27th Augt, 1761.

Note   The names of the signatories are not given here. They appear to vary with the copy used. Their authenticity is discussed on page 40.

THE CONSTITUTIONS OF 1762

Notes

1. These Constitutions are copied from a manuscript book found in the library of the Supreme Council for England and Wales. (See Chapter 5.) This is the earliest known version of this document.

2. The book was written in Kingston, Jamaica, by a Dutchman, H. A. Francken, and its authenticity is not in doubt as it is signed by him. As has been explained, these Constitutions were almost certainly prepared by Stephen Morin, possibly with the help of Francken, later than 1765 and probably earlier than 1767 when Francken went to N. America. The framework used for the Constitutions was the 1763 Statutes and Regulations of the Grand Lodge of France. It is not clear whether the Constitutions were originally written by Morin in French and then translated by Francken, or whether they were written by Morin in the 'English' he had learnt during his travels. In the event, it might have been either as the English is not easy to follow. The reader, if he has a knowledge of French, will see that many of the phrases are almost a literal translation of old French. As this is an original document, published for the first time, it is presented as unaltered as possible, subject to a few changes in capitals and punctuation. The original was not easy to decipher and a prolonged study might produce minor differences from the wording given below.

3. Many of the provisions of the Constitutions are unremarkable but they have three main importances:

> (a) They refute copies, previously published, which are different, usually more elaborate.
> (b) They prove that the Prussian connection, later developed into the Frederick legend, was an invention made by Morin in the West Indies.
> (c) The number of degrees in the rite has always been in doubt. The various articles, particularly the later ones, give much information about the degrees, their status and the honours due to their holders. The degrees, except possibly for the Sublime Prince of the Royal Secret (25°), may well be entirely of French development, possibly by the Emperors of the East and West, after 1763.
> The Rose-Croix degree is not mentioned, nor are there any Christian

references, except feast-days for meetings, though the title Prince Mason occurs frequently.

4.   In order to show the copying of the 1763 Statutes and Regulations of the Gd L of F by the author of the Constitutions, a few extracts from the French document are inserted in the more obvious cases. That there had to be alterations in ranks and titles will be appreciated.

THE GREAT STATUTES
AND REGULATIONS

Made in Prussia and France, Sept 7th, 1762. Resolved by the Nine Commissioners named by the Great Council of the Sublime Princes of the Royal Secret at the Great East of France. Consequently, by the deliberations dated as above, to be observed by the aforesaid Grand Council of the Sublime Princes of France and Prussia, and by all the particular & regular Councils spread over the two hemispheres.

Article 1.   The Sovereign Council of Sublime Princes is composed of all presidents of the Councils, particular & regular, constituted in the cities of Berlin and Paris; the Sovereign of Sovereigns, or his substitute general, or his representative, at their head.

Article 2.   The Sovereign Gnd Council of the Sub: Princes of the Royal Secret shall meet four times every year, and shall be called 'Gnd Council of quarterly communication' which shall be held the 25th of June, 27th December, 21st March and 7th September.

Article 3.   The 25th June, the Sovereign Grd Council shall be composed of all the presidents of Councils, particularly of Berlin and Paris, or their representatives, to assist [include] for that day only, with the two first Grd Officers, who are the Minister of State and the General of the army, who shall have the right to propose, and without a deliberative vote.
   [G.L. of France, 1763 Statutes—Art. 3.]
   Jour de St-Jean-Baptiste [24 June] Le lendemain de la St-Jean d'été la G∴L∴ sera composée de tous les maîtres de LL∴ assisté, pour ce jour seulement, de leurs deux surveillants, qui n'auront que le droit de proposer, sans avoir voix délibérative.

Article 4.   Every three years, on the 27th December, the Sovereign Gnd Council shall nominate 16 officers, viz. 2 representatives of the

Substitute-General, 2 grand officers who are the Minister of State and the General of the army, one Keeper of the Seals & Archives, one Grand Orator, one Grand Secretary General, one Secretary for Paris and Berlin, one other Secretary for the country and other parts, one Grd Architect, one Grd Hospitaller and 7 Inspectors, who reunited together under the orders of the Sover^n of Sovereigns, Prince President, or his Substitute-General, comprising 18 in number; to which shall irrevocably remain the number fixed of grand officers of the Sovereign Grand Council of the Subme. Princes of the Royal Secret, who cannot be chosen but among the presidents of the Councils particular of those of Princes of Jerusalem regularly constituted in Paris and Berlin and those constituted by grand inspectors or their deputies. And in case of default of the Sovereign and the Sublime Grd Council, shall make those nominations in the Grd Council composed of at least 10 President Princes.

Article 5.   Each Prince Grd Officer or Dignitary of the Sovereign Grd Council shall have a patent delivered to him of the dignity to which he shall be nominated in which shall be expressed the duration of his function, and counter-signed by all the Grand Officers and those of the Sovereign Grand Council of Suble Princes of the Royal Secret, crested and sealed proper.

Article 6.   Besides the four quarterly communications, a meeting shall be held once a month within the first ten days by the Grd Officers, and in dignity of Suble Prince only, a Council for that purpose to regulate the business of the Order, as well general as particular, but still subject to an appeal to the Grand Council of Communication.

Article 7.   In the meeting of the Council of Communication, and in that of the particular Council, all business shall be decided by a plurality of votes, the President shall have two votes and other members one. If in these meetings, by a dispensation, or as a deputy, any Prince Suble (who is not a member) is admitted he shall have no vote, nor give any advice unless desired by the President.

Article 8.   All business carried before the Sovereign Grand Council of the Suble Princes shall first be regulated in the Councils meetings and the regulations shall be a writ of execution provisionally, except the ratification of the Quarterly Communication.

Article 9.   When the Grand Council of Quarterly Communication is held the Grand Secretary General shall be obliged to bring all the current registers and to render an account of all the deliberations and regulations during the last quarter to be ratified, and if any should meet with opposition at the ratification, they shall nominate 9 Commissioners before whom the opposers shall deliver in writing the reasons of their opposition in order that the same may be answered in writing, and upon the report of the aforesaid Commissioners, the same to be enacted at the following meeting of the Council of Communication, and in the interim, the aforesaid deliberation of regulations shall continue to be a writ of execution by patent.

Article 10.   The Grand Secretary General shall keep a register for Paris and Berlin, and another for foreign parts, containing the names of the particular Councils, as they stand in seniority, by the dates of their constitutions, and a catalogue of the names, degrees, offices, dignities, civil qualities and residence of the members conformable to the accounts sent to him by our Inspectors and their Deputies, as well as the number of regular Lodges of Perfection, established under the government of our Inspectors or Councils abroad. The titles of the said lodges, the dates of their constitutions, with a catalogue of the names, degrees, offices, dignities, civil qualities and residence of the members conformable to the Statutes which shall be delivered to us by our Inspectors in the Grand Council of Communication.

Article 11.   The Grand Secretary shall likewise keep a register containing all the deliberations and regulations made by the Grand Council of Quarterly Communication in which shall be mentioned all the business transacted in the aforesaid Council, and all letters received and all the subject of the answers agreed upon.
   (G.L. of France, 1763 Statutes—Art. 11.]
   Registre des délibérations. Il sera en outre tenu par le secrétaire général de Paris, un registre contenant toutes les délibérations et réglements faits en L:. de conseil et de Communications de quartier, et les délibérations feront mention de toutes les affaires traitées dans les Loges, des Lettres reçues et des objets de réponses arrêtés.

Article 12.   The Grand Secretary General shall write in the margin the petitions, letters or memoirs which shall be read in Council, and the subject agreed upon for answers, he shall get them signed by the Substitute General or his representative, by the Secretary of the Jurisdiction; and the Keeper of the Grand Seals shall sign, stamp and send them. As these things cannot be done during the sitting of the Council, and it may be of a dangerous consequence sometimes to delay the aforesaid letters until the next Council, he shall produce the minutes of his answers in order that the same may be read in the next Grand Council and deliver the whole relative thereto to the Keeper of the Archives in order that such alterations shall be made as the Sovereign Grand Council shall think fit.

Article 13. The Council particular of Berlin or Paris or anywhere else shall not have power to send any letter, constitution or regulation unless they are empowered, properly stamped and sealed by the Sovereign Grand Council, or a Grand Inspector of the Order or his Deputy.

[G.L. of France, 1763 Statutes—Art. 13.]

Timbres et sceaux.—Il ne pourra être fait aux Loges, envoi d'aucuns [sic] Lettres, constitutions ou réglemens, qu'ils ne soient revêtus des timbres et sceau de la Grande Loge.

Article 14. The Grand Keeper of the Seals and Stamps cannot stamp or seal any letter(s) unless they are sent signed by the Secretary General and by two secretaries of different jurisdictions, neither can he stamp or seal any resolution unless the same be sent signed by the Substitute General or his representative and by the 3 aforesaid Grand Secretaries. Neither can he stamp or seal any Constitution unless likewise signed by the above three Grand Officers and other Princes to the number of seven at least, and those members of the Sovereign Grand Council of Princes.

[G.L. of France, 1763 Statutes—Art. 14.]

Observations au Garde des sceaux.—Le Garde des sceaux et timbre ne pourra timbrer ni sceller aucune lettre qu'elle ne soit signée du secrétaire gal, et des deux secrétaires du département, aucun réglement qu'il ne soit signé du substitut gal. ou son représentant et des d. trois secrétaires, ni aucune constitution qu'elle ne soit signée des officiers ci-dessus et autres maîtres, au nombre de neuf au moins, membres de la Grande L:. de Conseil.

Article 15. The Grand Treasurer, who ought to enjoy and be possessed on [of?] an independent fortune, shall be trusted with all the stock that shall be raised for the use of the Sovereign Grd Council and given in charity; and he shall keep a register very exact of every receipt and expenses, and clearly and distinctly set forth how and in what manner the cash has been expended, as well as that for the use of the Grand Council, as that of the Charity Fund. He shall give a receipt for each sum specifying them with the folios of his register and shall not pay any money but by an order in writing from the President and two Grand Officers of the Sovereign Grand Council.

Article 16. At the first meeting of the Grand Council after the 27th December, the Grand Treasurer shall render in his account.

Article 17. No orders for money upon the Grand Treasurer shall be valid unless those made at a full meeting of the Grand Council, and no money out of stock shall defray any of the charges at any of the Council meetings in ordinary but be paid out by the respective member or their own purses.

Article 18. Any memorial, petition or complaint that shall be brought before the Sovereign Grand Council whose President is present in the Grand Council, the said President (though a member of the Grand Council) has no voice in the debates of the Council's complaint, nor has he leave to speak for [in?] said debates, as paid complaints must all be brought in writing, unless the President of the Sublime Grand Council shall call and require some reclarishment [? clarification] (in the said debate) of the said President and member.

Article 19. The Substitute General and the 2 Grand Officers cannot be deprived of their offices but by the Grand Council of Quarterly Communication on legal complaints being made and brought in deliberation, and then their abdication shall be made in the full Grand Council. The Substitute General's place can only be filled up again by the appointment of the Sovereign of Sovereigns and Most Powerful Chief [*Très Puissant Chef*?] and the first two Grand Officers in the Grand Council of Quarterly Communication by a plurality of votes.

Article 20. Deputies of the Grand Council shall visit particular councils and these again shall visit Lodges of Perfection. Those Inspectors shall draw up a verbal process of said proceedings, signed by the officers in dignity of said Councils and Lodges, and the Protractor[?] shall attain [send?] them as soon as possible to the Sovereign Grand Council, directed to the Grand Secretary General. Those aforesaid Inspectors or viewers shall always preside at these Councils and Lodges they visit, and make their visits as often as they please without any opposition from any of the officers or members of said Councils or Lodges whatsoever under the penalty of disobedience and interdiction, for such is our pleasure.

Article 21. In the meeting of the Sovereign Grd Council of Quarterly Communication regularly called together, and if only 7 members present, they shall open the work at the usual hour: and those regulations, which shall be made and passed by a plurality of votes among them, shall have the same strength of the law as if other members had been present.

[G.L. of France, 1763 Statutes—Art. 21.]

Neuf officiers ouvrent la L∴.—Dans les LL∴. de conseil régulièrement convoquées lorsqu'il se trouvera neuf membres ils ouvriront les travaux à l'heurè dite, et les réglemens qui seront entre eux passés à la pluralité des voix, auront force de loi comme si les autres membres convoqués avaient été présents.

Article 22. At the meeting of the Sovereign Gd Council, if any member shall appear in an indecent manner, either being heated with liquor or otherwise commit any fault tending to destroy that harmony which ought to subsist in those respectable meetings, he shall be admonished for the first time; for the 2nd time, he shall be fined, whh fine he shall pay immediately; and for the 3rd offence he shall be deprived of his dignity and, if a majority of the votes of the Grand Council is for his expulsion, he shall be expelled.

[G.L. of France, 1763 Statutes—Art. 22.]

Indécence punie.—Dans le LL∴. de Conseil, si un membre se présente en état indécent par intempérance ou autrement, ou s'il commet quelques fautes graves capable de nuire à l'harmonie qui doit régner en L∴., il sera admonesté pour la 1re fois, pr la seconde il sera condamné à une amende payable sur le champ, et pour la 3é, il sera privé de sa dignité à laquelle la L∴. de conseil pourra nommer par voie de scrutin et il en demeurera exclu.

Article 23. If any of the Presidents of the other Gd. Councils, as members of the Sovereign Grand Council of Quarterly Communication, should be guilty of faults mentioned in the foregoing article, for the first time, he shall be fined a sum of money to be paid immediately, for the second fault, he shall be deprived of the general meeting for one year as also of his dignity; and for the third offence, he shall be expelled immediately for ever and lose his office, by the Sovereign of Sovereigns who shall immediately appoint another President in his room.

Article 24. The Sovereign Grand Council shall acknowledge none for a regular Council and Lodge of Perfection but those provided with

Constitutions issued by them or by a Grand Inspector or his Deputy. It shall be the same as regards the Knights Masons, Princes and Gd.E. & P.Ms. who might have been constituted improperly by those who were not regularly authorized to do so.

Article 25.   All petitions presented to the Sovereign Grd Council in order to obtain letters of Constitution either for establishing or to regulate a Council or Lodge shall be restored [forwarded?] vizt. for the country to the Inspectors. Such jurisdiction shall choose four commissioners to take all the necessary information which shall be sent to the Grand Inspector of the jurisdiction, with an exact list of the members who shall demand the execution of a Council or of a Lodge of Perfection because on the report of the commissioners and of the Grand Inspector, the Grand Council is to determine the demand of the aforesaid members. And, when it is for a foreign part, the Grand Inspector his Deputy shall be able and have power to erect, constitute, forbid, repeal or exclude according to his prudence; and shall make in writing a verbal process of their work and to be by them informed of all when they find a favourable opportunity. The aforesaid Inspector or his Deputy shall conform himself to the Sovereign Grand Council's laws and customs of our secret Constitutions. They shall be at liberty to choose Deputies, to despatch and authorize them with letters patent, the which shall have power and validity.

Article 26.   The Sovereign Grand Council shall not grant any letter of Constitution for the establishment of a Royal Lodge of Perfection, except the brother be at least a Prince of Jerusalem, and for the establishment of a Council of Knights of the East except a brother be at least a Knight of the East and West. But for the establishment of a Grand Council of Princes of Jerusalem, the brother must absolutely be in the degree of Knight and Prince of the Sun, and prove by authentick titles to have been lawfully and regularly received, and that he has always enjoyed a free state and lived decent or free from reproach by a sound and approved conduct at all times, to be submissive to the decrees and mandates issued by the Sovereign Council of Princes of which he desires to be the chief.

Article 27.   The Sovereign Grand Council of the Sublime Princes shall not grant any letters patent or constitutions unless they receive £10 sterling money for the supply of the person employed. The Grand Inspectors of the East shall conform themselves in the like case, besides they shall not deliver any commission or warrant to any Prince before he has signed his submission in the register of the Grand Secretary General or, for foreign parts, to the Inspector or his Deputy as is necessary, the submission he writes to be signed by the Brother.

Article 28.   If the Inspectors or Deputies shall think proper to visit in any place over the two Hemispheres, either Grand Councils or Princes of Jerusalem, Councils of Knights of the East or Lodges of Perfection or any other Lodge and when they are known and furnished with authentic titles and decorated with the ornaments of their dignities either at the door of the Grand Council of Knights of the East or Lodges of Perfection, they shall be received with all the honours that are due to them and shall enjoy in all places all their privileges and prerogatives, and the Inspectors as well as the Kts Prince Masons when they shall visit a Royal Lodge of Perfection or any other lodge whatsoever, the Sovereign Prince Grand Master or Grand Wardens of such Lodges shall send 5 officers or deputies in dignity to introduce the Princes Insprs. with all the honours due to him in any lodge in such manner as will be fully explained hereafter.

Article 29.
1ST.   The Princes of Jerusalem being the valorous Princes Sublime and Chiefs of Masonry Renewed, owe no Honor but to the Sublime Noachites, Knights of the Sun, Kadosh and Sublime Princes of the Royal Secret, our Illustrious Chiefs.

2ND.   The Princes of Jerusalem have a right and privilege to annul and repeal all that might be done inconsistant to the orders & laws in a Council of Knights of the East, and also in a Royal Lodge of Perfection and in any other lodges whatsoever, provided nevertheless that there is not present any of the Sublime Princes of a superior degree.

3RD.   When a Prince of Jerusalem shall be announced to be at the door of a Royal Lodge &c. as his titles and ornaments will demonstrate, the I.P. [Illustrious Prince] of such Lodge shall send four brother officers, deputies in dignity, to introduce and attend him. When he enters cover'd, his sword drawn in his right hand; with the Sign of Battle on him, his shield on his left arm and cuirass'd if he pleases, when he comes between the wardens in the west with the 4 deputies, he first salutes the S.P. Master, then in the North and South, and then the wardens with his sword, after which the Prince visitor shall make the sign of the lodge which is open, which shall be repeated by the Master and all the Bretheren after which the Master shall say, To order and by one knock, all the Bretheren from the north and south shall form the arch with their swords through which he passes with a grave face till he arrives by the Throne, when the Master shall offer him his seat which he may accept and command the works. [proceedings ?] The Master shall then render him an account of everything relative to the Order &c. and then if he thinks proper, shall deliver the seat to the Master again in order to continue the work begun. If the Prince Visitor chuses to retire before the lodge is closed, and having informed the Master of it, he shall receive the thanks for his visit, and invite him to come often, offering him all service in the power of the said lodge. After this compliment is paid, the Master shall strike one great stroke and say, To Order Bretheren: which is repeated in the west, when all the bretheren in the north and south shall form the arch as before, through which the Prince Visitor goes back until he comes between the two Wardens, where he turns to the east and salutes the Master, the north, south and the Wardens, and then walks to the door w^h is thrown wide open (which must have been done also when he enters) and when he is conducted out of the doors by the 4 deputies they return in [into?] the Lodge & continue the works.

4THLY.   The Princes of Jerusalem cannot enjoy these privileges when there are any kn^{ts} of higher degrees, such as Noachites, kn^{ts} of the Sun, or of the white & black Eagles, or a Sublime Prince of the Royal Secret present, but may make their entry with all their honours if the Sublime Prince present agrees to it.

5THLY.   A Prince of Jerusalem shall be stiled Valorous Prince, a knight of the Sun, Sovereign Prince, and a Sublime Prince of the Royal Secret, Illustrious Sover^{gn} of Sovereigns. A k^{nt} of the East, Excellent; who has the right, when no Prince of Jerusalem, &c is present, to the inspection of the Constitutions of any Royal Lodge; and to make peace among the Bretheren if there should be any coolness subsisting, to exclude the obstinate and those that will not submit to these Statutes and Regulations.

6THLY.   The most Valorous Princes of Jerusalem shall have a right, as well as the knights of the East & West to sit down with their hatts on during the works in the Royal Lodges of Perfection. The knights of the East or of the Sword have also that right; nevertheless they cannot enjoy these privileges but when they are know [as?] such and come properly decorated with the attributes of their dignities, &c.

7THLY.   Five Valorous Princes of Jerusalem shall have power to form a Council of Knights of the East everywhere, where none is establish^d and they shall be judges, but be obliged to give notice to the

Sovereign G^rd Councils of their proceedings, or give the same to the nearest Inspector or his Deputy. They are authorized to do so by the power that has been given to their illustrious predecessors by the People of Jerusalem at the return of a very glorious Embassy &c., &c.

Article 30. In order to establish rightly all the particular Councils, and to have among all the true Knights and Princes Masons a regular correspondence, every particul^r council shall once a year send a particular catalogue to the Grand Council of all the particular, regular and authorized councils, also the names of the officers belonging to them. They shall also give, in the course, of the year, notice of any interesting changes that shall have happened in the said catalogue.
[G.L. of France, 1763, Statutes—Art. 30.]
Tableau General—Pour établir entre toutes les LL:. regulières et entre tous les vrais maçons une correspondence regulière, il sera tous les ans envové par la G.L:. de France à chaque L:. particulière le Tableau général de toutes les LL:. de France, ainsi que celui des officiers de la G.L. de France. et il sera donné avis, dans le cours de l'année de tous les changements intéressans qui pourraient survenir dans les d[its] tableaux.

Article 31. The better to maintain good order and discipline, the Sovereign Grand Councils of the Sub^lme Princes of the Royal Secret shall only meet every year to proceed on Masonic work, when none shall be admitted to the Sub^lme and final degree of Masonry but the 3 oldest knights of the Sun, who shall be proclaimed in the different councils and the G^rd Lodges of Perfection.

Article 32. Holy days to be kept by the Knights of Princes Masons.
The Princes of Jerusalem shall privately celebrate vizt.

1ST. The Holy Day on the 20th of March when their ancestors made their entry into Jerusalem.

2ND. They shall celebrate the 23rd day of September when they shall give thanks to the Lord for the re-building of the Temple.
The Knights of the East shall solemnize the only day of Redification [? *Ré-édification*=rebuilding] of the Temple of the Living God, the 22nd of March and the 22nd of September the Equinoctial days or renewing the long & short days in memory that the Temple was built twice.
All the Prince Masons are obliged to go to the Council of the

Knights of the East and the work is not to be opened but with the necessary ceremonies.

The Grand Elect Perf^t & Sublime shall solemnize the 24th June and the 26th of September, the Dedication of the first Temple, the day of the month when the knights and perfect Masons shall be decorated with their ornaments.

These Statutes are to be observed by all our Inspectors and Deputies, and cause the same to be read and received in all private chapters, as well as in the Grand Council whatsoever.

At the Great East, under the Celestial Canopy &c. the day and year above written.

THE CONSTITUTIONS OF 1786

Note The Latin version of 1834 was translated into French by Charles Laffon de Ladebat. The version below is an English translation of the latter. It may therefore differ slightly in wording from the translation normally found in America, which seems to be a direct translation from the Latin. The Preface to these Constitutions is given on pages 72 and 84.

UNIVERSI TERRARUM ORBIS SUMMI ARCHITECTONIS
GLORIA AD INGENIIS.

CONSTITUTIONS AND STATUTES
OF
THE GRAND AND SUPREME COUNCILS
of
Grand Inspectors General, Patrons, Chiefs and
Commissioners
of
THE ORDER OF THE 33°.
and last degree of the Ancient and
Accepted Scottish Rite
and
REGULATIONS
for the government of all Consistories,
Councils, Colleges and other Masonic
bodies under the jurisdiction of the
aforesaid Councils.
IN THE NAME OF THE VERY HOLY AND GREAT ARCHITECT
OF THE UNIVERSE.

ORDO   AB   CHAO.

With the approbation, in the presence of and under the auspices of His August Majesty FREDERICK (Charles) II, King of Prussia, Margrave of Brandenburg, etc., Very Puissant Monarch, Grand Protector, Grand Commander etc., of the Order etc., etc., etc.,

The Sovereign Grand Inspectors General in Supreme Council assembled.

Have, after deliberation, sanctioned the following decrees which are, and ever will be, their CONSTITUTIONS, STATUTES AND REGULATIONS for the government of the Consistories and other Masonic Lodges under the jurisdiction of the said Inspectors General.

ARTICLE I.

All the articles of the CONSTITUTIONS, Statutes and Regulations laid down in the year 1762 by the nine Commissioners of the Grand Councils of Prince Masons of the Royal Secret, which are not contrary to the present regulations, are retained and will be observed; those which are contrary will be abrogated and considered as if expressly abolished.

ARTICLE II

$ I.   The thirty-third DEGREE confers on Masons, who are legally invested with the position, the titles, position, privileges and authority of Sovereign Grand Inspectors General of the ORDER.

$ II.   The particular aim of their mission is to instruct and enlighten their brethren; to institute among them Charity, Unity and Fraternal Love; to maintain correctness in the work of each degree and to ensure that this is observed by all the Members; to ensure respect and, on all occasions, to respect and defend the Tenets, Doctrines, Institutions, Constitutions, Statutes and the Regulations of the ORDER, and especially those of High Masonry, and finally to apply themselves everywhere to works of Peace and Benevolence.

$ III.   A meeting of members of this Grade is entitled a COUNCIL OF THE THIRTY-THIRD DEGREE or of Puissant Grand Inspectors General of the ORDER: this Council being composed as follows:

1°. In places correct for the establishment of a Supreme Council of this Degree, the most senior Inspector in rank is herewith authorized to promote another brother to the same dignity, after having assured himself that the latter has truly merited it by his character, his knowledge and the ranks with which he is invested, and he will administer the oath to him.

2°. These two brothers jointly and in the same manner confer the degree on another brother.

$ IV.   THE SUPREME COUNCIL will then be constituted.

But no other candidates will be admitted unless they obtain an unanimous vote, each member giving his vote aloud, starting with the youngest, that is the most recently joined.

One negative vote among the members deliberating, if the reasons are considered adequate, will reject the candidate. This rule will be observed in all similar cases.

ARTICLE III.

$ I.   In the circumstances given above, the two first brethren raised to this degree have the *right* to the first two officers of the SUPREME COUNCIL, that is: the Very Puissant Sovereign Grand Commander, and the Very Illustrious Lieutenant Grand Commander.

$ II.   If the first of these officers dies, abdicates or absents himself permanently, he will be replaced by the second Officer who will choose his own successor from among the other Grand Inspectors.

$ III.   If the second officer abdicates, dies or absents himself permanently, the first officer will take as his successor another brother of the same rank.

$ IV.   The Very Puissant Sovereign will also nominate the Illustrious Minister of State of the Holy Empire, the Illustrious Grand Master of Ceremonies and the Illustrious Captain of the Guard: and he will designate in the same manner, brethren to fill other vacant duties or which become vacant.

ARTICLE IV.

Every Mason, possessing the necessary qualities and capacity who is raised to this Sublime Degree, will pay in advance, into the hands of the Very Illustrious Treasurer of the Holy Empire, a contribution of *ten gold Fredericks*, or of *ten gold Louis, old money*, or the equivalent in the money of the country.

When a brother is initiated to the thirtieth, thirty-first or thirty-second degree, a sum of the same value and kind will be required from him for each step.

Th SUPREME COUNCIL will supervise the administration of these funds and will use them for the benefit of the ORDER.

ARTICLE V.

$ I.   EACH SUPREME COUNCIL will consist of nine Sovereign Grand Inspectors General of the thirty-third degree, of which four at least must profess the dominant religion of the country.

$ II.   When the Very Puissant Sovereign Grand Commander and the Lieutenant Grand Commander of the ORDER are present, three members will be enough to compose the SUPREME COUNCIL for the transaction of the business of the ORDER.

$ III.   In each great Nation, Kingdom or European Empire, there will only be one SUPREME COUNCIL of this degree.

In the States and Provinces which compose North Amerca [*Amérique Septentrionale*] either on the mainland, or in its islands, there will be two Councils, situated as far as possible from each other.

In the States and Provinces which compose South America [*Amérique Méridionale*] either on the mainland, or in its islands, there will also be two Councils as far as possible from each other.

There will only be one Supreme Council in each Empire, Sovereign State or Kingdom of Asia, Africa, etc., etc.

ARTICLE VI.

The SUPREME COUNCIL does not always exercise its authority directly over Degrees below the seventeenth or *Knight of the East and West*. According to circumstances and situations, it can delegate it, even tacitly; but its right cannot be waived and all the Lodges and all Councils of Perfect Masions, whatever their degree, are hereby required to recognize, in those who have received the thirty-third degree, the authority of the Sovereign Grand Inspectors General of the Order, to respect their prerogatives, to give them the honours to which they are entitled, to obey them and finally to submit with confidence to all the demands they make for the good of the ORDER, in virtue of its laws, of the present Grand Constitutions and the authority delegated to its Inspectors, whether this authority be general or special or even temporary and personal.

ARTICLE VII.

EVERY COUNCIL and every Mason of a degree above the sixteenth has the right of appeal to the SUPREME COUNCIL of Sovereign Grand Inspectors General who can allow him to appear before them and be heard in person.

When it concerns an 'affair of honour' between Masons irrespective of degree, the matter will be brought directly before the SUPREME COUNCIL who will decide in the first and last instance [i.e. without appeal?].

ARTICLE VIII.

A Grand Consistory of Prince Masons of the Royal Secret will choose its President from among the holders of the thirty-second degree who compose it; but in every case, the acts of the Grand Consistory will have no authority until they have first been sanctioned by the SUPREME COUNCIL of the thirty-third degree, which, after the death of his August Majesty the King, Very Puissant Monarch and Commander General of the ORDER, will inherit the Supreme Masonic authority and will exercise it throughout the whole of the

State, Kingdom or Empire which will have been placed under its jurisdiction.

ARTICLE IX.

In countries under the Jurisdiction of a SUPREME COUNCIL of Sovereign Grand Inspectors General, regularly constituted and *recognized by all other SUPREME COUNCILS*, no Sovereign Grand Inspector General or Deputy Inspector General can exercise his authority unless he has been recognized by the same SUPREME COUNCIL and received its approval.

ARTICLE X.

No Deputy Inspector General, even if he has been admitted and received his patent or whether by virtue of the present Constitutions, he is in due time admitted, may confer on anyone the degree of Knight Kadosh or other higher degree, or give patents.

ARTICLE XI.

The degree of *Knight Kadosh*, as well as the thirty-first and thirty-second degrees, will only be conferred on Masons who have been judged worthy, and that in the presence of at least three Sovereign Grand Inspectors General.

ARTICLE XII.

When it pleases the Holy and Great Architect of the Universe to call to HIMSELF his August Majesty the King, Very Puissant Sovereign Grand Protector, Commander and True Keeper of the ORDER etc., etc., etc., each SUPREME COUNCIL of Sovereign Grand Inspectors General, already regularly constituted and recognized, or who will in due course be constituted and recognized by virtue of these present Statutes will be, by absolute right, legally invested with all the Masonic authority of which his August Majesty is now invested. Each SUPREME COUNCIL will use this authority when it is necessary and wherever it may be, throughout the country placed under its jurisdiction; and if, for reasons of illegality, it is necessary to protest, whether about Patents or the powers given to Deputy Inspectors General, or on any other subject, a report will be sent to all the SUPREME COUNCILS of the two hemispheres.

ARTICLE XIII.

$ I. Every SUPREME COUNCIL of the thirty-third Degree can delegate one or more of the Sovereign Grand Inspectors General of the ORDER who belong to it, to found, constitute and establish a

COUNCIL of the same degree in all the countries referred to in the present Statutes, on conditions that they will obey punctiliously what is laid down in the third paragraph of Article II above, as well as in other parts of the present Constitutions.

$ II. The SUPREME COUNCIL can also give power to its Deputies to issue patents to Deputy Inspectors General, who must at least have regularly received all the degrees possessed by a Knight Kadosh, delegating each part of their supreme authority as may be necessary to constitute, direct and supervise Lodges and Councils from the fourth to the twenty-ninth degree inclusive *in countries where there are no other lodges or Councils of the Sublime Degree*, legally constituted.

$ III. The manuscript ritual of the Sublime Degrees will only be entrusted to the two senior officers in each COUNCIL, or to a brother charged with constituting a Council of the same degree in another country.

ARTICLE XIV.

In all masonic ceremonies of the Sublime Degrees and in every solemn procession of Masons possessing these degrees, the SUPREME COUNCIL will walk last and the two first officers will follow after all the other members, being immediately preceded by a great Standard and the Sword of State (*Glaive*) of the ORDER.

ARTICLE XV.

$ I. A SUPREME COUNCIL must meet regularly during the first three days of each third new moon. It will meet more often if the business of the ORDER requires it or if there is an urgency.

$ II. In addition to the solemn feasts of the ORDER, the SUPREME COUNCIL will have three special ones each year: on the Calends (first day) of October, the 27th of December and the Calends (first day) of May.

ARTICLE XVI.

$ I. In order to be recognized and to enjoy the privileges attached to the thirty-third degree, each Sovereign Grand Inspector General will be provided with Patents and credentials of which an example can be found in the ritual of the Degree. These letters will be given to him on condition that he pays into the Treasury of the Holy Empire the sum which each SUPREME COUNCIL will decide for its jurisdiction, as soon as it is constituted. The said Sovereign Grand Inspector General will also pay a Frederick or a Louis, ancient money, or the equivalent in the coin of the country, to the Illustrious Secretary as payment for his work, for sending the above-mentioned letters and for affixing the seal.

$ II.   Every Sovereign Grand Inspector General will keep, in addition, a Register of his actions: each page of this will be numbered, the first and last page being so marked and initialled to prove his identity. The Grand Constitutions, the Statutes and the General Regulations of the sublime Art of Freemasonry will be inscribed in this Register.

The Inspector will be held responsible for entering all his actions as they occur, or risk repudiation or even suspension.

Deputy Inspectors General are required to do the same or incur the same penalties.

$ III.   They will show each other their Registers and their Patents, and they will inform each other of the places where they are both known. (*Mutuellement reconnus*)

ARTICLE XVII.

A majority of votes is necessary to legalize the actions of Sovereign Grand Inspectors General, in places where there is a SUPREME COUNCIL of the third-third degree legally constituted and recognized. In consequence, in a country under a SUPREME COUNCIL, no single one of these Inspectors can act on his own authority, at least not without having obtained the authority of the said SUPREME COUNCIL, and in the case of an Inspector belonging to another Jurisdiction, at least of having been recognized by a declaration, to which is applied the name of EXEQUATUR.

ARTICLE XVIII.

All the money received to meet the expenses—*that is to say the fees of* candidates (*Receptions*)—and which are collected to cover the initiation expenses of the Degrees above the sixteenth up to and including the thirty-third, will be paid into the Treasury of the Holy Empire to the custody of the Presidents and Treasurers of the Councils and of the Sublime Lodges of those Degrees, as well as to the Sovereign Grand Inspectors General, of their Deputies, of the Illustrious Secretary and Illustrious Treasurer of the Holy Empire.

The SUPREME COUNCIL will regulate and supervise the administration and use of these sums. It will render each year a faithful and correct account and will ensure that this is brought to the notice of the Lodge under it.

ORDERED, MADE and APPROVED in *Grand* and SUPREME COUNCIL of the thirty-third Degree, regularly constituted, convoked and assembled, with the approbation and in the presence of His Very August Majesty, Frederick, second of that name, by the Grace of God, King of Prussia, Margrave of Brandenburg, etc., etc., etc., Very Puissant Monarch, Grand Protector, Grand Commander, Universal Grand Master and True Keeper of the Order.

The day of Calends—first of May A.L. 5786 and of the Christian era, 1786.

(Signed)

:	(?)	:	Stark	:	(?)
:	(?)	:	H. Willhelm	:	D'Esterno
:	(?)	:	Woellner	:	

APPROVED and given at our Royal Residence at Berlin, the day of the Calends—first May, year of Grace 1786, and of our reign the 47th.

Seal   Signed   Frederick.

Note The signatures shown as (?) were reported as no longer legible.

Signature of Frederick the Great. This signature does not appear on any known high degree document.

JOHN KNIGHT'S MANUSCRIPT NOTEBOOK, 1811

Notes

(a)   This Appendix covers the connection between the notebook and the high degree rituals of the A & A Rite. The reader interested in other early high degree rituals should consult the original Ms in the Library of Grand Lodge, or other notebooks in the same series in the Masonic Library at Hayle, Cornwall. All extracts from the notebook are included by permission of the Board of General Purposes of the UGL.

(b)   Words which John Knight considered as 'secret' in the notebook are in a simple code viz a = c, e = h, i = m, o = p, u = r. The heading of the book thus appears as:

FREE MASONRY

From the

Hnthrhd   Apprhntmch

to   the

Rpsy   Crrsmcn

or

Nh   plrs   rltrc.

The Degrees start on page 85.

1.   *Entered Apprentice.* 'Our own way, or as usual.'

2.   *Fellow-Cft.*   –do–

3.   *Mark Man*, or Foreman of the Fellow-Cfts. 'No preparation necessary or required now, but it should be given before the Master Mason's degree.' The Ob. S.T. and W. are given.

4.   *Master Mason.* 'the usual way'.

5.   *Mark Master or Mark Mason or Scot man of Mk Masonry.* Ob, S.T. and W. are given. A similarity with the present degree is the jewel.

6.   *Master of Arts and Sciences* (or Passing the Chair). No details are given.

7.   *Architects.* Given in some detail. The wording indicates direct translation from the French i.e. Most Mighty Master (*Très Grand*

Maître), Venerable Wardens (*Vénérables Surveillants*) Respectable Brothers (*Respectables Frères*) or the word covered (*couverte*) for tyled. The degree is close to the 4° of Little Architect or Apprentice *Ecossais* in *Les Plus Secrets Mystères*. The legend includes the immolation of the heart of Hiram and the candidate being thrown upon a Blazing Star and the letter G. The inference is that the degree came to England though de Lintot's 4°, and does not resemble any degree in the A & A Rite. The Architect's duties are to 'give plans and elevations'.

8. *Grand Architecht*. A continuation of the degree above. The architect's duties are to 'give plans and elevations'. An oddity is that the W. is 'Harodim' while other 'secrets' come from early French high degrees.

9. *Excellent* or 81 Deputy Grand Masters. The legend is 'to decorate the Holy Sanctuary of the Temple' i.e. is much the same as the Secret Master 4° in the A & A Rite. Much of the wording is almost a copy of No 5 in *Les Plus Secrets Mystères*. The Architect's duties are 'to inspect the plans and elevations'.

10. *Super Excellent* or 9 Supreme Deputy Grand Masters. This is still a continuation of the architect theme, but no details are given, except that the work 'is to inspect and survey the Sacred Utensils'. The secrets are anachronistic as the candidate, in giving them, copies the instructions given to Moses to 'smite' the Egyptians i.e. the curing of his leprous arm, the plague of serpents and the turning of water into blood, while the word jumps from Exodus 4 to the Song of Solomon—I am the Rose of Sharon and the Lily of the Valley.

The degrees numbered 7 to 10 are a series dealing with the building of the Temple and its decoration after the death of Hiram. As explained earlier, there are no ostensible reasons for the use of the word 'Exellent' in the titles and that it may be an association with the French *Elu*. There is, however, no 'vengeance' theme as in the modern *Elu* degrees (9°–10°) in the A & A Rite. That came into the degrees later than *Les Plus Secrets Mystères* version.

11. *Red Cross*. Knight divides the degree into two parts. The first is the legend of Cyrus, King of Persia, and Zerubbabel. It is thus the first half of the Knight of the East in *Les Plus Secrets Mystères* and of the 15° in the A & A Rite. There is no description of the second half, merely 'for a full description of the degree, see the Super-Excellent Book.' It must, however, have covered the degree of Prince of Jerusalem 16° of the A & A Rite and there is a crossing of the bridge ceremony leading from one degree to the next.

Those familiar with Scottish rituals will recognise the Babylonian Pass of the R.A. Some of the English Allied degrees are also concerned.

12.–17. *Royal Arch*. The degree is divided into five parts, Preparing, Dedicated, Decorated, Advanced and Circumscribed Points. These are the stages in the rebuilding of the Temple under Zerubbabel and, from the brief account given, seem to have little resemblance to present degrees. A student of the R.A. may find more elsewhere in Knight's notebooks, as it ends 'For a full explanation of this degree, see the Royal Arch Book, J.K.'

18. *Royal Ark Masons, Marioners, or Noachites, also sometimes called the Prusian Masons*. The degree is very close to the first part of the 21° in the A & A Rite but John Knight's degree stresses the humiliation of Noah and the punishment of Ham for mocking his father's drunkenness.

> , 'Cursed be Ham, and he shall be a slave to his brothers for his mocking.
> Blessed be Shem, and Ham shall be his slave.
> Blessed be Japhet, and Ham shall be his slave.'

In spite of the title for the degree, there is no reference to the usual second part of the legend i.e. Prussia and Frederick the Great. There is also no resemblance to the modern Royal Ark Mariner degree.

19. *Knights Templar*. The degree is only given in outline. It seems to be similar to parts of the modern degree but is mixed with the Malta theme. There is no resemblance to the Kadosh degrees of the A & A Rite.

20. *Mediterranean Pass*. The legend is that the password was the reward to knights who had served valiantly in the Holy Land and who wished to return to their homes. It precedes the Malta degree, as one would expect, but has nothing to do with St Paul. The sign is, however, 'as if speaking through a trumpet'. Later in his notebook, Knight lists some additional degrees and one of these is 'Knight of St Paul' and its legend is the shipwreck off Melita; this word being the password of the degree.

21. *Knights of Malta or Malta Orders*. This has no connection with the modern degree but 'The Origin and Explanation of the E. W. N. & S. Knights' which is given in full is rather like early Kadosh degrees and could be a prototype of the first half of the present Malta traditional history. Short descriptions of the four knighthoods cover 22. to 25. in the notebook.

26. *Rosy-Crusian or Ne Plus Ultra*. The ceremony is given in full. The ritual is one of the many versions of this degree which were in circulation at this period. All are much the same and contain the same essentials. The jewel, as described is similar to that now used. An interesting rubric is:

All Rosy-Crusians write their names and Age 33 years, also the Candidate, before admittance, send in his name wth age 33. Viz A.B. Aged 33 years. The two officers [there were only two in the ceremony, the Most Wise Sovereign and an Orator in theory, but actually there was a Master of Ceremonies who conducted the candidate] write their names under, altho' one will do..........A.B.   C.D.

For Summons, sign by A.B. Most Wise.

For Certificates   A.B. Most Wise   C.D. Orator

The practice of 'aging' candidates for the 18° as 33 years old appears in early rituals of the Rite and was continued until near the end of the XIX century.

The sign that John Knight shows above for the Orator is that of the Deputy Grand Master i.e. the head of the local Knights Templar Conclave. All these signs show the close association between the high degrees of the Knights Templar and the Rose-Croix, and their development from the Royal Arch. It is generally accepted that Thomas Dunckerley was responsible for the use of these signs, even if he did not invent them himself, except possibly the Rose-Croix signature sign. The signature sign of the Knight Templar was Templus Hierosolyma Eques, the E(Eques) on the right of the triple tau being the sign of Knighthood. It is possible that the Rose-Croix sign is an elementary monogram of F.H. and C., but this is no more than speculation; as is the thought that the tears below the Templar monogram mourn the death of Jacques de Molay.

On pages 183 to 185 of Knight's book are the names and biblical references to the following 'Sundry Orders called Masonic Orders' viz. Link, Wrestle, Prussian Blue, Red Cross, Black Cross, White Cross, Elysian Knights or Orders of Death, Priestly Order of Seven Pillars, Sepulchre, Patmos or Order of Philippi, Knight of St John of Jerusalem, Knight of St Paul. It seems that the English were almost as prolific in inventing high degrees as were the mid-XVIII century French!

MAJOR SHIRREFF'S CHARTER FOR A LODGE OF PERFECTION

By the Glory of the Great Architect of the Universe—*Lux ex Tenebris*. From the East of the Grand Court of the Most Valiant Princes and Masons of the Royal Secret, &c., &c., under the Celestial Canopy of the Zenith which Answers to Fifty-one Degrees, Thirty Minutes.

To Our Illustrious and Most Valiant Knights and Princes of Free and Accepted and Perfect Masons of all Degrees over the Surface of the Two Hemispheres.

Greeting: I, Charles Shirreff, Esq., of Whitchurch, in the County of Salop, Grand Elected Perfect and Sublime Mason, Knight of the East and Prince of Jerusalem, &c., &c., Patriarch, Noachite Knight of the Sun and of the White and Black Eagle, &c., &c., Prince of the Royal Secret, Deputy Grand Inspector General over all Lodges, Chapters, Councils, and Grand Councils of the Superior Degrees of Ancient and Modern Masonry over the Surface of the Two Hemispheres. By Patent from Major Augustine Prevost at St Augustine, in the Province of East Florida, North America, under the special protection of the most puissant Princes and in their place and stead Do Certify and Attest to all Free and Valiant Princes of Free and Accepted Masons, &c., &c., That our Dear Brothers James Heseltine, Esq., Grand Treasurer to the Grand Lodge of London; William White, Esq., Grand Secretary to the Grand Lodge of London; John Allen, Esq., Provincial Grand Master for the County of Lancashire, and Past Junior Grand Warden to the Grand Lodge of London; James Galloway, Esq., Past Junior Grand Warden to the Grand Lodge of London; and George Sweetingbourg, a Past Master and Assistant to the Grand Secretary of the said Grand Lodge of London, and known to be perfect Masters, and arrived to the Degree of Perfection, or the Ultimate of Symbolick Masonry to which Sublime Degree I have initiated them. Now be it known that the said Brethren having with firmness and constancy sustained the brightness of the Grand Luminary, given me the most solid proofs of their Fervency, Constancy and Zeal in the support of the Royal Craft and of their submission to the Supreme Tribunal of the Sovereign Princes of the Royal Secret, &c., &c., I, the said Charles Shirreff have and by these Presents as Deputy Inspector General and Grand Master over all Lodges of the Royal Arch and Perfection, &c., &c., Do Grant this my Warrant of Dispensation and Constitution to them the said James Heseltine (as the Master); William White, Esq.; John Allen, Esq.; James Galloway, Esq.; and Mr. George Sweetingbourg, and do authorize them to meet and form a Lodge from the fourth Degree of Secret Master to the fourteenth Degree called Perfection, or the Ultimate of Symbolick Masonry, as occasion may require On conditions that the aforementioned Brethren, viz., Heseltine, White, Allen, Galloway, and Sweetingbourg in all things do fully conform and act agreeably to all the Rules, Statutes, Laws, and Regulations prescribed by the Bye-Laws now intrusted to their Charge for the government of the different Degrees above-mentioned. In full assurance of which and in virtue of the authority intrusted to me as aforesaid, I do hereby give and grant them full power to Congregate, meet, and to Initiate all those whom they shall find into the afore-mentioned Degrees, or any of them, Agreeably to the Laws and Regulations laid down for the government of the said several Degrees.

Given under my Hand and Seal at London, this 6th day of May, in the year of Our Lord, 6788.

I accept this Dispensation,

(Signed)   JAS. HESELTINE.

Seal

(Signed)   C.SHIRREFF, D.G.I.G.

Note   Shirreff states that he was given the high degrees by Major August*ine* Prevost about 1775. J. Fairbairn Smith assumes that this was the August*in* Prevost who received his high degrees in Albany, New York, about 1767/68. This claim seems doubtful in view of the spelling in the Charter and it is possible that the giver of the high degrees was the cousin who spelt his name August*ine*. This Prevost could have been in Florida about 1775 and it is more likely that he would have been a major. The 'Albany' Prevost was an Adjutant and Captain/Lieutenant, position and rank held by those normally 'rankers' or without means, therefore unlikely to have purchased a majority by 1775.

Bibliography

Anon. Manuscript Volume in French, c. 1790, contains some 26 early rituals. In Library of Supreme Council, London. (Referred to in text as *London French Ms.*)

J. V. Andrae (?) *Fama Fraternitatis or a Discovery of the Fraternity of the Most Noble Order of the Rosy Cross.* c. 1615.

C. N. Batham. Chevalier Andrew Michael Ramsay, a new Appreciation. *AQC* 81, 1968. (*Ars Quatuor Coronatorum* or the Transactions of the Quatuor Coronati Lodge).

Avocat Barbier. Journal, 1717.

S. H. Baynard Jr. *History of the Scottish Rite of Freemasonry*, Supreme Council Council 33°, 1938.

Alain Bernheim. *Contribution à la Connaissance de la Genèse de la première Grande Loge de France.* Transaction of Loge Villard de Honnecourt, 1974. *Présentation des Problèmes Historique du Rite Ecossaise Ancien et Accepté.* Renaissance Traditionelle No. 61, Jan 1985.

G. E. W. Bridge. *A & A R. The Intermediate Degrees, 1°–17°*, 1960.

R. Carlile. *Manual of Freemasonry* c. 1825.

H. Carr. *Early French Exposures 1737–1751.* (Referred to in text as *Early French Exposures.*)

D. Caywood. Waller Rodwell Wright, *AQC* 85, 1972.

N. Choumitzky. *Etienne Morin, Bulletin de la Grande Loge Nationale et Regulière Loge Saint-Claudius No. 21*, 1927.

F. J. Cooper. R.W.Bro. William Tucker, Prov G.M. of Dorsetshire 1846–53, *AQC* 83, 1970.

W. J. Chetwode Crawley. Two Corner Stones laid in the Olden Time, *AQC* 24, 1911. The Templar Legends in Freemasonry, *AQC* 26, 1913.

Ron Chudley. *Thomas Dunkerley, a Remarkable Freemason*, 1982.

Rev N. Barker Cryer. A Fresh Look at the Harodim, *AQC* 91, 1979.

Frederick Dalcho. *Orations*, 1808, Dublin Edition.

P. J. Dawson. The Chevalier Ruspini, *AQC* 91, 1979. John Christian Burckhardt. Leicester Lodge of Research 1982.

de Bérage. *Les Plus Secrets Mystères des Hauts Grades de la Maçonnerie Dévoilés ou le Vrai Rose-Croix, Traduit de l'Anglois; suivi du Noachite, Traduit de l'Allemand. A Jerusalem MDCCLXVII.* (Referred to in the text as *Les Plus Secrets Mystères.*)

Brest de la Chaussée. *Mémoire Justificatif du F:: de la Chaussée*, 1773.

Baron de Tschoudy. *L'Etoile Flamboyante*, 1766. *G.I.G.E. Chevalier Kados, connu sous les titres du Chevalier Elu, du Chevalier l'Aigle Noir*, c. 1769.

G. S. Draffen. Some Further Notes on the Rite of Seven Degrees, *AQC* 68, 1955.

Encyclopaedia Britannica. Article on Frederick II, the Great, of Prussia.

J. G. Findel. *History of Freemasonry*, 1866.

H. A. Francken. Manuscript book of Rituals and the 1762 Constitutions, 1771. (In the Library of the Supreme Council, London). Manuscript book of Rituals and Regulations for a Lodge of Perfection, 1783. (In the Library of the Supreme Council, Northern Jurisdiction USA.) Referred to in the text as *Francken* with date.

R. F. Gould. *History of Freemasonry*, 1886–8. Thomas Manningham MD Dep GM *AQC* 5, 1892. Albert Pike, *AQC* 4, 1891.

A. Graham. *History of the Lodge No. 1 at Whitchurch*, 1902.

G. Greiner. German Freemasonry in the Present Era, *AQC* 9, 1896.

R. M. Handfield-Jones. Pamphlet on *History of the United, Religious and Military Orders of the Temple, and St John of Jerusalem, 1730–1824*, 1938.

E. L. Hawkins. Adoptive Masonry and the History of the Mopses, *AQC* 24, 1911.

C. W. Heckthorn. *The Secret Societies*, 1965.

A. R. Hewitt. The A & A Rite, Another Francken Manuscript Rediscovered, *AQC* 89, 1977.

G. P. Hills. Notes on some Masonic Personalities at the end of the 18th Century, *AQC* 25, 1912. Notes on the Rainsford Papers in the British Museum, *AQC* 26, 1913.

Jeremiah How. Freemasons' Manual 1862.

A. C. F. Jackson. Freemasonry in Jersey, Part I, *AQC* 86, 1973. Early Statutes of the Knights Templar, *AQC* 89, 1977. *A & A R, The Intermediate Degrees 19°–29° and a Resumé of the 30°.* 1981. *A Commentary on the Rose-Croix Ritual*, 1983. Joseph Glock. *AQC* 94, 1981. *The Scripture References to the Rose-Croix Ritual*, 4th Ed. 1984. The Effects of Rosicrucianism on Freemasonry, *AQC* 97, 1984.

P. R. James. The Royal Cumberland Lodge at Bath, 1732–1785, *AQC* 59, 1946. The Crucefix–Oliver Affair, *AQC* 74, 1961.

Alice Joly. *Un Mystique Lyonnais et les Secrets de la Franc-Maçonnerie 1730–1824*, 1938.

B. E. Jones. *Freemasons' Guide and Compendium*, 2nd Edition, 1956.

Flavius Josephus. *The Works of Flavius Josephus, Antiquities of the Jews*, Translated by William Whiston, 1818.

J. Heron Lepper (with) Philip Crossle. *The Ritual History of the 32° in Ireland. History of the Grand Lodge of Ireland*, Vol. 1, 1925.

R. S. Lindsay. *Report on the Institutions and Grand Regulations of 1763*, 1948. *The Scottish Rite for Scotland*, 1957.

Alain le Bihan. *Francs-Maçons Parisiens du Gd. Orient de France (fin du XVIII Siècle)*, 1966. *Loges et Chapitres de la Grande Loge et Grand Orient de France (2e Moitié du XVIII Siècle)*, 1967. *France-Maçons et Ateliers Parisiens de la Grande Loge de France au XVIII Siècle*, 1973.

A. E. Mackey. *An Encyclopaedia of Freemasonry*, Revised Edition, 1913. *History of Freemasonry*, Vol. VII, 1895 (written by W. R. Singleton).

Nancy Mitford. *Frederick the Geat*, 1970.
Paul Naudon. *Les Origines Réligieuses et Corporatives de la Franc-Maçonnerie*, 1972. *Histoire, Rituels et Tuileur des Hauts Grades Maçonniques*, 3rd Ed. 1984.
J. G. Osborne. *History of Freemasonry in West Cornwall from 1765 to 1828*, 1901.
Rev A. W. Oxford. *The Origin and Progress of the Supreme Council of the Ancient and Accepted Rite (Scottish) for England and Wales, the Dominions and Dependencies of the British Crown*, 1933.
Albert E. Pike. *The Ancient and Accepted Rite of Freemasonry*, 1872.
A. C. Powell. *A History of Freemasonry in Bristol*, 1910. (With J. Littleton). *The Bye-Laws of the Baldwyn Rite*, 1936.
William Preston. *Illustrations of Masonry*, 1772, and later editions.
J. B. P. L. Pyron. *Abrégé Historique de l'Organization en France des Trente-trois dégrés du Rite Ecossais Ancien et Accepté, 1814*.
Freemason's Quarterly Review Magazine. Various numbers, 1843–1854. Edited by R. T. Crucefix until his death in 1850.
Henry Sadler. *Thomas Dunckerley, His Life, Labours and Letters*, 1891.
Louis Guillemain de Saint-Victor (?). *Recueil Précieux de la Maçonnerie Adonhiramite, contenant les Trois Points de la Maçonnerie Ecossoise, le Chevalier d'Orient, le Vrai Rose-Croix, qui n'ont jamais été imprimés, précédés des trois Elus et suivis des Noachite ou le Chevalier Prussien*, 1785. (Referred to in the text as *Recueil Précieux*.)
F. W. Seal Coon. *An Historical Account of Jamaican Freemasonry*, 1976.
N. H. S. Sitwell. Some Mid-Eighteenth Century French Manuscripts, *AQC* 40, 1927. *Early Ecossism and the Chevalier d'Orient* Ms. No. 13383–24. In the Quatuor Coronati Library.
G. W. Speth. The English Lodge at Bordeaux *AQC* 12, 1890.
J. Fairbairn Smith. *The Rise of the Ecossais Degrees*. Chapter of Research of the Grand Chapter of R.A. Masons, Ohio, Vol. 10, 1965.
Sup. Council for E. & W. *Rules, Regulations and Lists of Members of the A & A R for E & W*, 1986.
J. T. Thorp. *French Prisoners' Lodges*, 1935.
G. M. Trevelyan. *Illustrated English Social History*, 1944.
J. E. S. Tuckett. The Early History of Freemasonry in France *AQC* 31, 1918. The Origin of Additional Degrees, *AQC* 32, 1919.
P. Tunbridge. Emmanuel Zimmermann, founder of the Rose Croix in Ireland, *AQC* 79, 1966.
A. E. Waite. *Encyclopaedia of Freemasonry*, 1923. *The Brotherhood of the Rosy Cross*, 1924.
W. Waples. In Introduction to the Harodim, *AQC* 60, 1947. *The Royal Kent Chapter of the Knights of the Pelican and Eagle and Sovereign Princes of the Rose Croix of HRDM No. 8*, 1958. (With W. G. Bird.)
E. Ward. An Impartial Survey of the Baldwyn Rite, *AQC* 71, 1958. Early Masters' Lodges and their relation to Degrees, *AQC* 75, 1962.
William Wonnacott. The Rite of Seven Degrees in London, *AQC* 39, 1931.
Rev A. F. A. Woodford. *Kenning's Masonic Cyclopaedia*, 1878.

Lionel Vibert. Some Early *Elu* Manuscripts, *AQC* 44, 1931.
Harold V. B. Voorhis. *The Story of the Scottish Rite of Freemasonry*, 1965.
John Yarker. The High Grades in Bristol and Bath, *AQC* 17, 1904.
Francis A. Yates. *The Rosicrucian Enlightenment*, Paladin Edition, 1975.

Index

Compiled by Frederick Smyth 32°
Member of the Society of Indexers

Lodges, etc, are under the English Constitutions unless otherwise designated and, unless a location is given, meet (or met) in London. Masonic bodies still in existence are usually indexed under their modern titles and numbers; * indicates that a lodge or similar number is in no current series or register (eg, in the English Craft, it predates the last closing-up of lodge numbers in 1863).

Page numbers in **bold type** denote the more important references, those in *italics* illustrations or their captions; *passim* (eg, 40–50 *passim*) conveys that the subject is referred to not continuously but in scattered passages throughout the pages; 'q.' stands for 'quoted'.

Abbreviations used include: (A) for the Antients; (IC), (SC), (GLNF), for the Irish, Scottish and regular French Constitutions; AAR for the Ancient & Accepted (Scottish) Rite; RP for the Rite of Perfection; SC and SGC for Supreme Council and Sovereign Grand Commander respectively, for England & Wales unless otherwise indicated; Pr for Provincial; others, such as GM, GL, L and KT, are (it is hoped) self-evident.

Neither the Chronology (Appendix I) nor the Bibliography are indexed.